"REG'LAR FELLERS"

IN THE

ARMY

By Gene Byrnes

COACHWHIP PUBLICATIONS

Greenville, Ohio

It is an extreme pleasure to present this photographic evidence of America's military power which is being demonstrated so effectively in the present war. To the officers and men of the United States Army who made the photographs in this book possible and to the Army Signal Corps for its splendid cooperation I wish to express my thanks and appreciation.

Gene
Byrnes

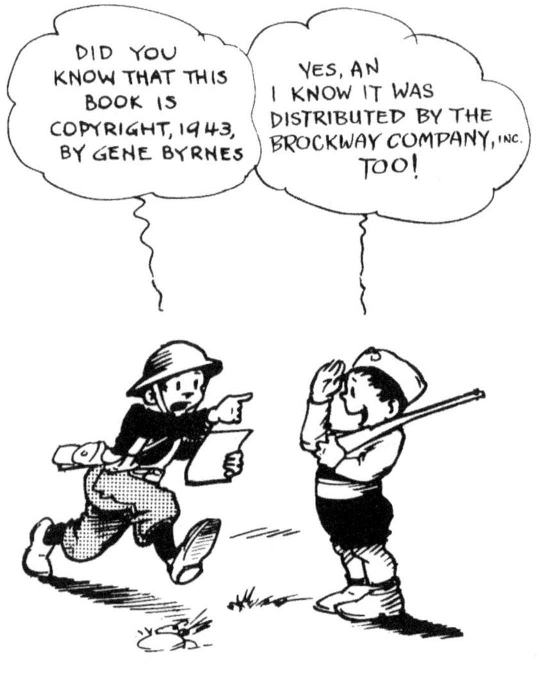
DID YOU KNOW THAT THIS BOOK IS COPYRIGHT, 1943, BY GENE BYRNES
YES, AN I KNOW IT WAS DISTRIBUTED BY THE BROCKWAY COMPANY, INC. TOO!

"Reg'lar Fellers" in the Army, by Gene Byrnes

Published 1943
Eugene Francis Byrnes (1889-1974)

ISBN 1-61646-286-8
ISBN-13 978-1-61646-286-4

CoachwhipBooks.com

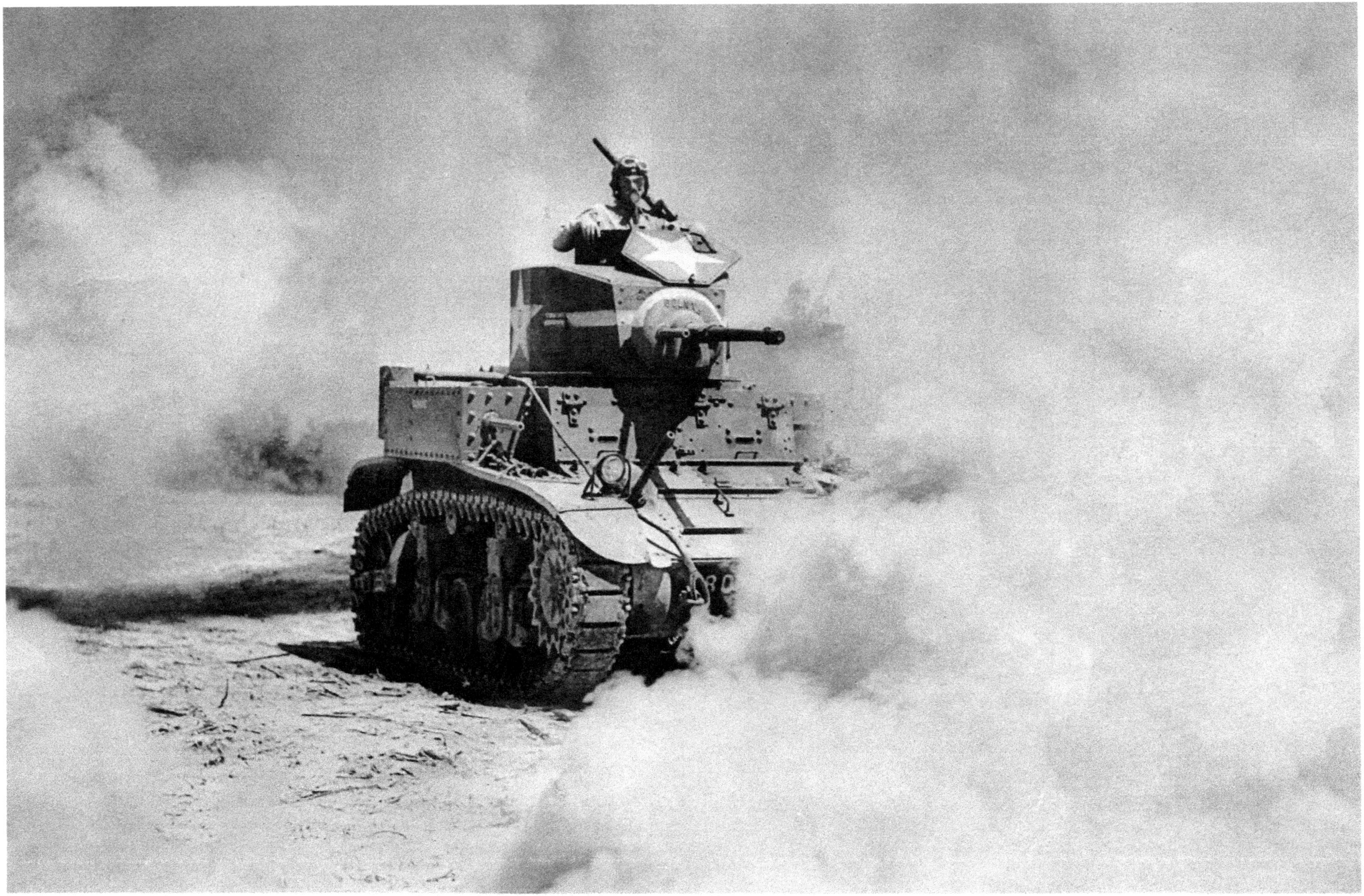

Official Photo: U. S. Army Signal Corps

Light tanks of the 80th Armored Regiment under cover of a smoke screen

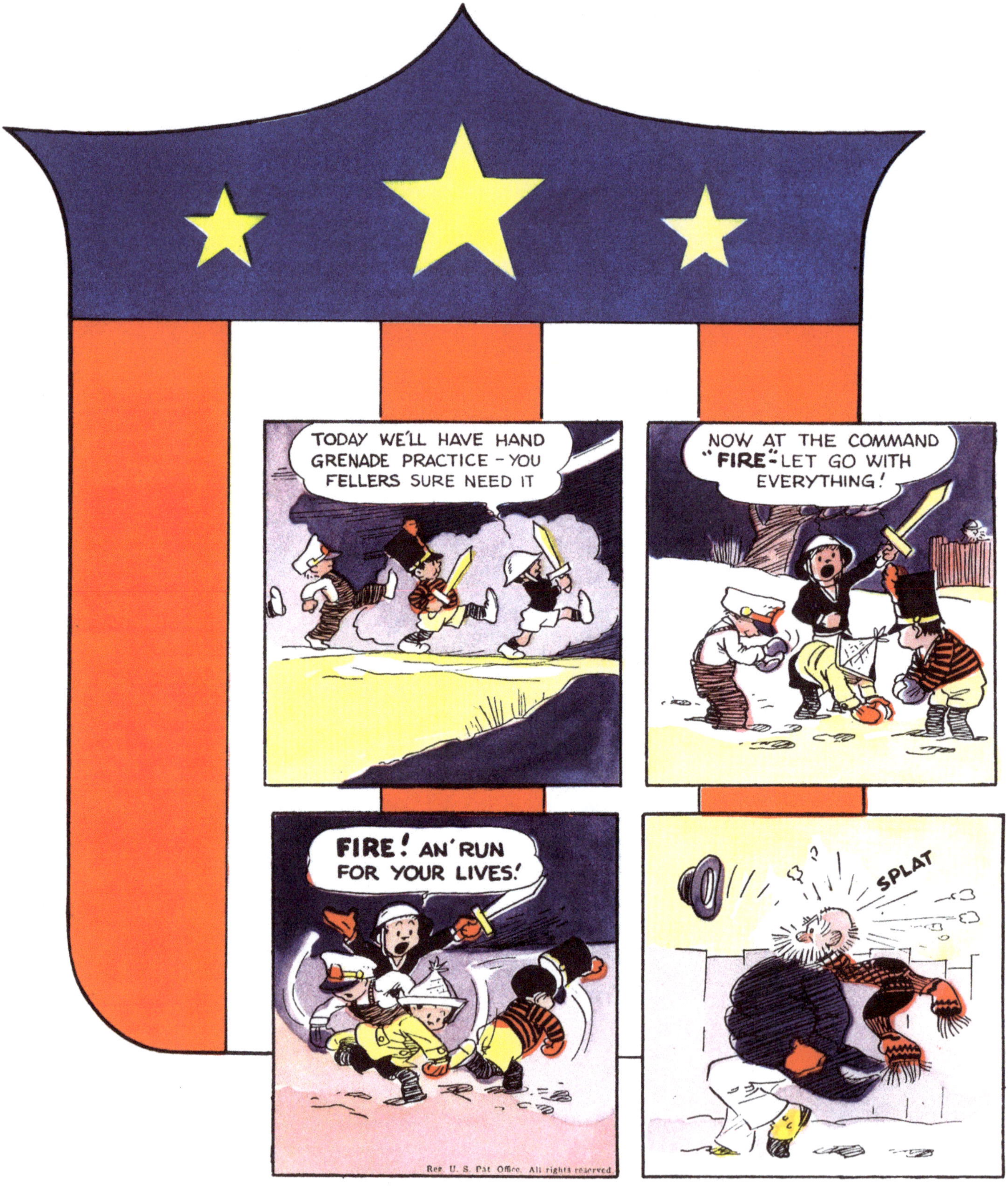
TODAY WE'LL HAVE HAND GRENADE PRACTICE - YOU FELLERS SURE NEED IT
NOW AT THE COMMAND "FIRE"-LET GO WITH EVERYTHING!
FIRE! AN' RUN FOR YOUR LIVES!
Reg. U. S. Pat. Office. All rights reserved
SPLAT

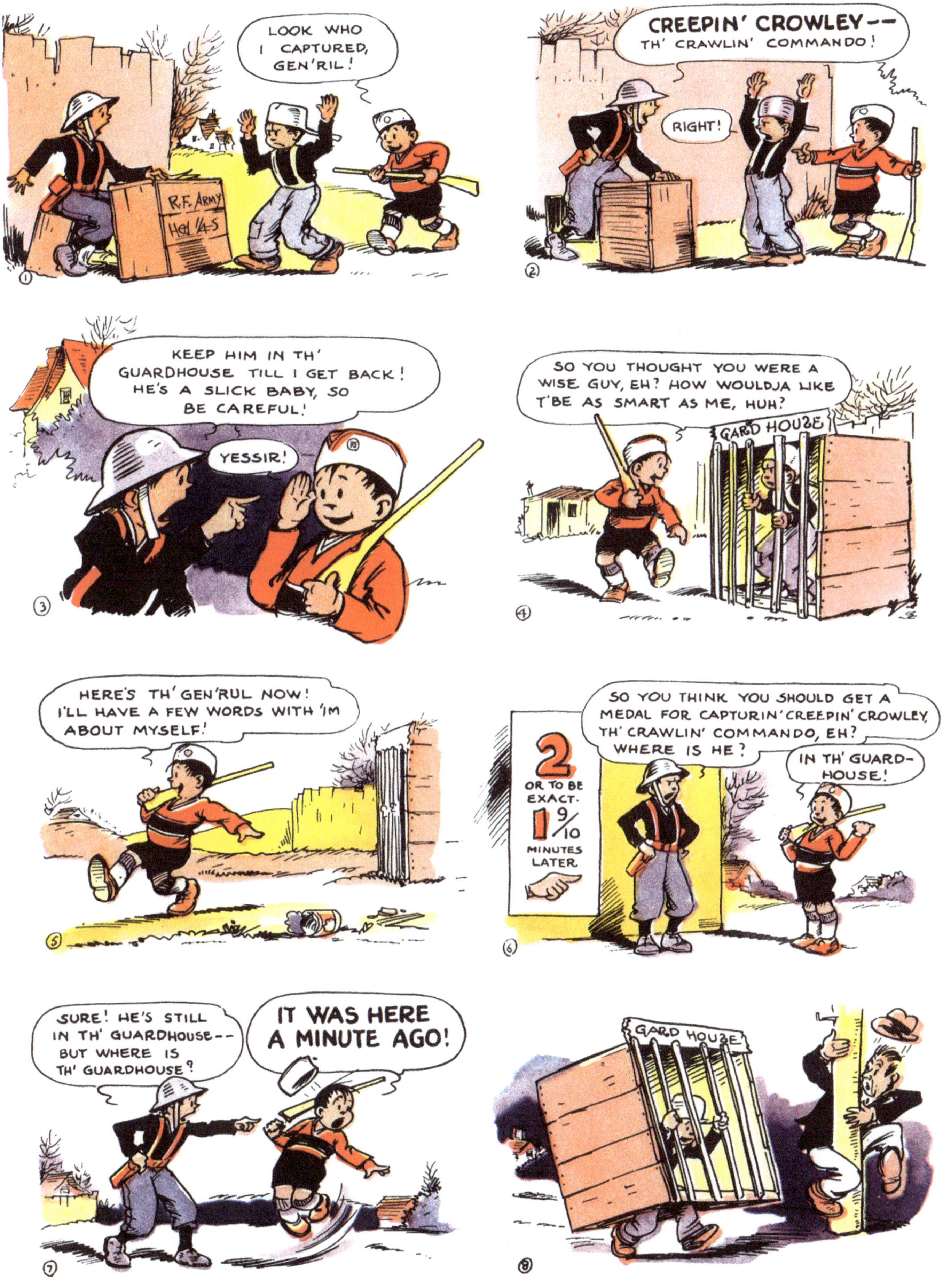
LOOK WHO I CAPTURED, GEN'RIL!
R.F. ARMY
HQ 1/4-5
CREEPIN' CROWLEY-- TH' CRAWLIN' COMMANDO!
RIGHT!
KEEP HIM IN TH' GUARDHOUSE TILL I GET BACK! HE'S A SLICK BABY, SO BE CAREFUL!
YESSIR!
SO YOU THOUGHT YOU WERE A WISE GUY, EH? HOW WOULDJA LIKE T'BE AS SMART AS ME, HUH?
GARD HOUZE
HERE'S TH' GEN'RUL NOW! I'LL HAVE A FEW WORDS WITH 'IM ABOUT MYSELF!
2 OR TO BE EXACT. 1 9/10 MINUTES LATER
SO YOU THINK YOU SHOULD GET A MEDAL FOR CAPTURIN' CREEPIN' CROWLEY, TH' CRAWLIN' COMMANDO, EH? WHERE IS HE?
IN TH' GUARD-HOUSE!
SURE! HE'S STILL IN TH' GUARDHOUSE-- BUT WHERE IS TH' GUARDHOUSE?
IT WAS HERE A MINUTE AGO!
GARD HOUZE

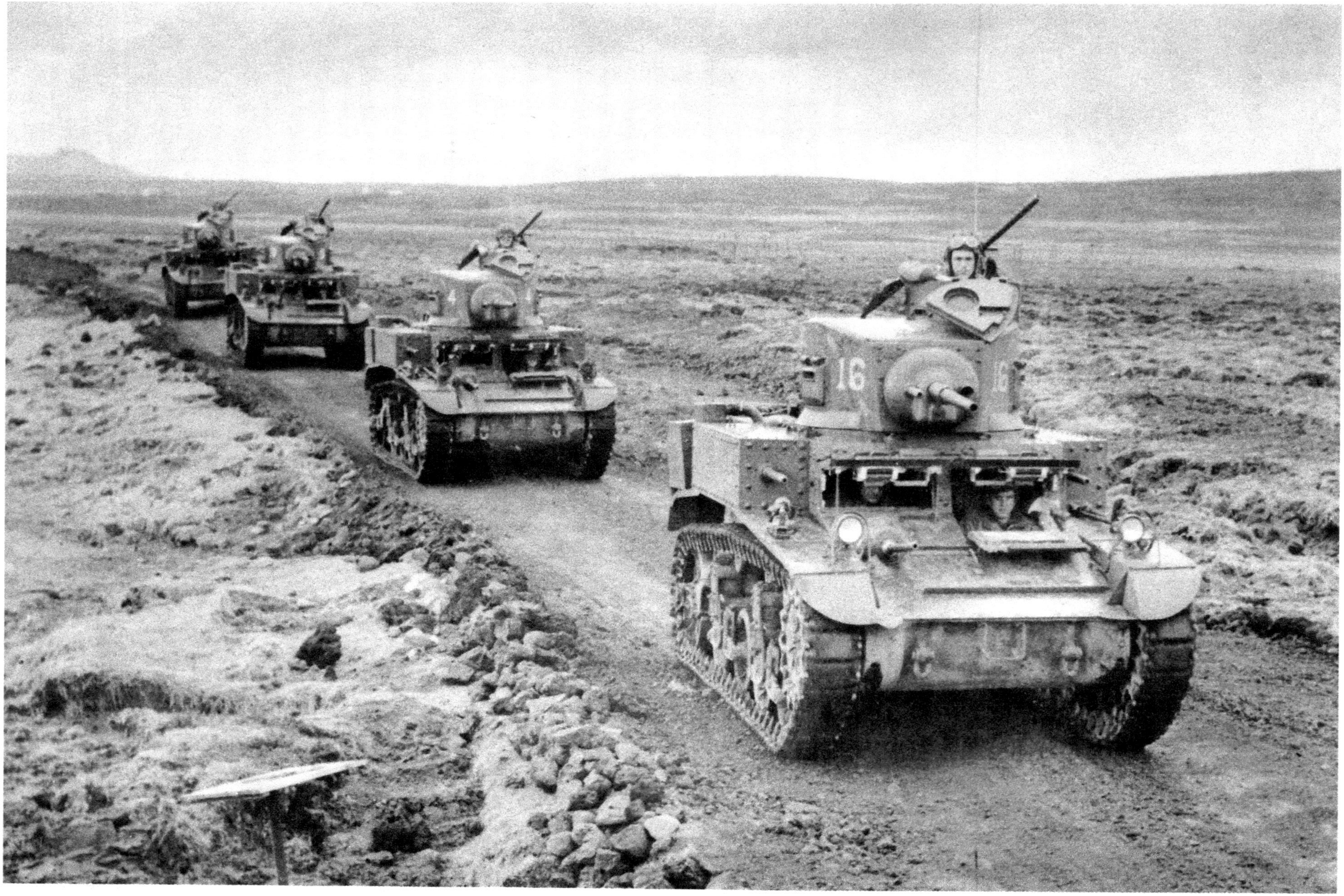
16
16

Official Photo: U. S. Army Signal Corps

U. S. Army tanks coming in after a day's practice in the lava fields of Iceland

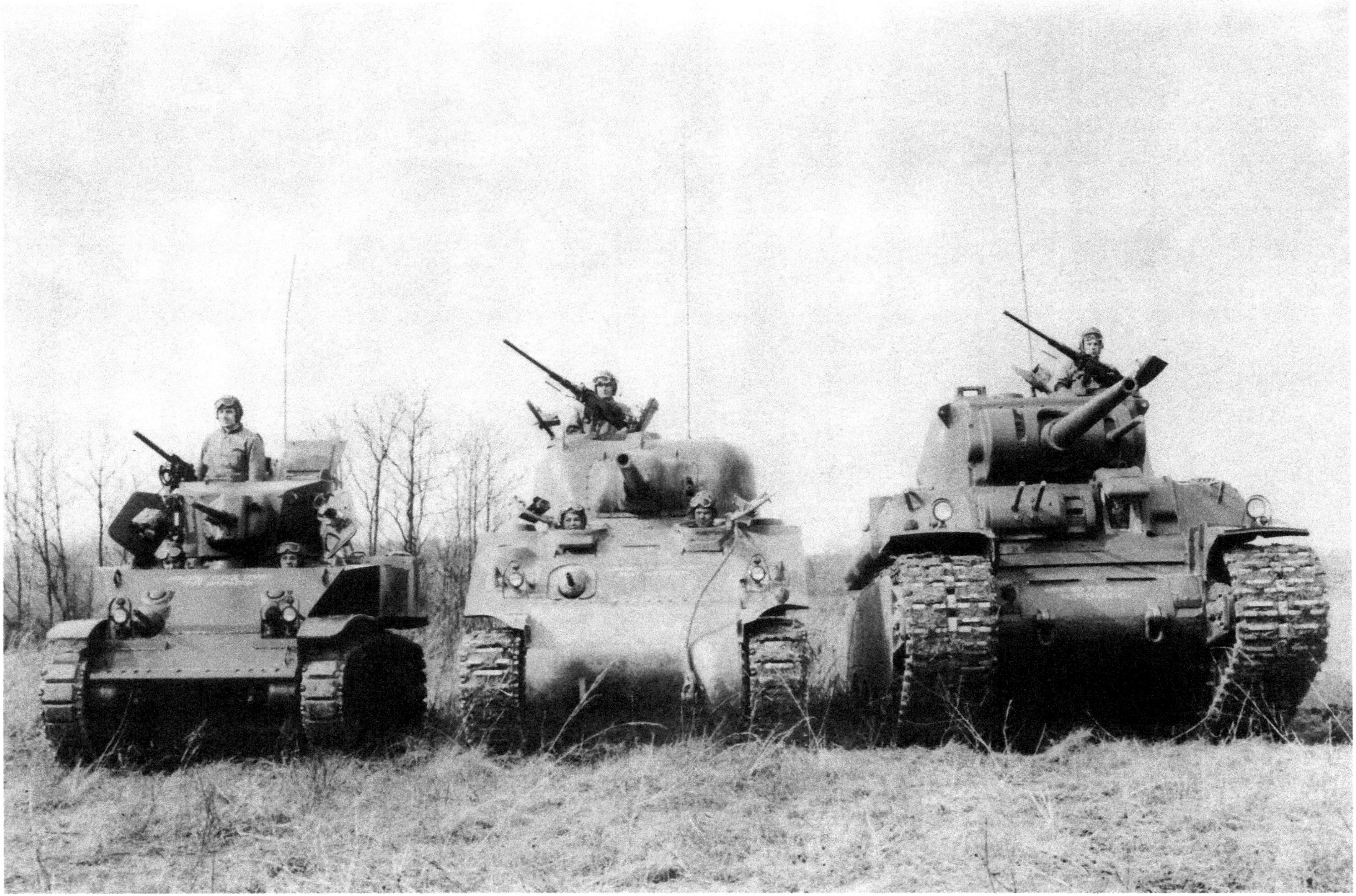

Official Photo: Hq. U. S. Armored Force Signal Section

Shown here are three of the most formidable members of the Armored Command's fighting family. From left are, the M-5 light tank, the M-4 medium tank and the M-6 heavy tank

R. F. ARMY
Anti AirCRAft
unit

TANK
CORPSe
D.S.

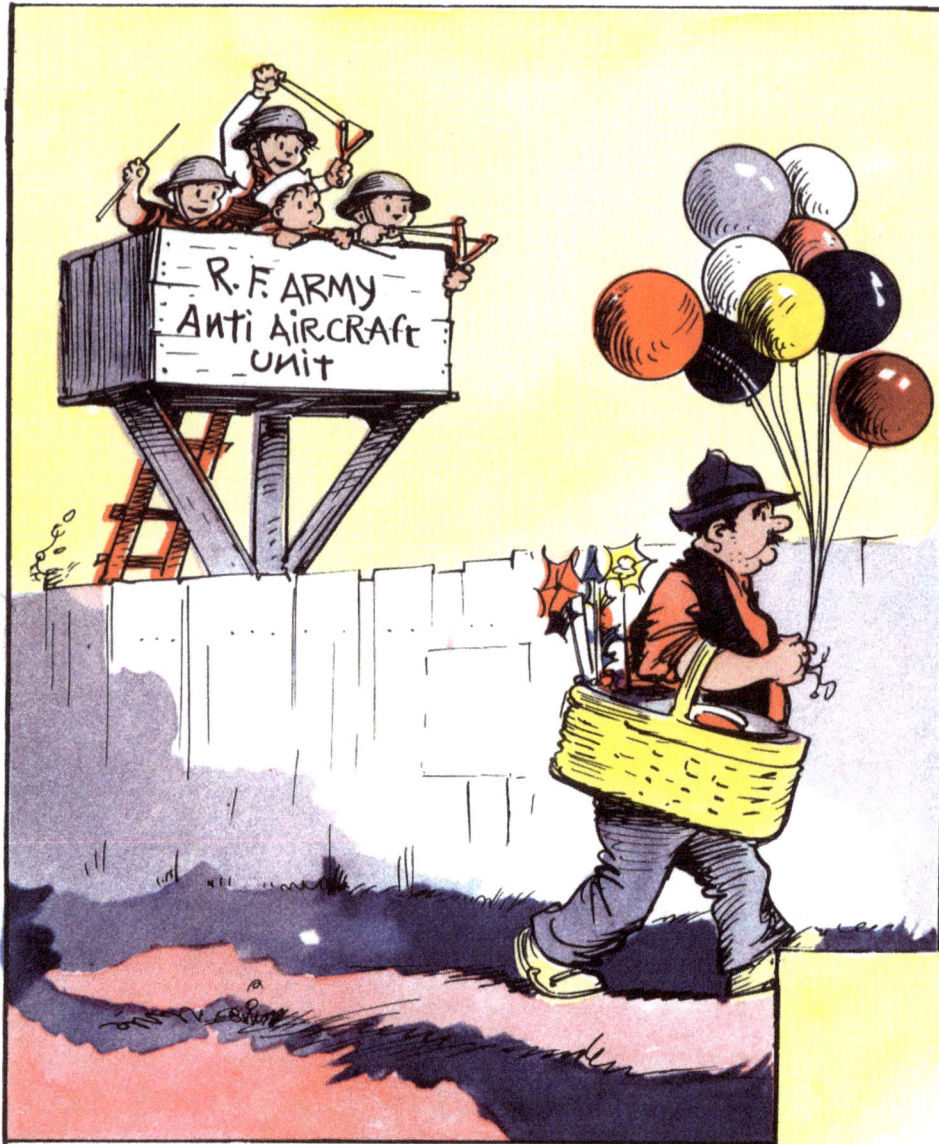

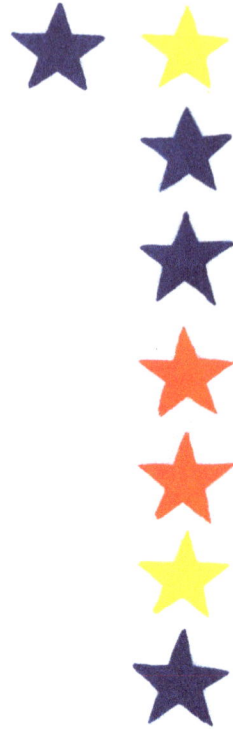

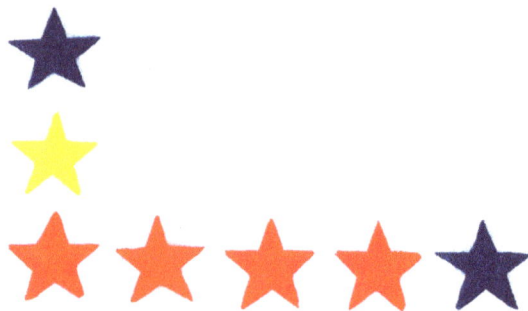

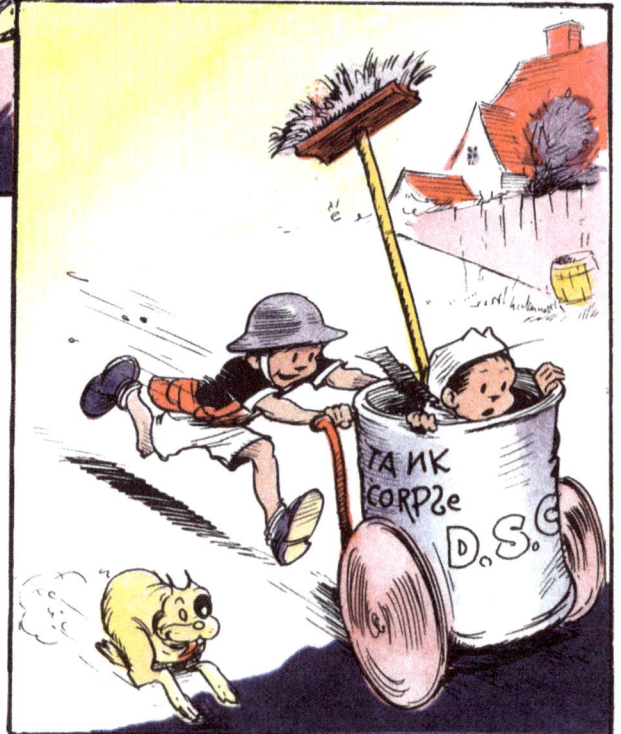

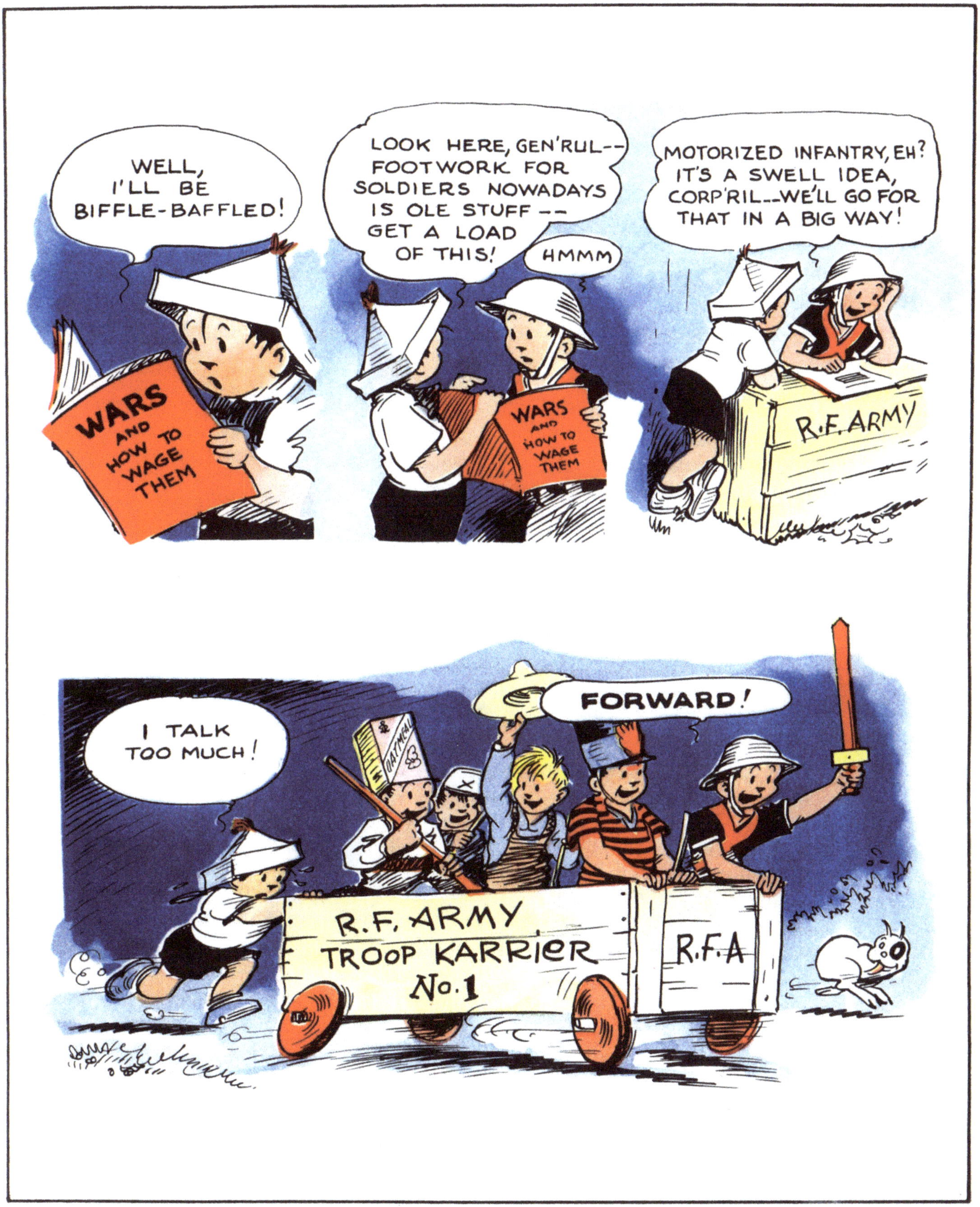
WELL, I'LL BE BIFFLE-BAFFLED!
WARS AND HOW TO WAGE THEM
LOOK HERE, GEN'RUL-- FOOTWORK FOR SOLDIERS NOWADAYS IS OLE STUFF -- GET A LOAD OF THIS!
HMMM
WARS AND HOW TO WAGE THEM
MOTORIZED INFANTRY, EH? IT'S A SWELL IDEA, CORP'RIL--WE'LL GO FOR THAT IN A BIG WAY!
R.F. ARMY
I TALK TOO MUCH!
FORWARD!
OATMEAL
R.F. ARMY
TROOP KARRIER
No. 1
R.F.A

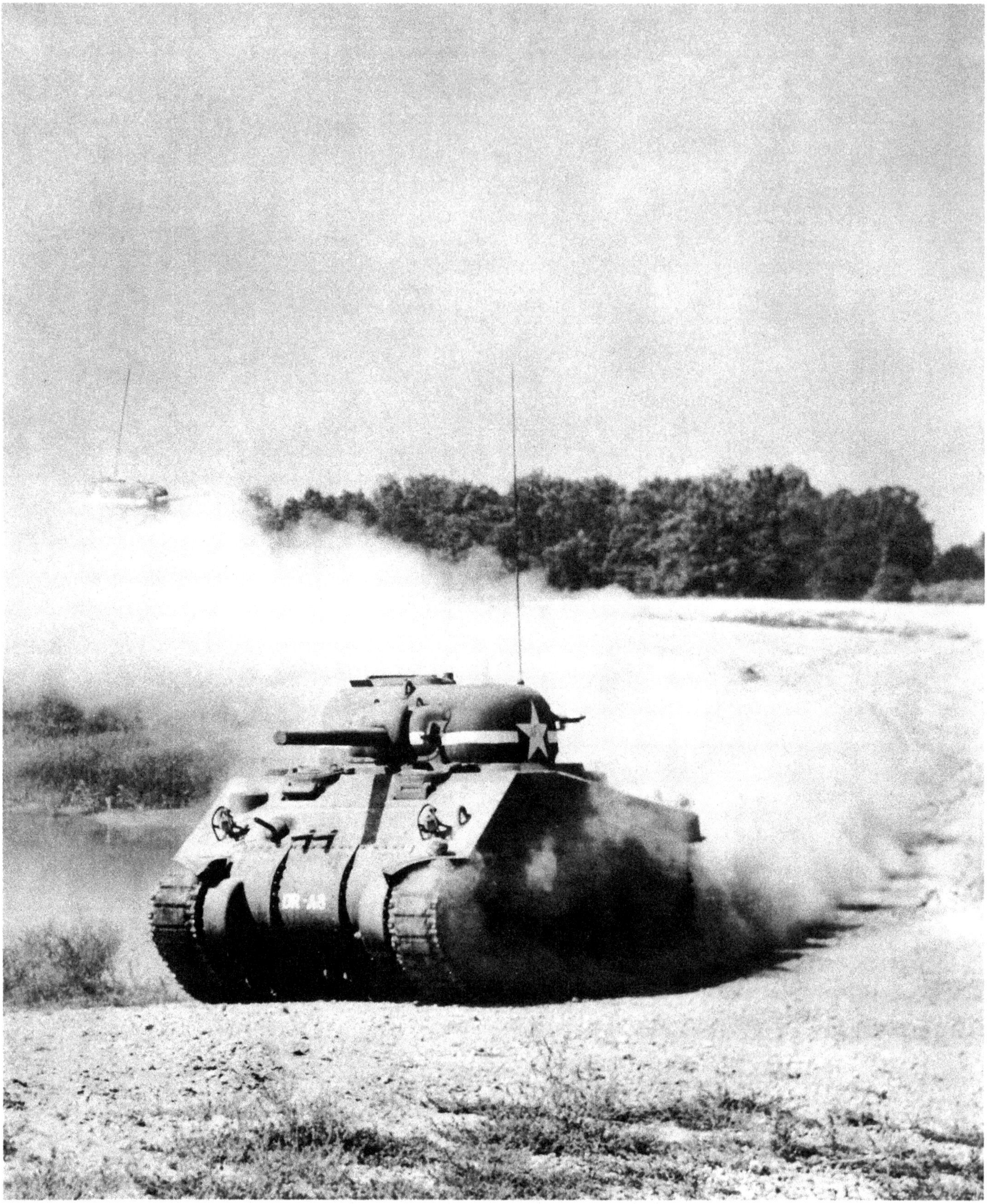

Official Photo: U. S. Army Signal Corps

A medium tank going at high speed makes a sharp turn during maneuvers. Considering their size and weight these machines are exceptionally fast

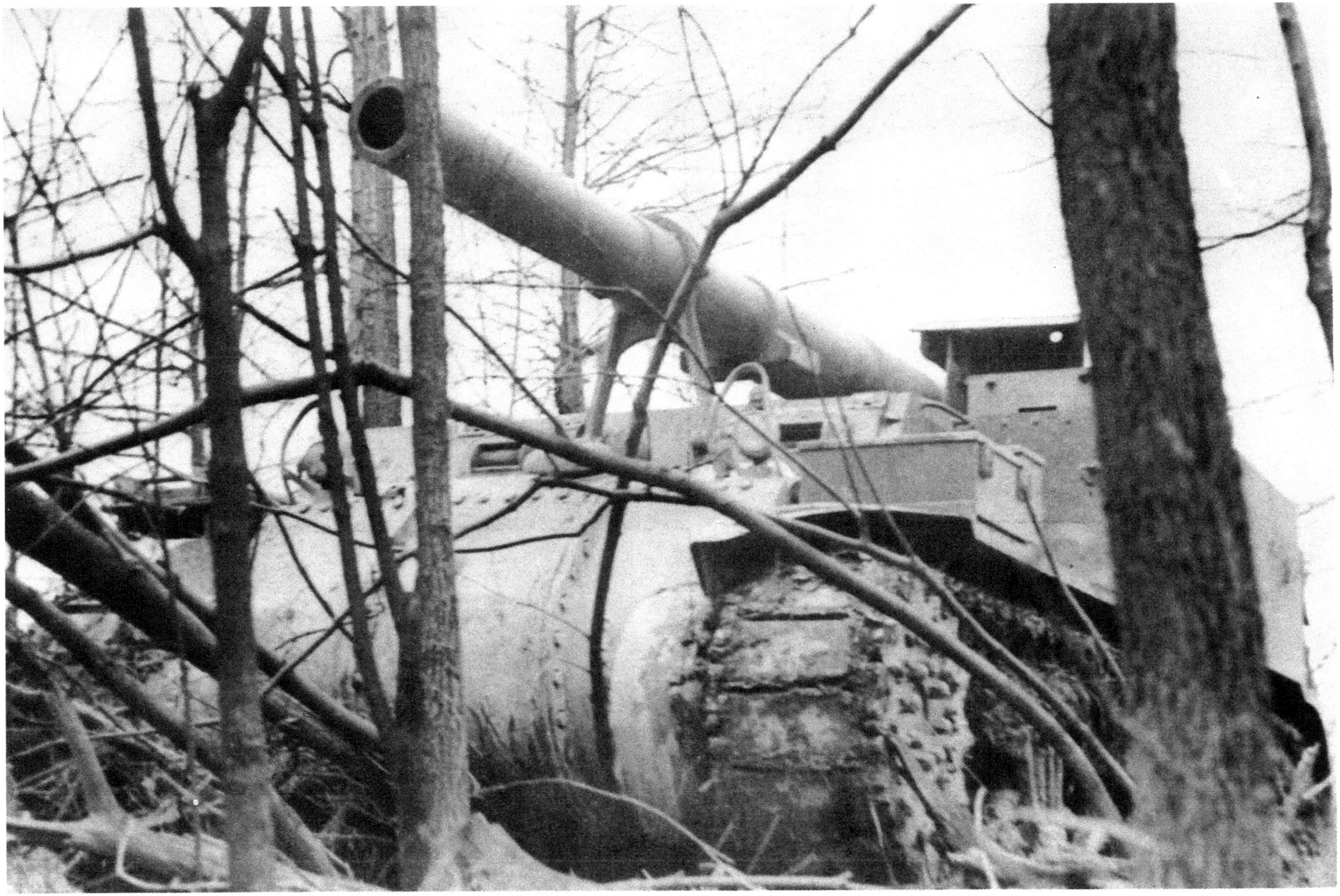

Official Photo: U. S. Army

Under way through rough terrain, the M-12 ploughs up a hillside and through a dense thicket. Trees of the size shown are no barrier to this versatile weapon which can work in any country suitable for operations of a medium tank

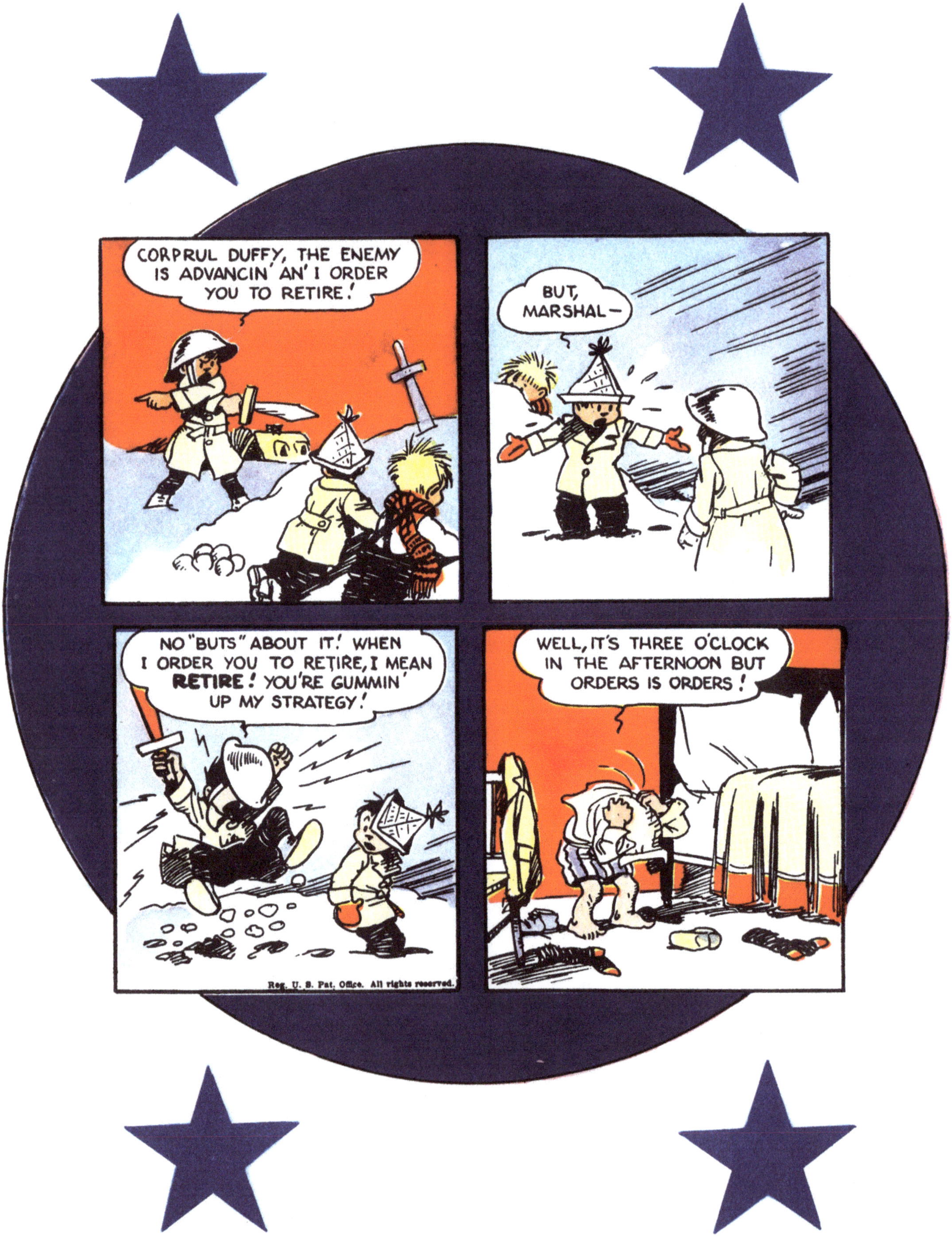
CORPRUL DUFFY, THE ENEMY IS ADVANCIN' AN' I ORDER YOU TO RETIRE!
BUT, MARSHAL—
NO "BUTS" ABOUT IT! WHEN I ORDER YOU TO RETIRE, I MEAN **RETIRE**! YOU'RE GUMMIN' UP MY STRATEGY!
Reg. U. S. Pat. Office. All rights reserved.
WELL, IT'S THREE O'CLOCK IN THE AFTERNOON BUT ORDERS IS ORDERS!

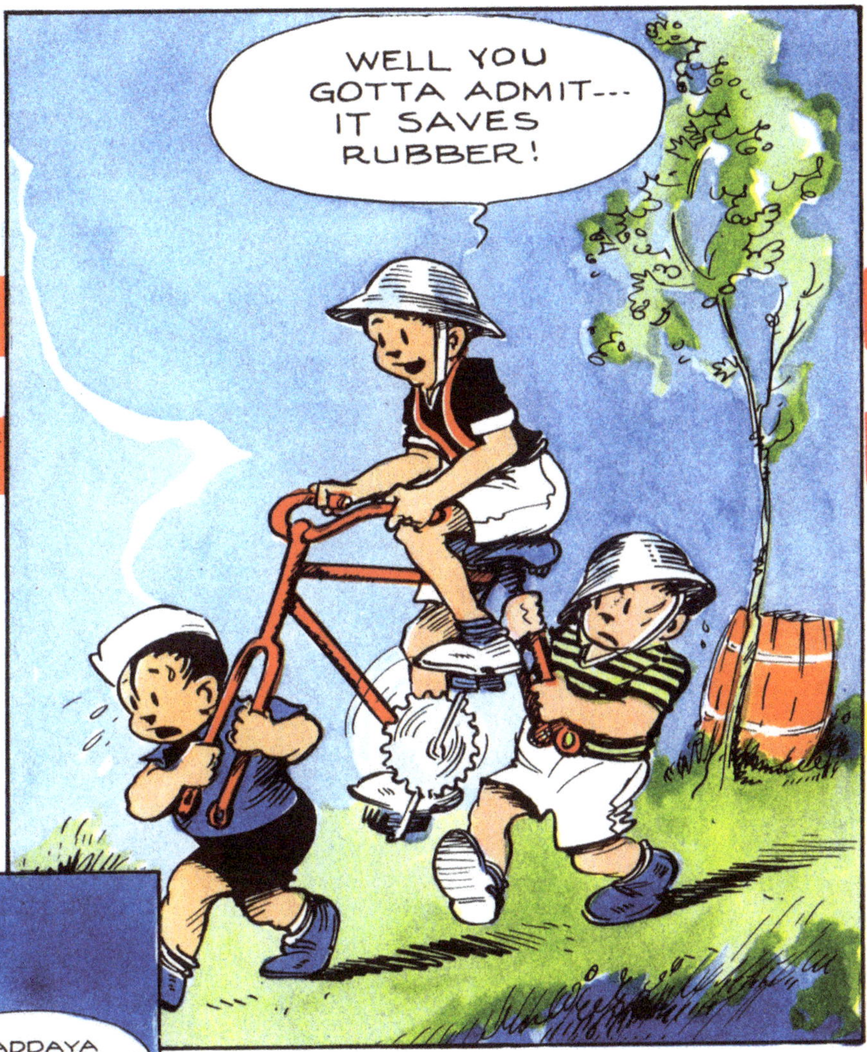
WELL YOU GOTTA ADMIT--- IT SAVES RUBBER!

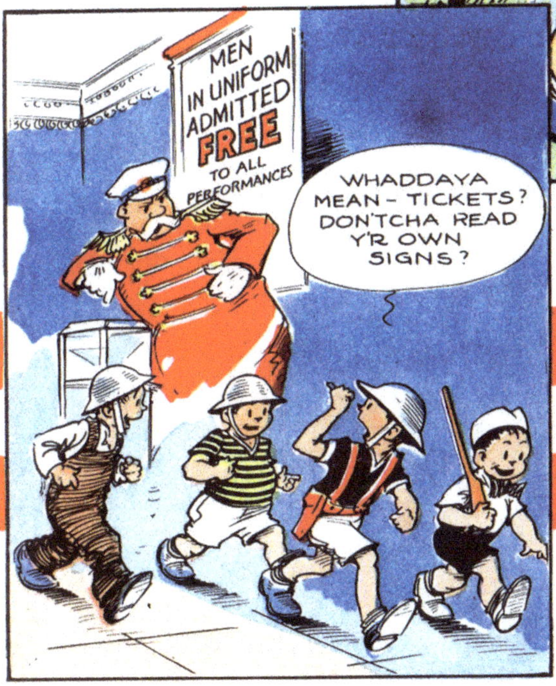
MEN IN UNIFORM ADMITTED FREE TO ALL PERFORMANCES
WHADDAYA MEAN - TICKETS? DON'TCHA READ Y'R OWN SIGNS?

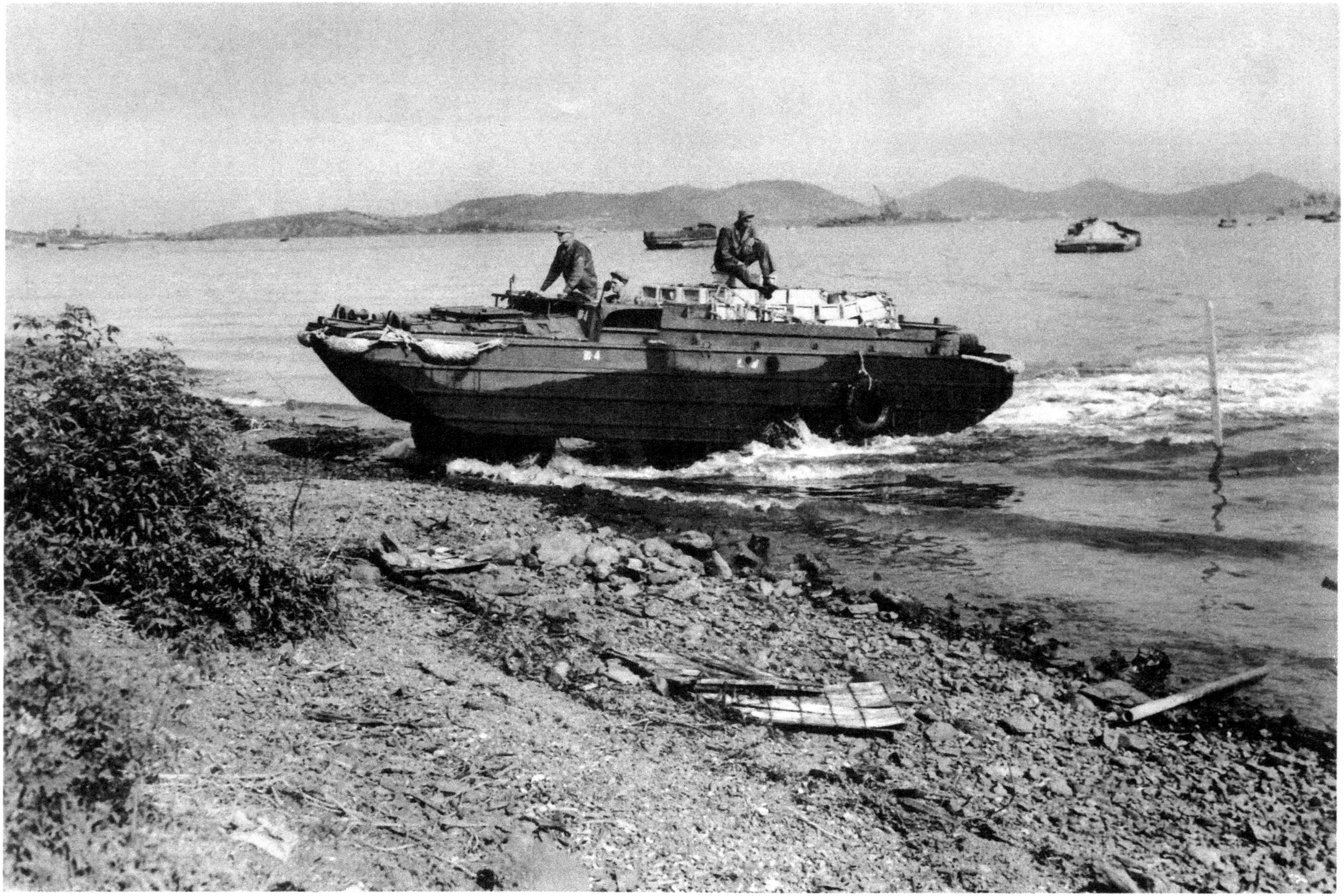

Official Photo: U. S. Army Signal Corps

This amphibian truck runs equally well afloat or ashore. Upon reaching land the propellors are switched off and the truck rolls up the beach on six rubber tired wheels. It can easily be operated by one man

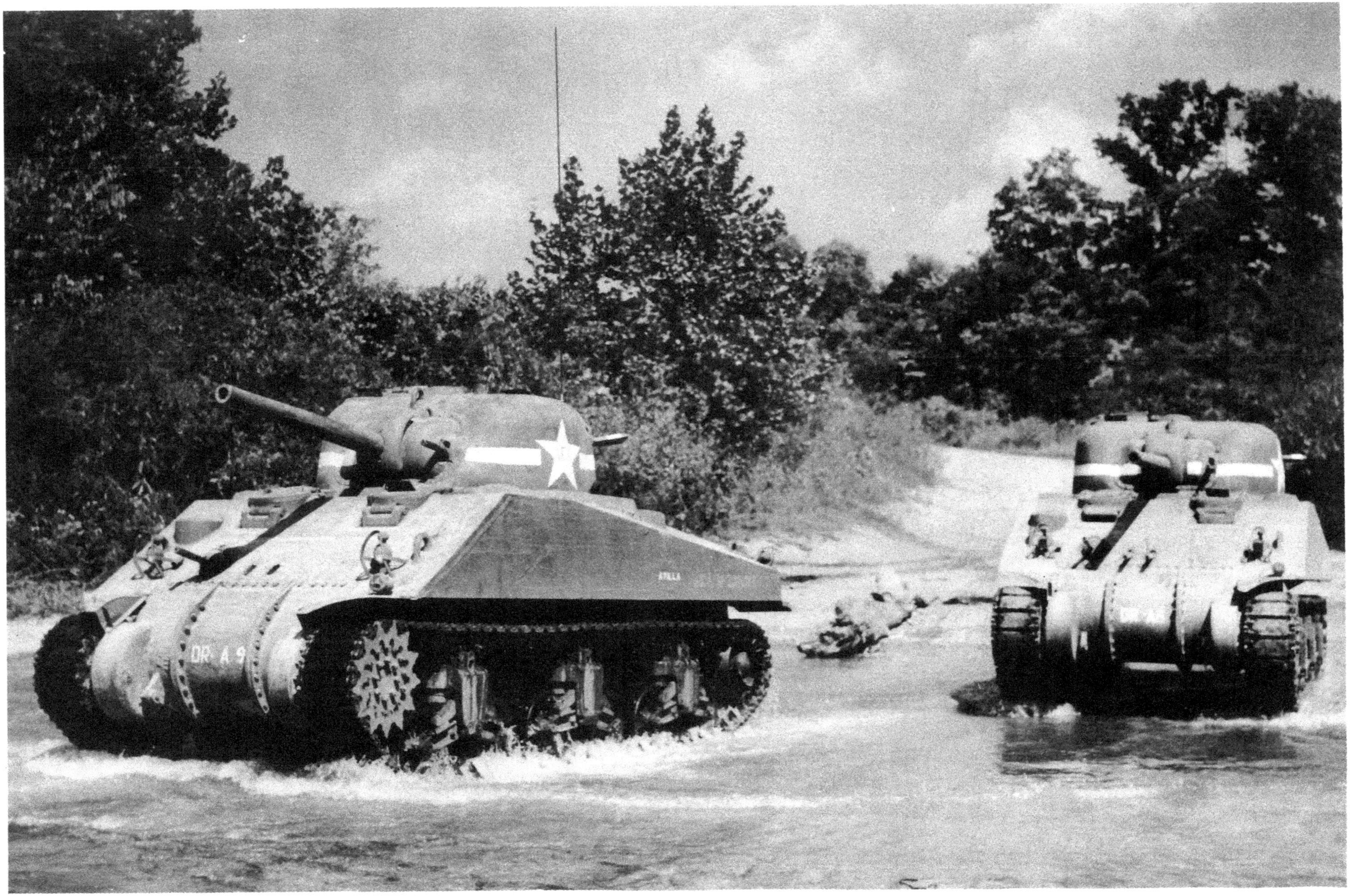
DR A 9

Official Photo: U. S. Army Signal Corps

A couple of medium tanks plunging across a stream while on army maneuvers in Kentucky

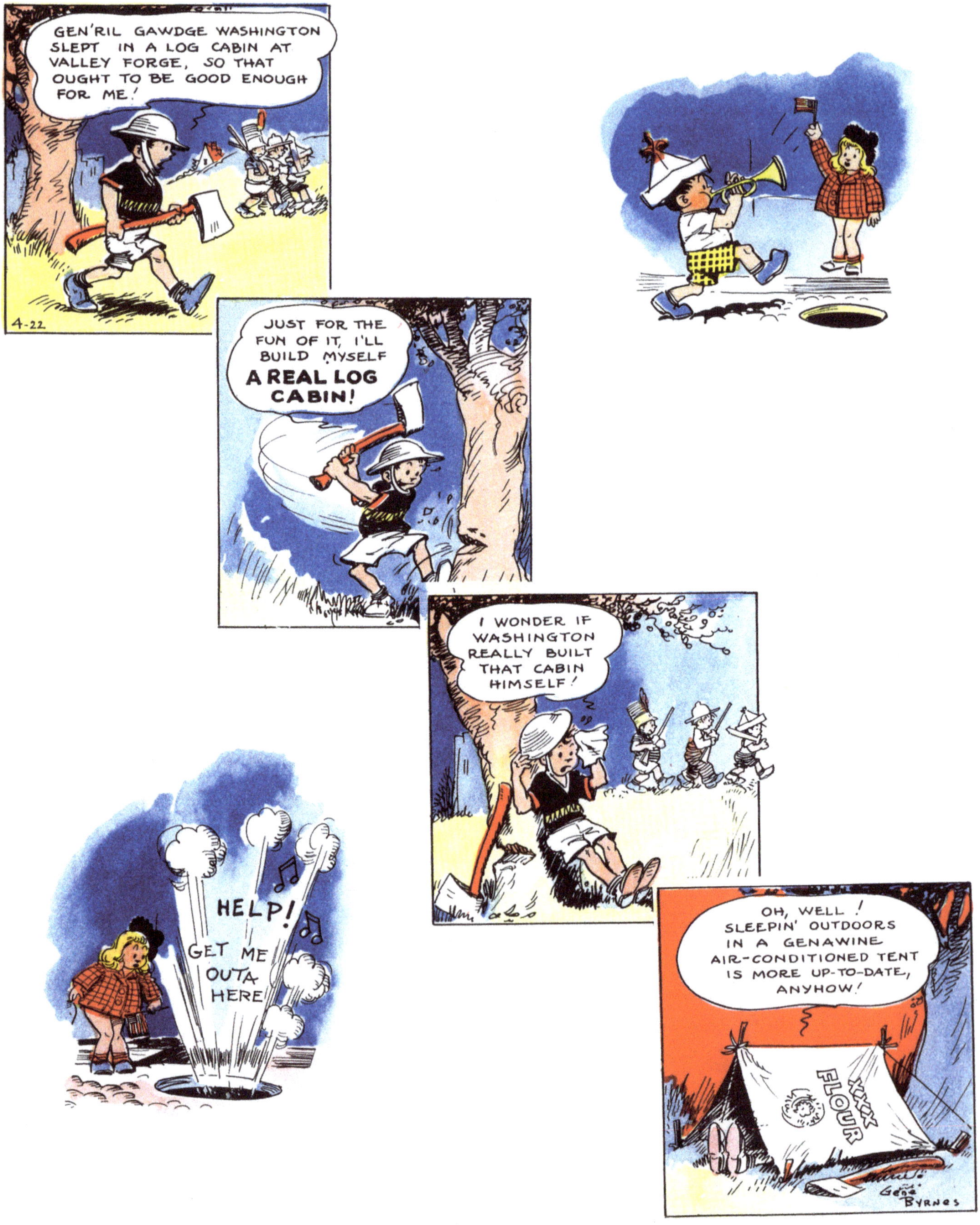
GEN'RIL GAWDGE WASHINGTON SLEPT IN A LOG CABIN AT VALLEY FORGE, SO THAT OUGHT TO BE GOOD ENOUGH FOR ME!
4-22
JUST FOR THE FUN OF IT, I'LL BUILD MYSELF A REAL LOG CABIN!
I WONDER IF WASHINGTON REALLY BUILT THAT CABIN HIMSELF!
OH, WELL! SLEEPIN' OUTDOORS IN A GENAWINE AIR-CONDITIONED TENT IS MORE UP-TO-DATE, ANYHOW!
XXX FLOUR
GENE BYRNES
HELP!
GET ME OUTA HERE

TH' RUSSIANS ARE USIN' CAVALRY AN' DOIN' A LOT O' GOOD WITH IT!
SO?
ROUND UP TH' ARMY, CORP'RIL, WE'LL GO IN FER A LITTLE CAVALRY DRILL!
WHAT'LL WE USE FER NAGS?
COUNIHAN'S CARNIVAL

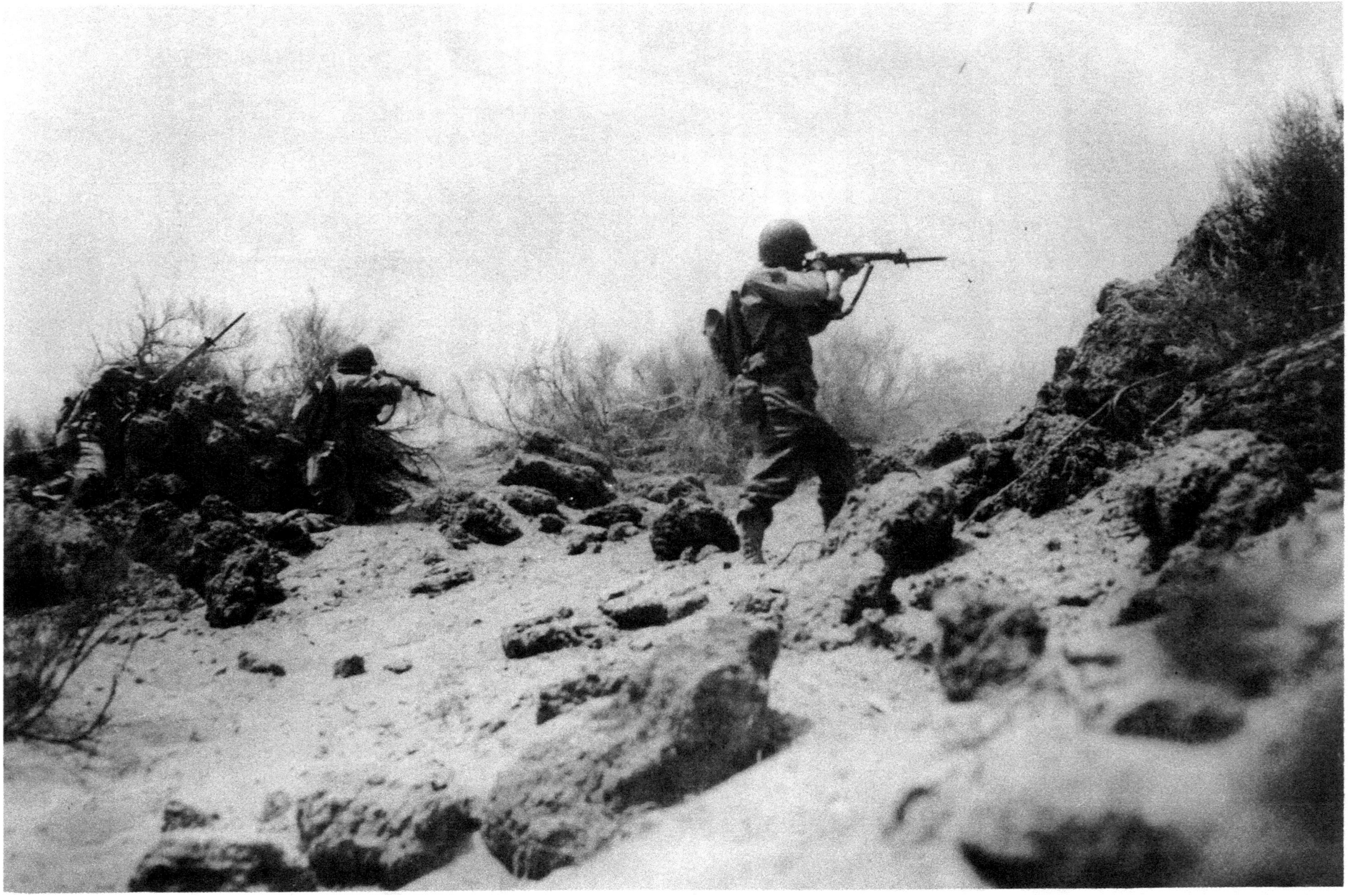

Official Photo: U. S. Army Signal Corps

American Soldiers advancing in the Sicilian campaign

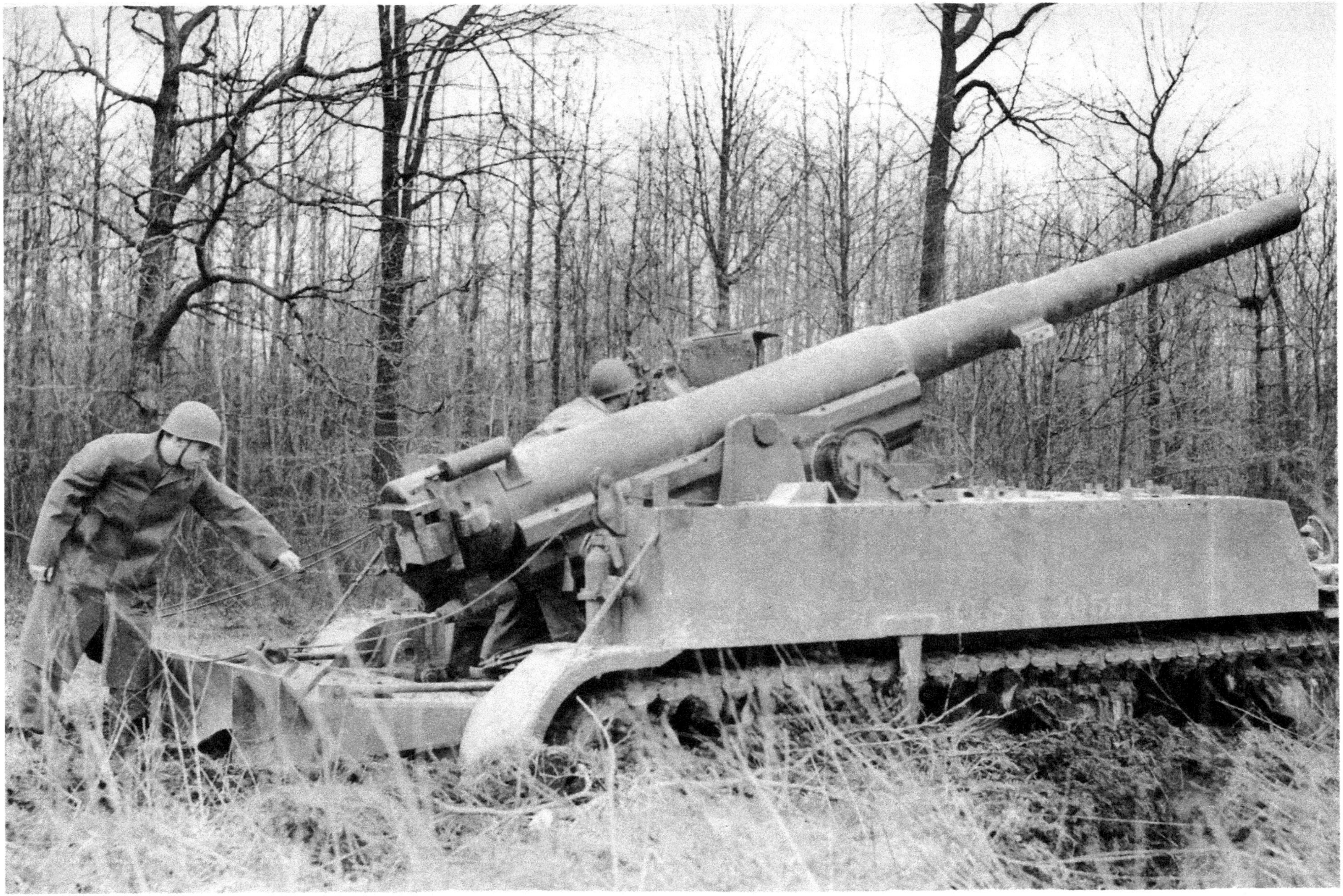

Official Photo: U. S. Army

A 155 mm. gun mounted on an M-3 tank chassis ready for action. This gun can fire a 95 pound shell more than ten miles

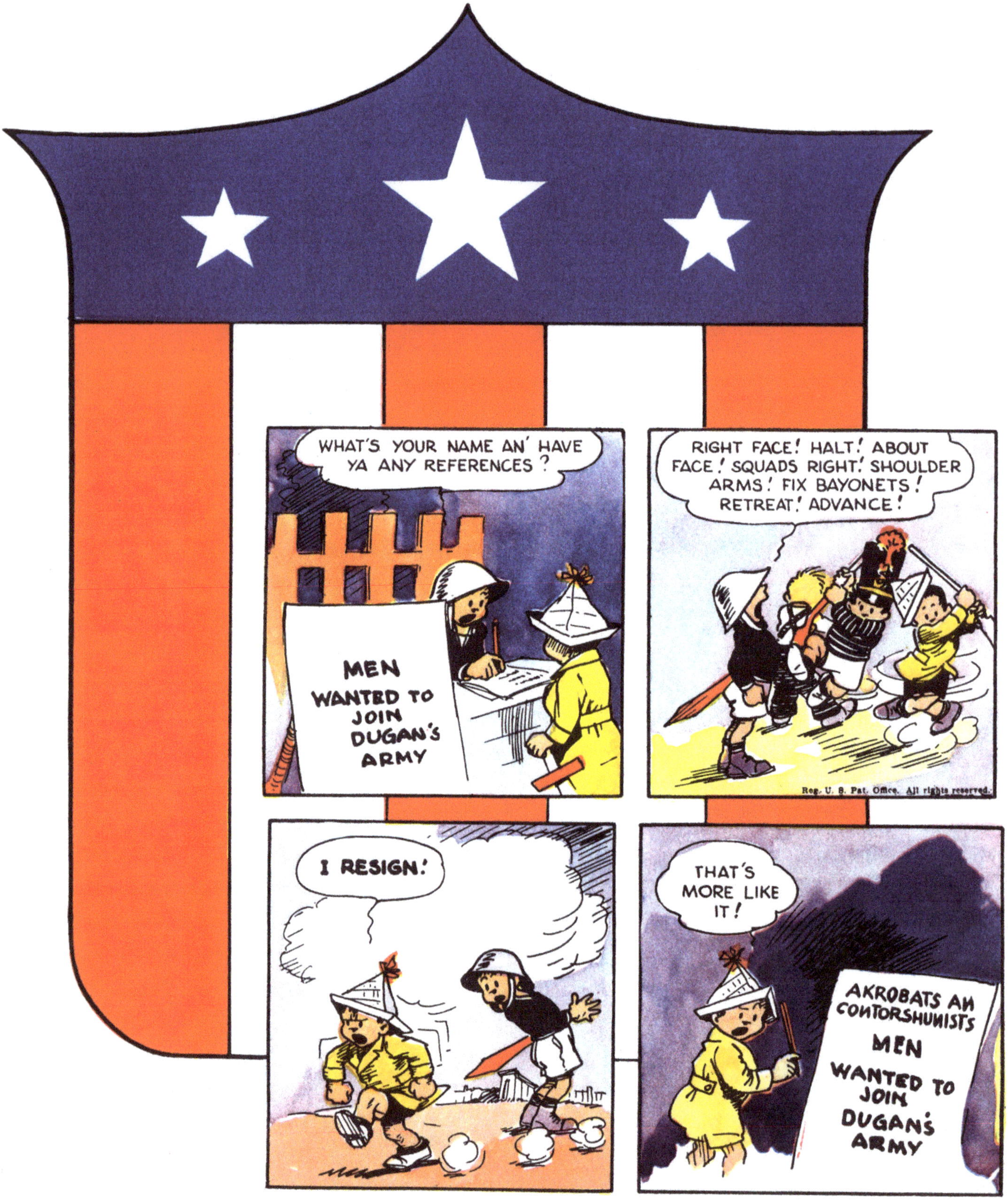
WHAT'S YOUR NAME AN' HAVE YA ANY REFERENCES?
MEN WANTED TO JOIN DUGAN'S ARMY
RIGHT FACE! HALT! ABOUT FACE! SQUADS RIGHT! SHOULDER ARMS! FIX BAYONETS! RETREAT! ADVANCE!
Reg. U. S. Pat. Office. All rights reserved.
I RESIGN!
THAT'S MORE LIKE IT!
AKROBATS AN CONTORSHUNISTS
MEN WANTED TO JOIN DUGAN'S ARMY

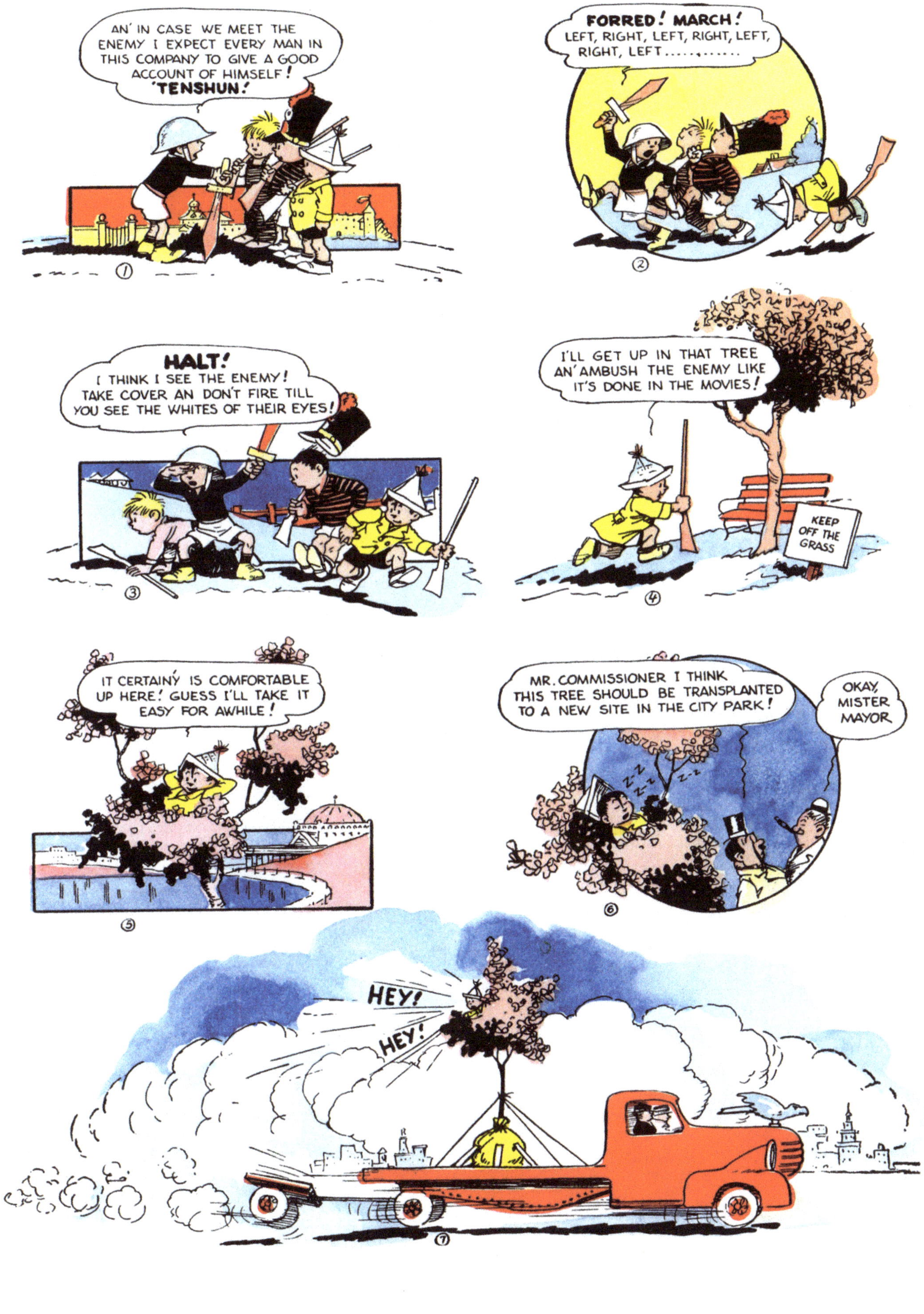
AN' IN CASE WE MEET THE ENEMY I EXPECT EVERY MAN IN THIS COMPANY TO GIVE A GOOD ACCOUNT OF HIMSELF! 'TENSHUN!
1
FORRED! MARCH! LEFT, RIGHT, LEFT, RIGHT, LEFT, RIGHT, LEFT........
2
HALT! I THINK I SEE THE ENEMY! TAKE COVER AN DON'T FIRE TILL YOU SEE THE WHITES OF THEIR EYES!
3
I'LL GET UP IN THAT TREE AN' AMBUSH THE ENEMY LIKE IT'S DONE IN THE MOVIES!
KEEP OFF THE GRASS
4
IT CERTAINY IS COMFORTABLE UP HERE! GUESS I'LL TAKE IT EASY FOR AWHILE!
5
MR. COMMISSIONER I THINK THIS TREE SHOULD BE TRANSPLANTED TO A NEW SITE IN THE CITY PARK!
OKAY, MISTER MAYOR
6
HEY!
HEY!
7

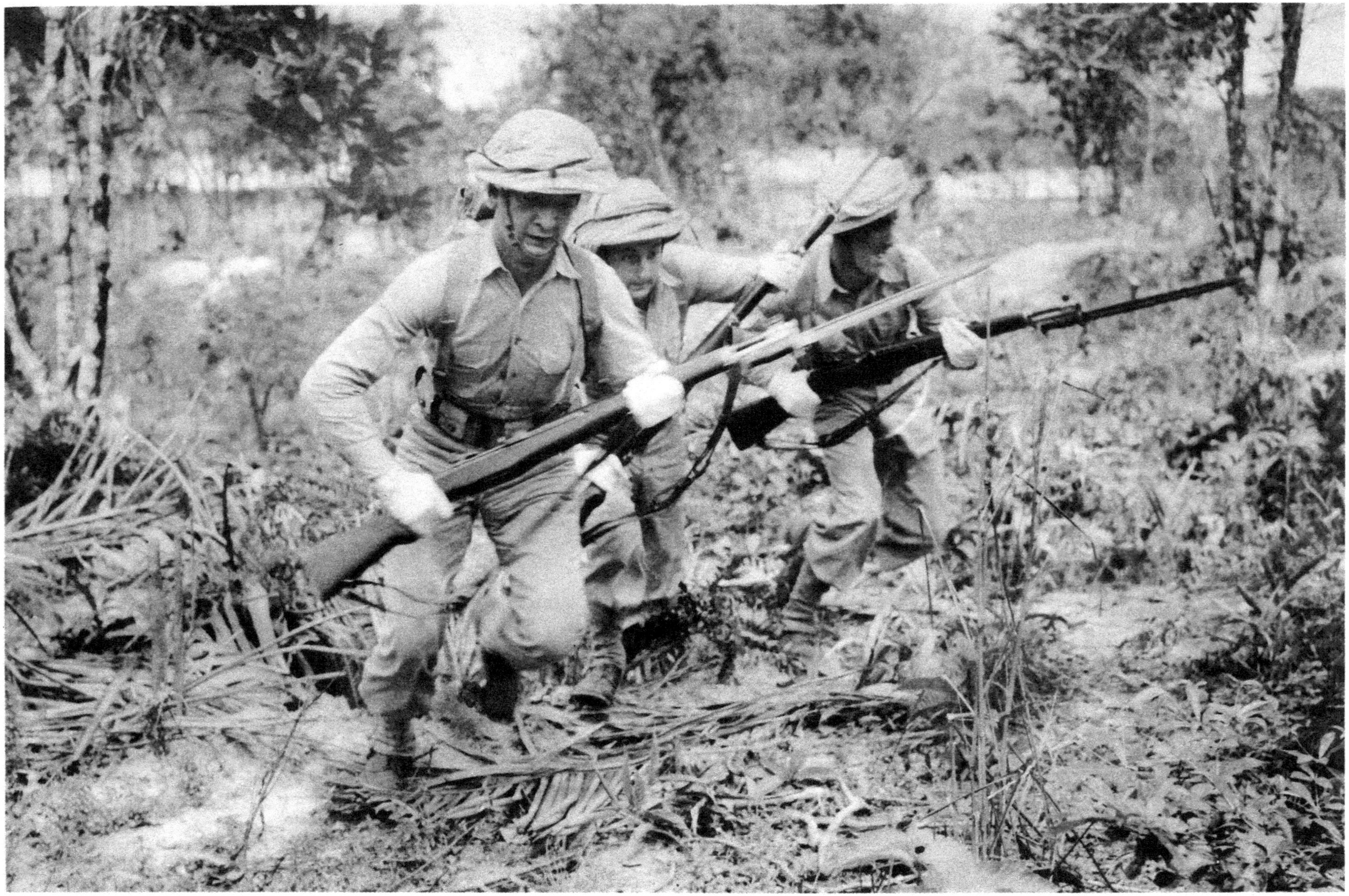

Official Photo: U. S. Army Signal Corps

''Somewhere in the Caribbean Area,'' troops of the U. S. Armed Forces in course of their vigorous training for ''bush'' warfare, are acclimating themselves to the intense heat prevalent in these tropical outposts. . . . Photo shows soldiers with mosquito-helmets and in full battle rig, charging thru the jungle growth

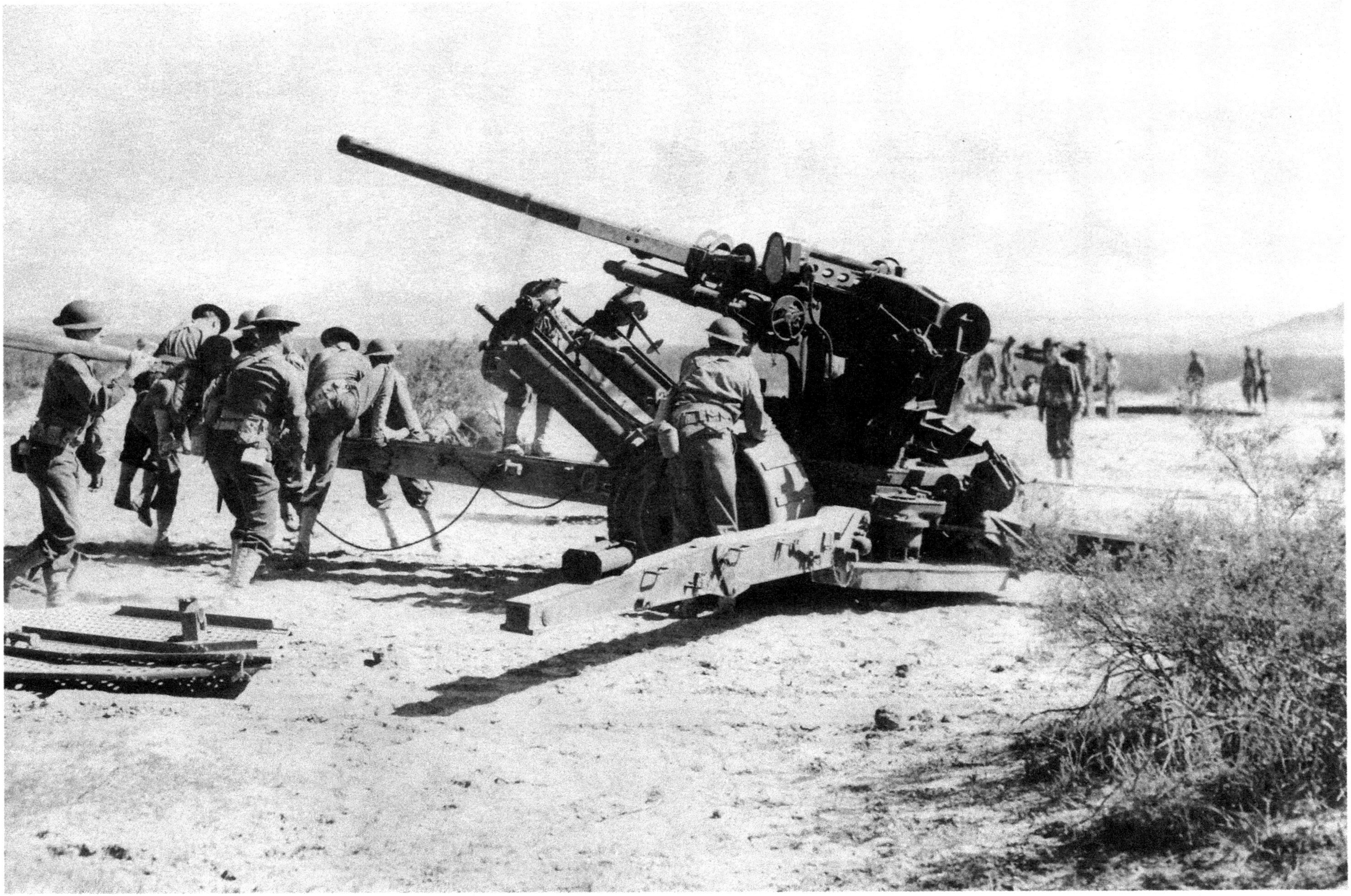

Official Photo: U. S. Army Signal Corps

A coast-artillery anti-aircraft unit in training in the California desert

WHAT DO YOU MEAN BY KEEPING YOUR PRISONERS IN MY **PANTRY**?
COOKIES
JAM

HEY GEN'RIL! WHY ARE WE RETREATIN'?
THIS AIN'T A RETREAT! WE'RE JUS' **ADVANCIN'** AT TH' DOUBLE QUICK IN TH' DIRECTION WE CAME FROM!

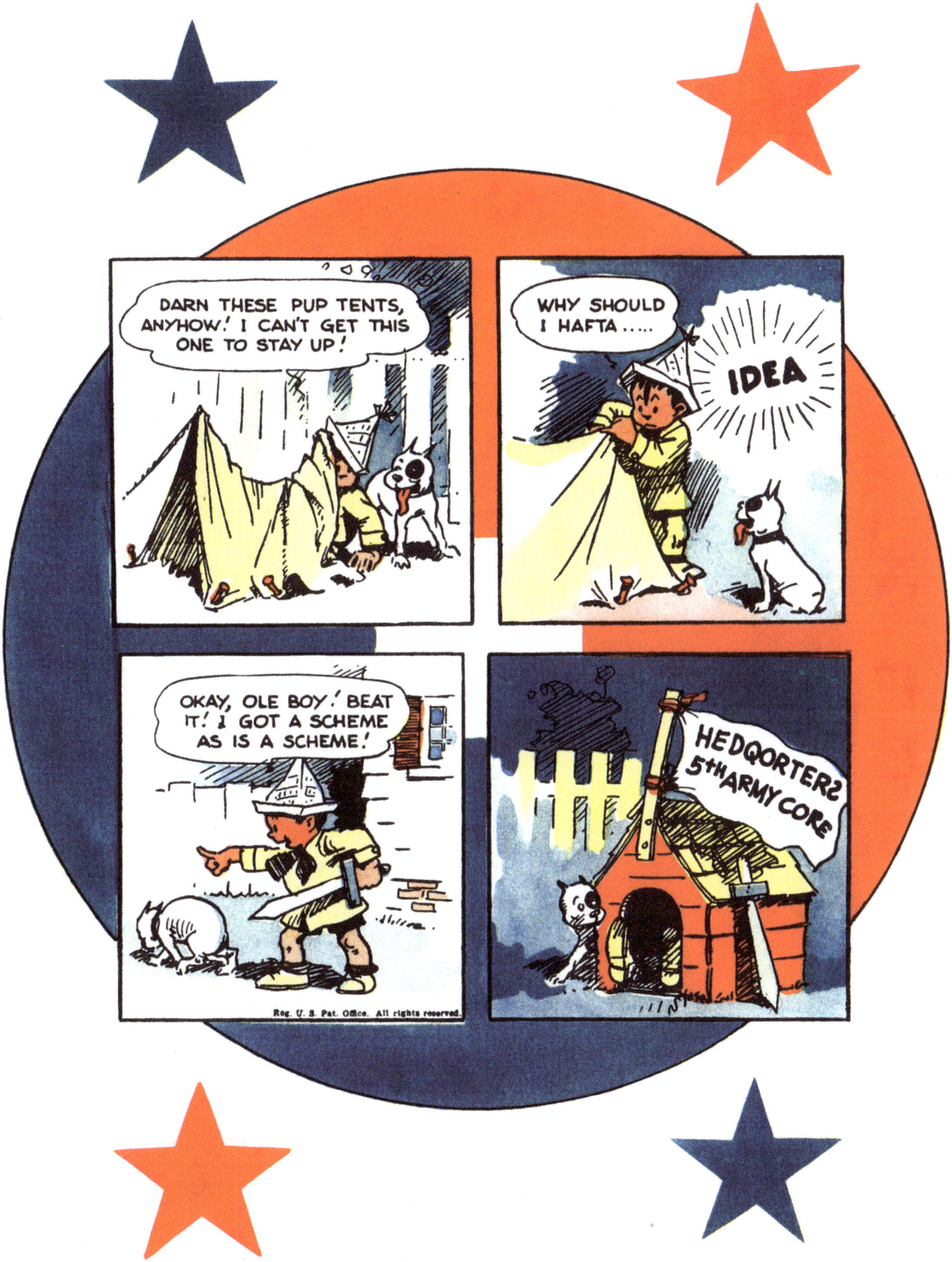
DARN THESE PUP TENTS, ANYHOW! I CAN'T GET THIS ONE TO STAY UP!
WHY SHOULD I HAFTA.....
IDEA
OKAY, OLE BOY! BEAT IT! I GOT A SCHEME AS IS A SCHEME!
Reg. U. S. Pat. Office. All rights reserved.
HEDQORTERS 5th ARMY CORE

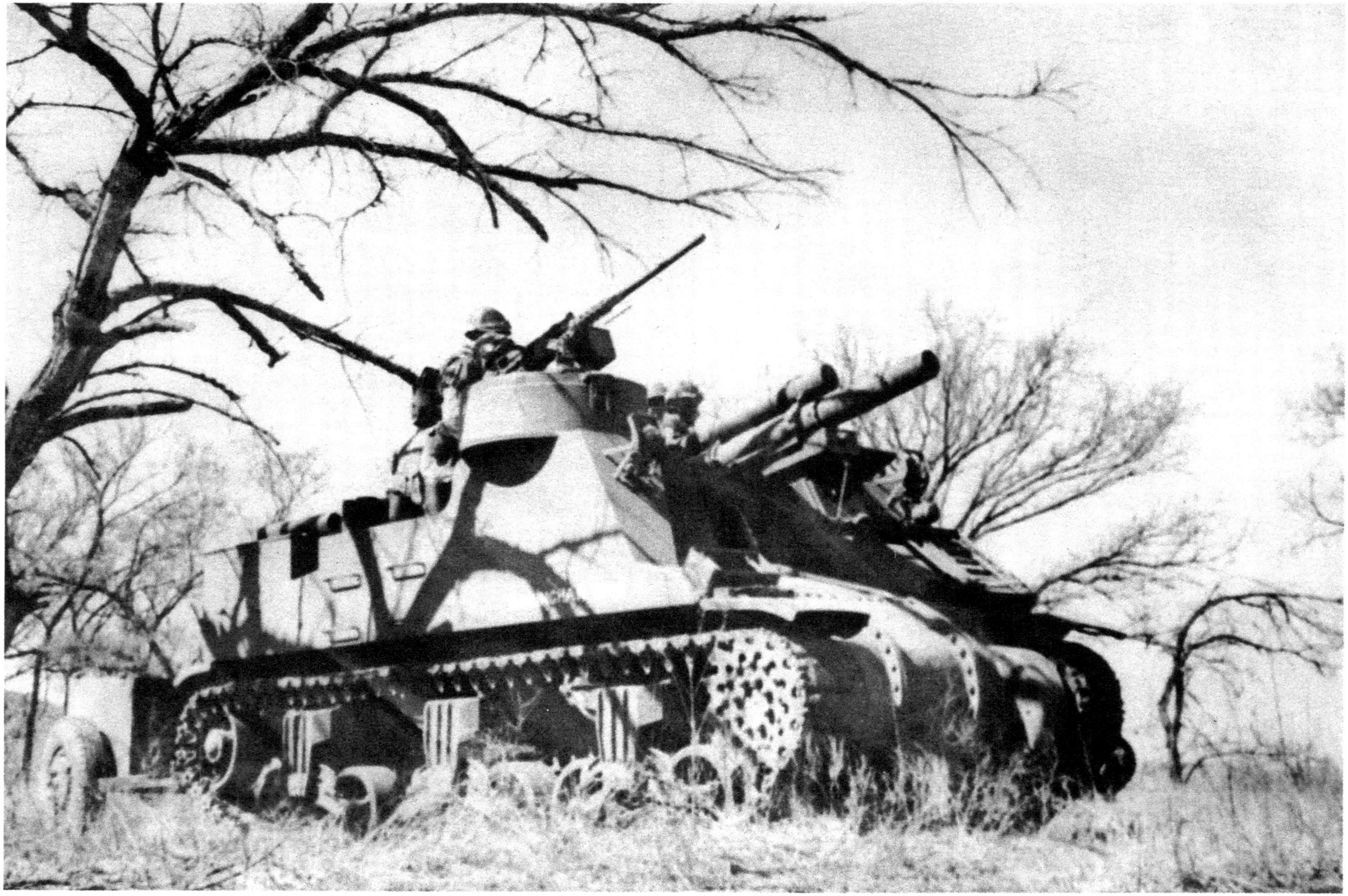

Official Photo: U. S. Army Signal Corps

M-7, Self-propelled Field Artillery on maneuvers at Fort Sill, Oklahoma, . . . "Birmingham Bess" awaits the signal to advance

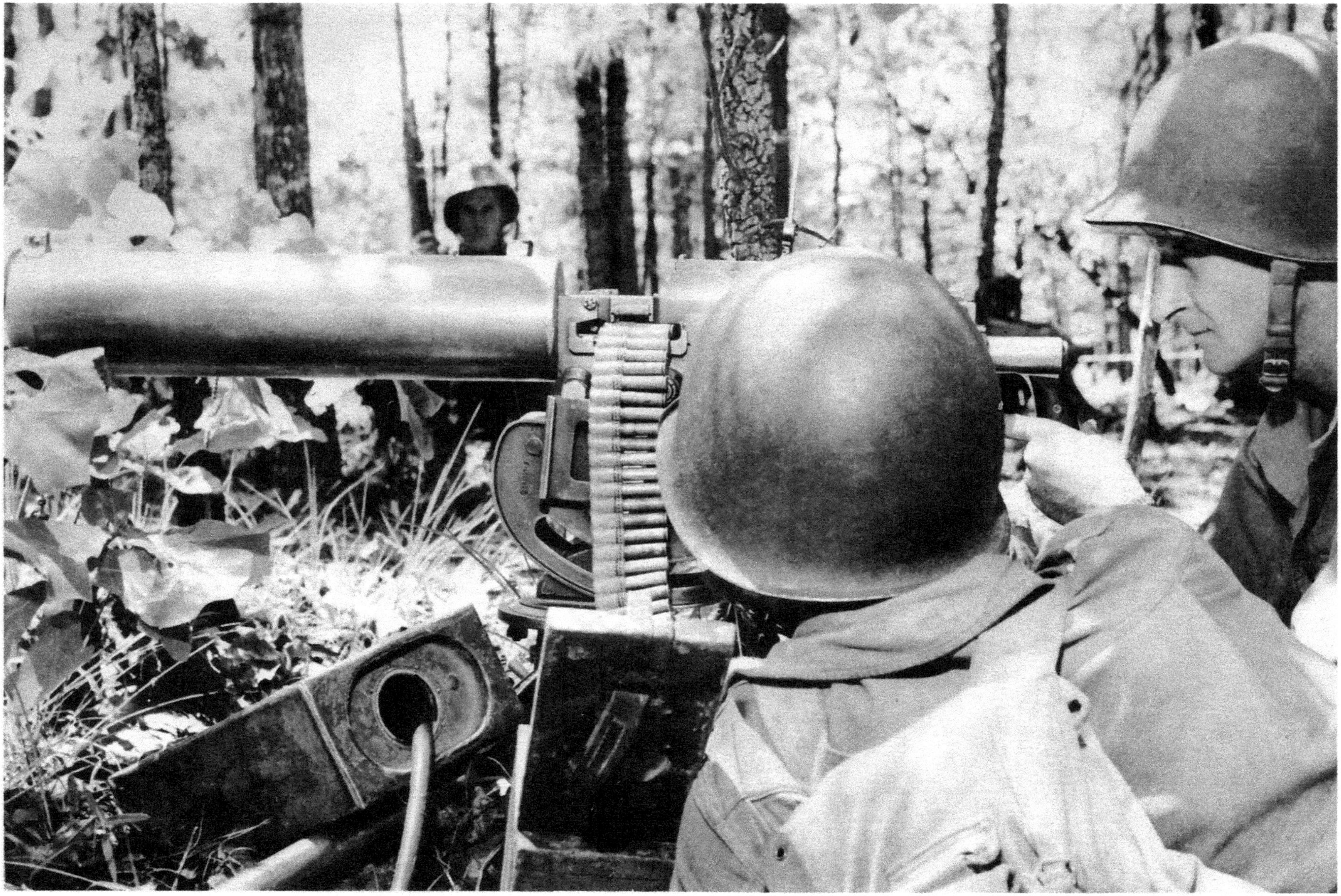

Official Photo: U. S. Army

The Browning Machine Gun, water-cooled, is a .30 calibre weapon weighing 90 pounds and with a cyclic rate of fire of 500 rounds per minute. The water-cooled barrel allows longer periods of sustained fire before the gun has to be dismantled. It is operated by a five-man squad and can be stripped for field repairs with a cartridge for a tool

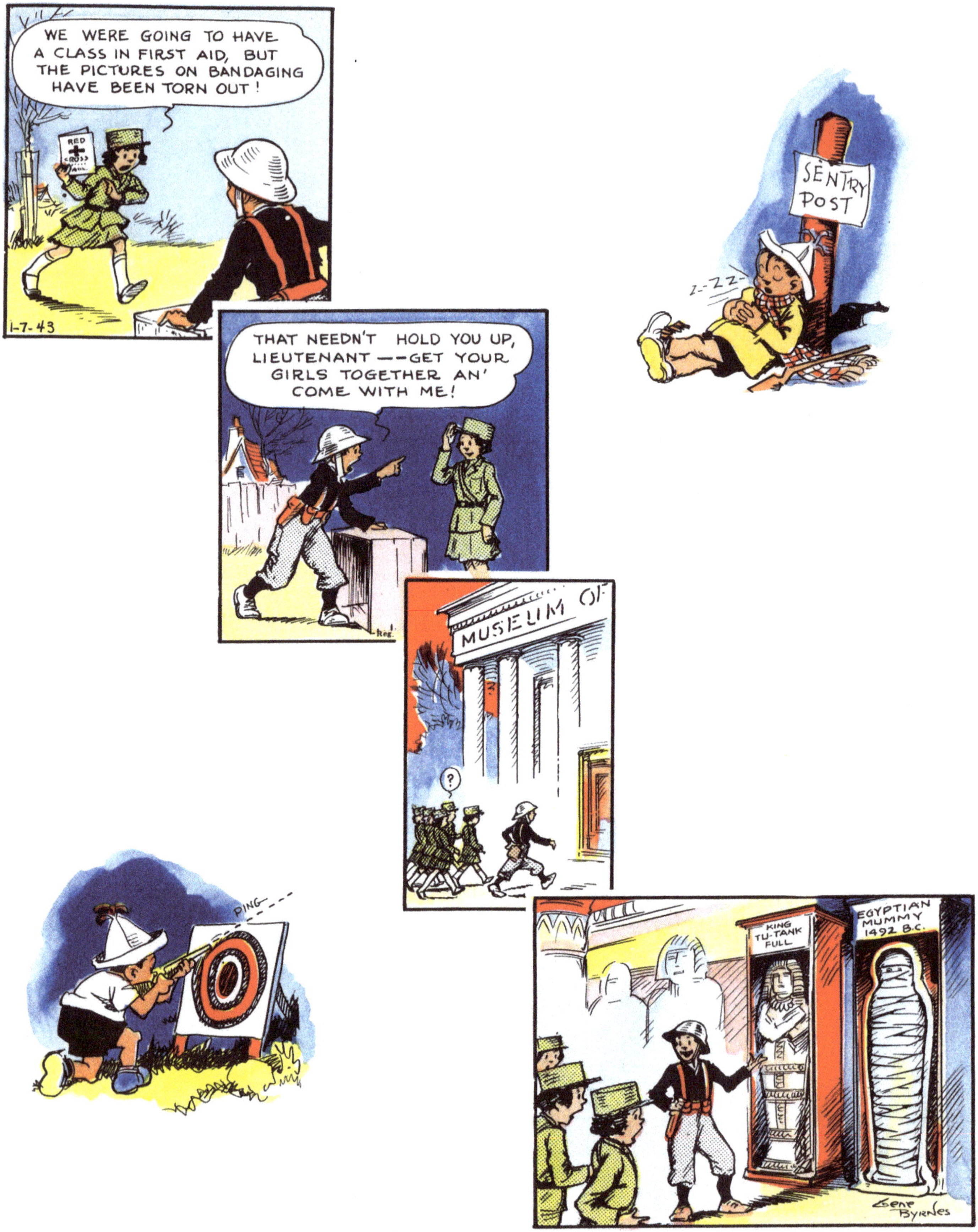
WE WERE GOING TO HAVE A CLASS IN FIRST AID, BUT THE PICTURES ON BANDAGING HAVE BEEN TORN OUT!
1-7-43
SENTRY POST
Z-Z-Z
THAT NEEDN'T HOLD YOU UP, LIEUTENANT --GET YOUR GIRLS TOGETHER AN' COME WITH ME!
MUSEUM OF
?
PING
KING TU-TANK FULL
EGYPTIAN MUMMY 1492 B.C.
GENE BYRNES

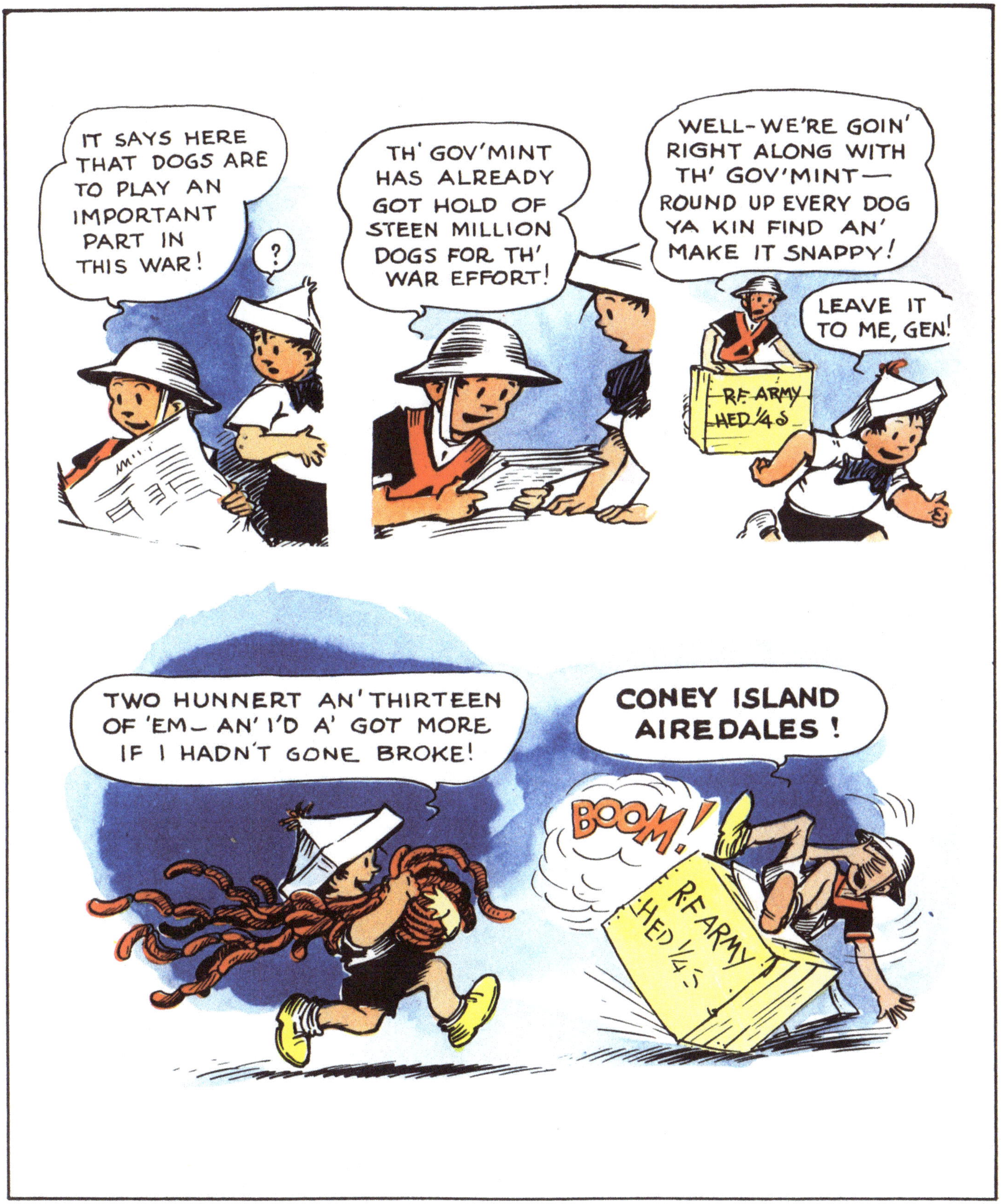
IT SAYS HERE THAT DOGS ARE TO PLAY AN IMPORTANT PART IN THIS WAR!
?
TH' GOV'MINT HAS ALREADY GOT HOLD OF STEEN MILLION DOGS FOR TH' WAR EFFORT!
WELL-WE'RE GOIN' RIGHT ALONG WITH TH' GOV'MINT— ROUND UP EVERY DOG YA KIN FIND AN' MAKE IT SNAPPY!
LEAVE IT TO ME, GEN!
R.F. ARMY HED 1/4 S
TWO HUNNERT AN' THIRTEEN OF 'EM— AN' I'D A' GOT MORE IF I HADN'T GONE BROKE!
CONEY ISLAND AIREDALES!
BOOM!
R.F. ARMY HED 1/4 S

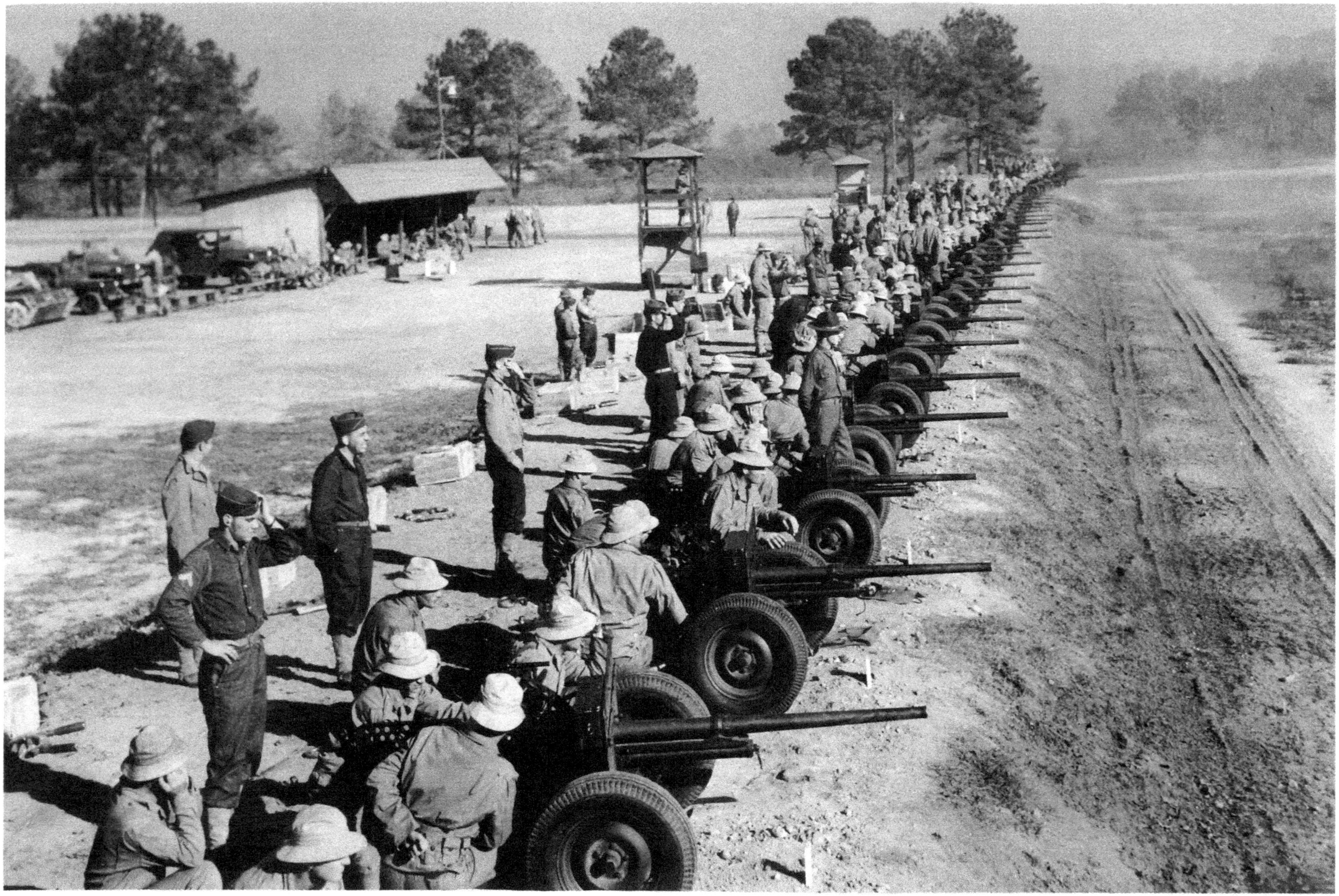

Official Photo: U. S. Army Infantry School

A regiment of 37 mm. anti-tank guns lined up on the target range at a Southern training camp

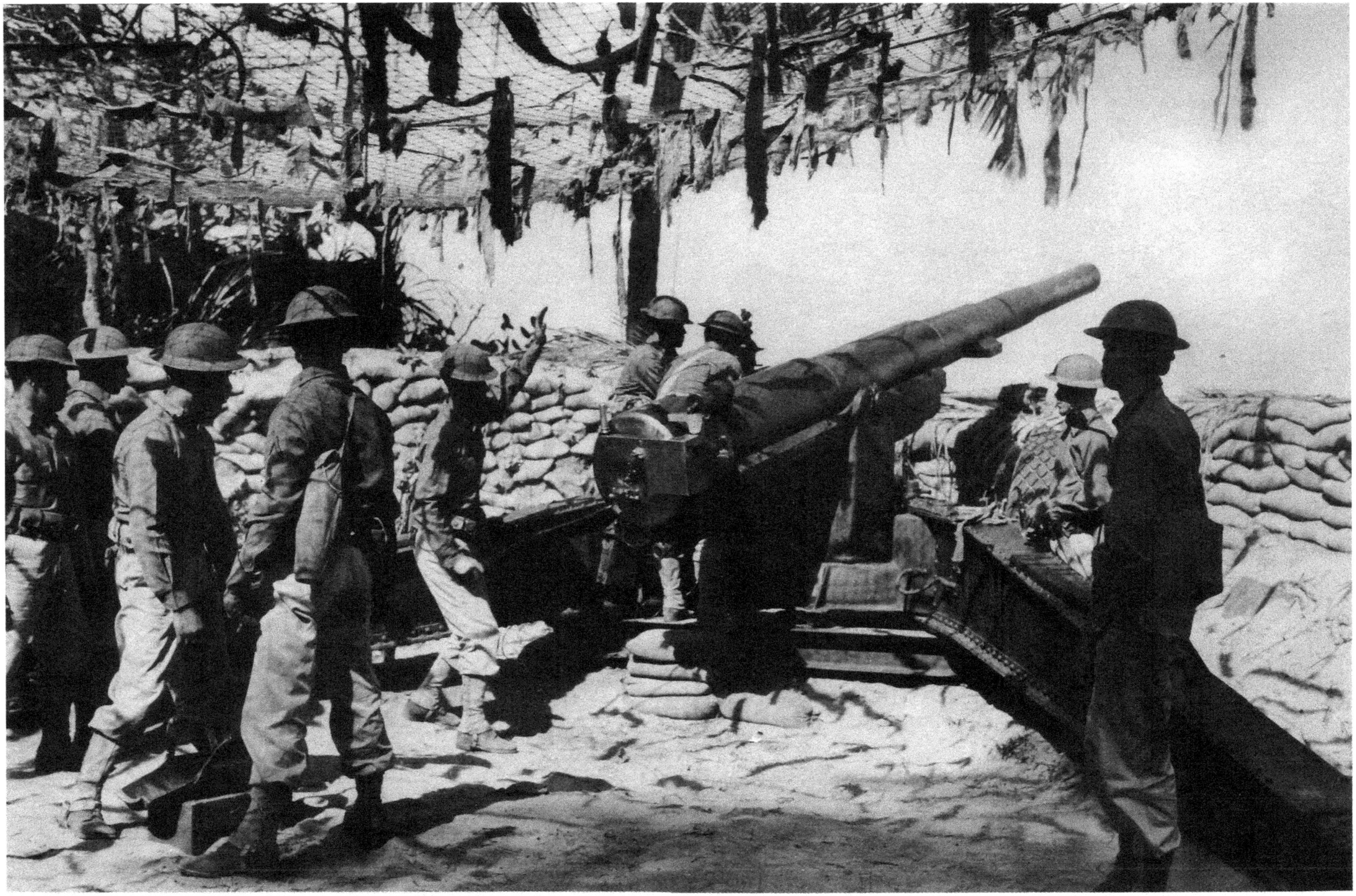

Official Photo: U. S. Army Signal Corps

A camouflaged coast defense gun at a Puerto Rican army base. The gun crew stands by awaiting the command to fire

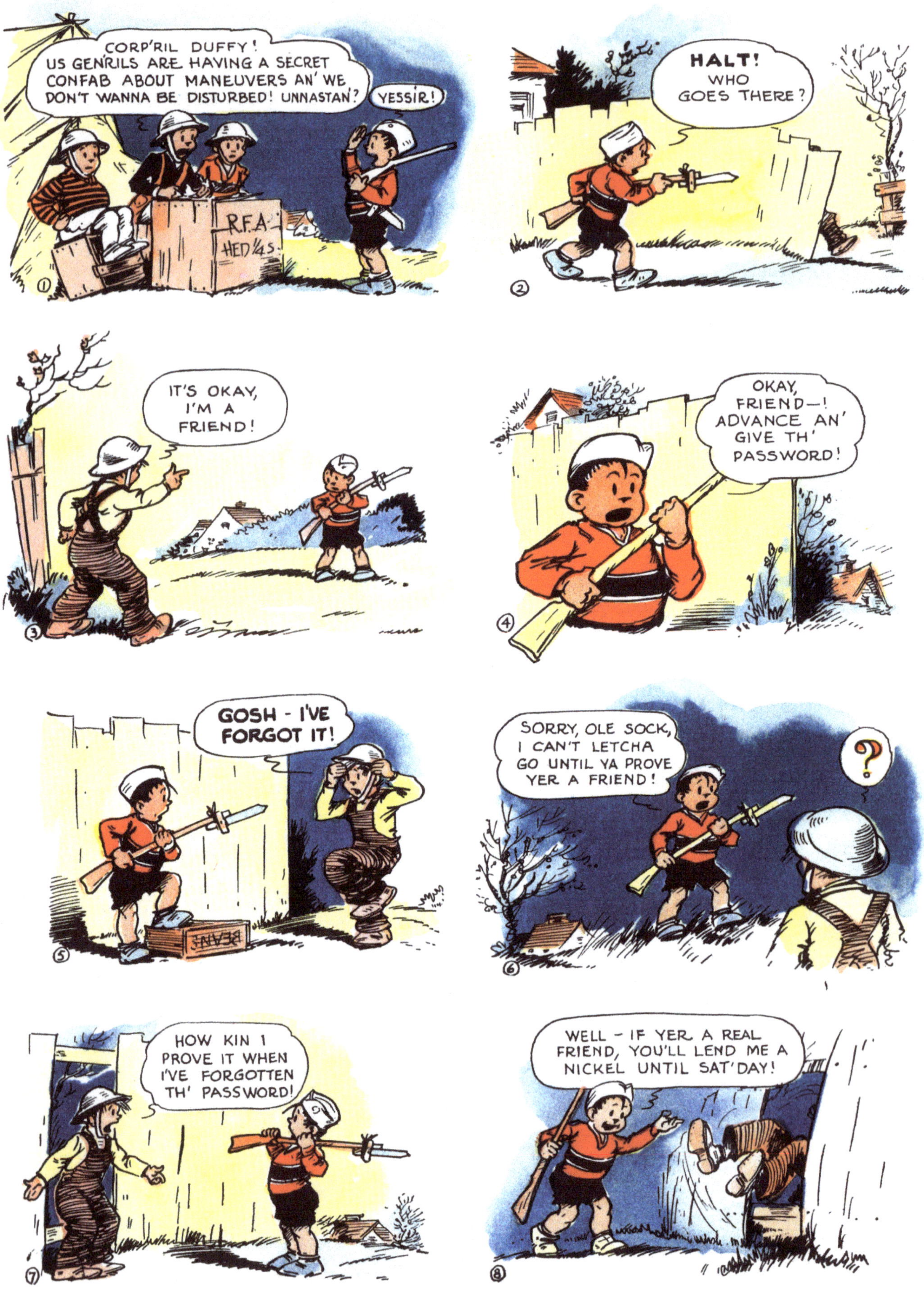
CORP'RIL DUFFY! US GEN'RILS ARE HAVING A SECRET CONFAB ABOUT MANEUVERS AN' WE DON'T WANNA BE DISTURBED! UNNASTAN'?
YESSIR!
R.F.A. HED'Q'S.
HALT! WHO GOES THERE?
IT'S OKAY, I'M A FRIEND!
OKAY, FRIEND—! ADVANCE AN' GIVE TH' PASSWORD!
GOSH - I'VE FORGOT IT!
SORRY, OLE SOCK, I CAN'T LETCHA GO UNTIL YA PROVE YER A FRIEND!
?
HOW KIN I PROVE IT WHEN I'VE FORGOTTEN TH' PASSWORD!
WELL - IF YER A REAL FRIEND, YOU'LL LEND ME A NICKEL UNTIL SAT'DAY!

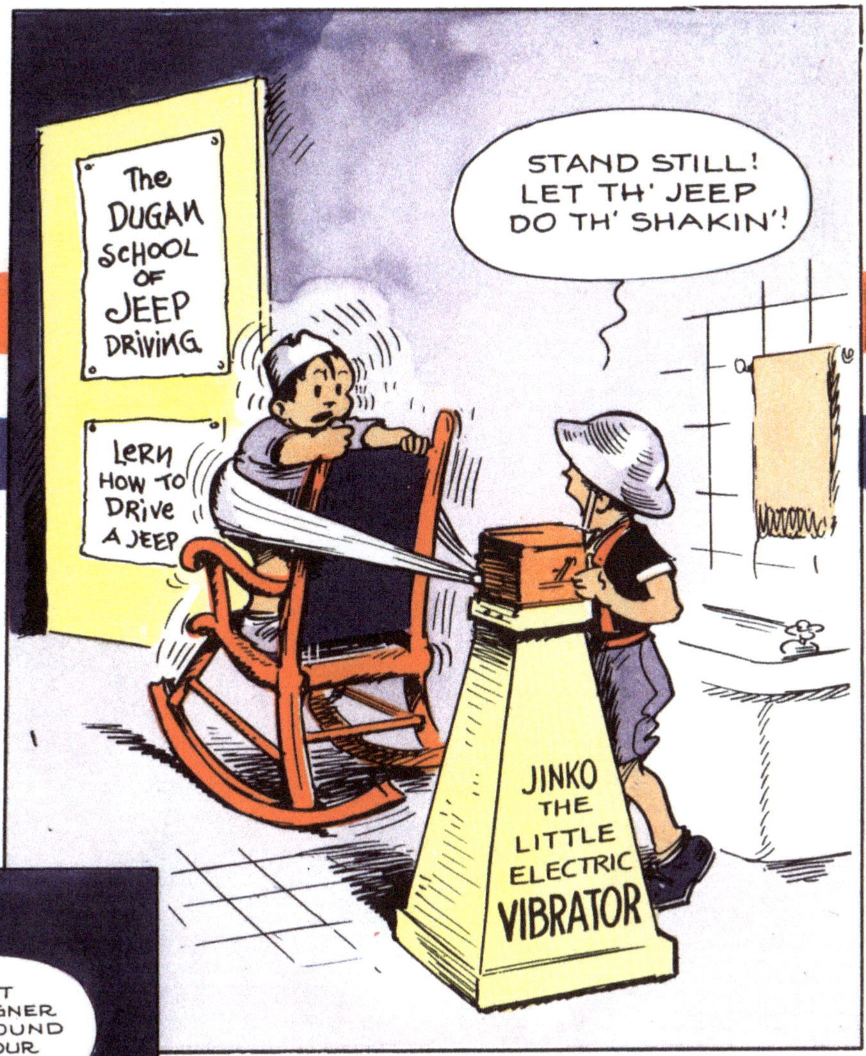
The DUGAN SCHOOL OF JEEP DRIVING
LERN HOW TO DRIVE A JEEP
STAND STILL! LET TH' JEEP DO TH' SHAKIN'!
JINKO THE LITTLE ELECTRIC VIBRATOR

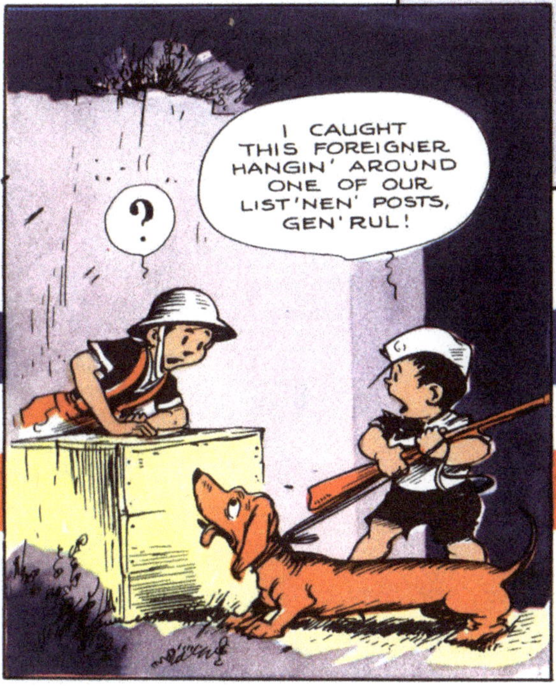
?
I CAUGHT THIS FOREIGNER HANGIN' AROUND ONE OF OUR LIST'NEN' POSTS, GEN'RUL!

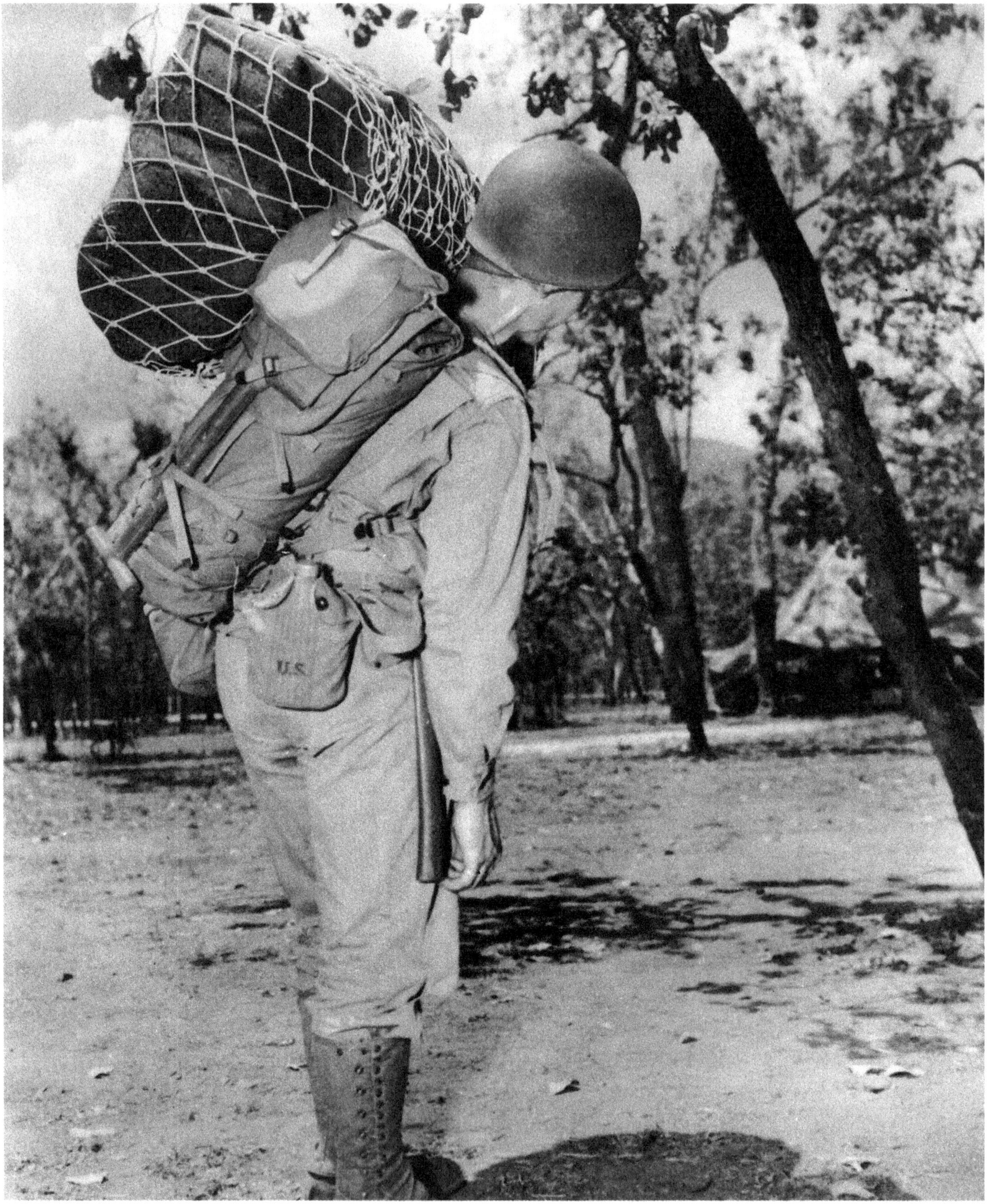

Official Photo: U. S. Army Signal Corps

A soldier in Australia carrying 50 lbs. of portable hospital equipment wrapped in hammock made of netting which is later used as a bed. This is in addition to full pack

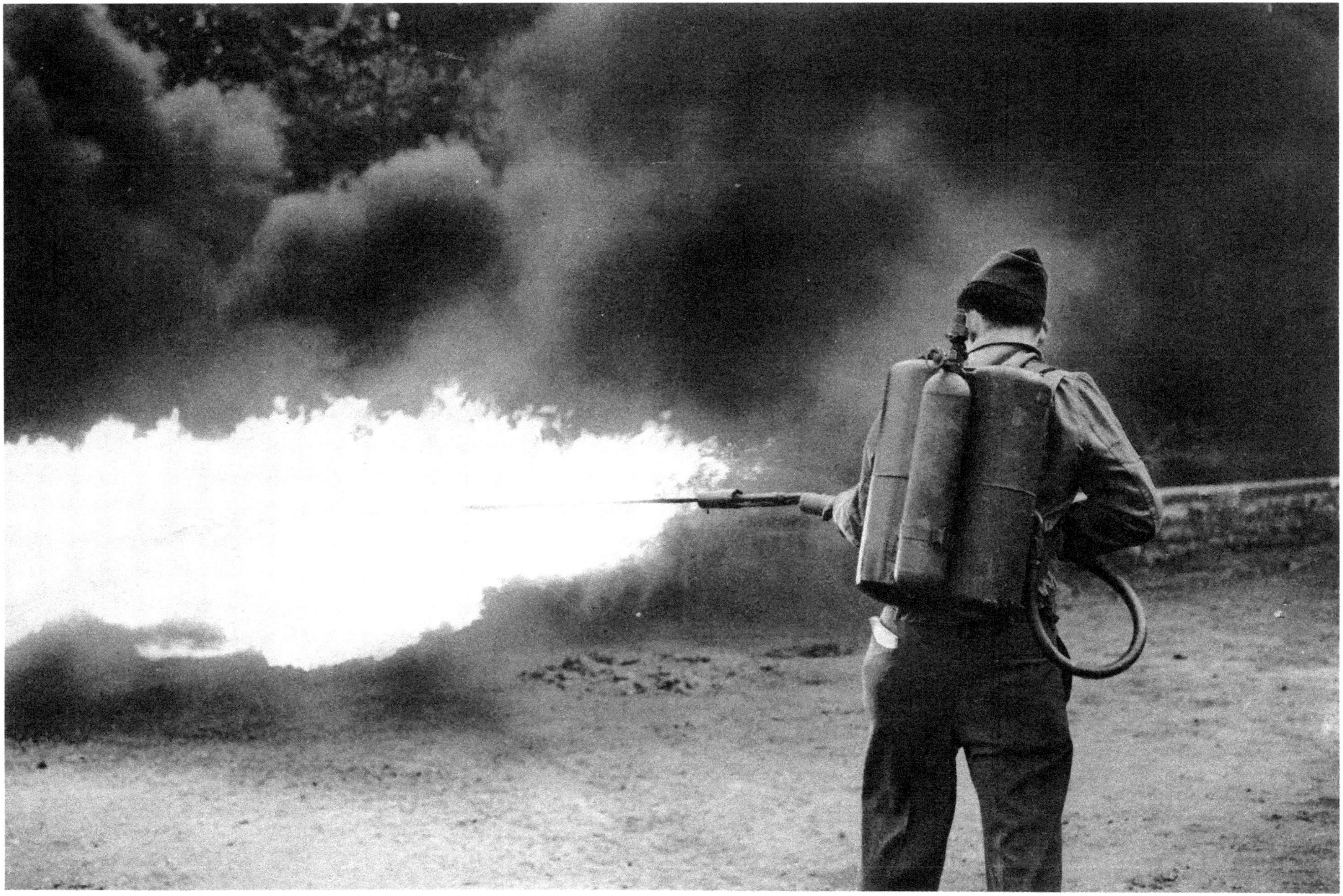

Official Photo: U. S. Army Signal Corps

A demonstration of a flame thrower in action in Northern Iceland. This terrifying weapon is very effective in wiping out machine gun nests and pill boxes

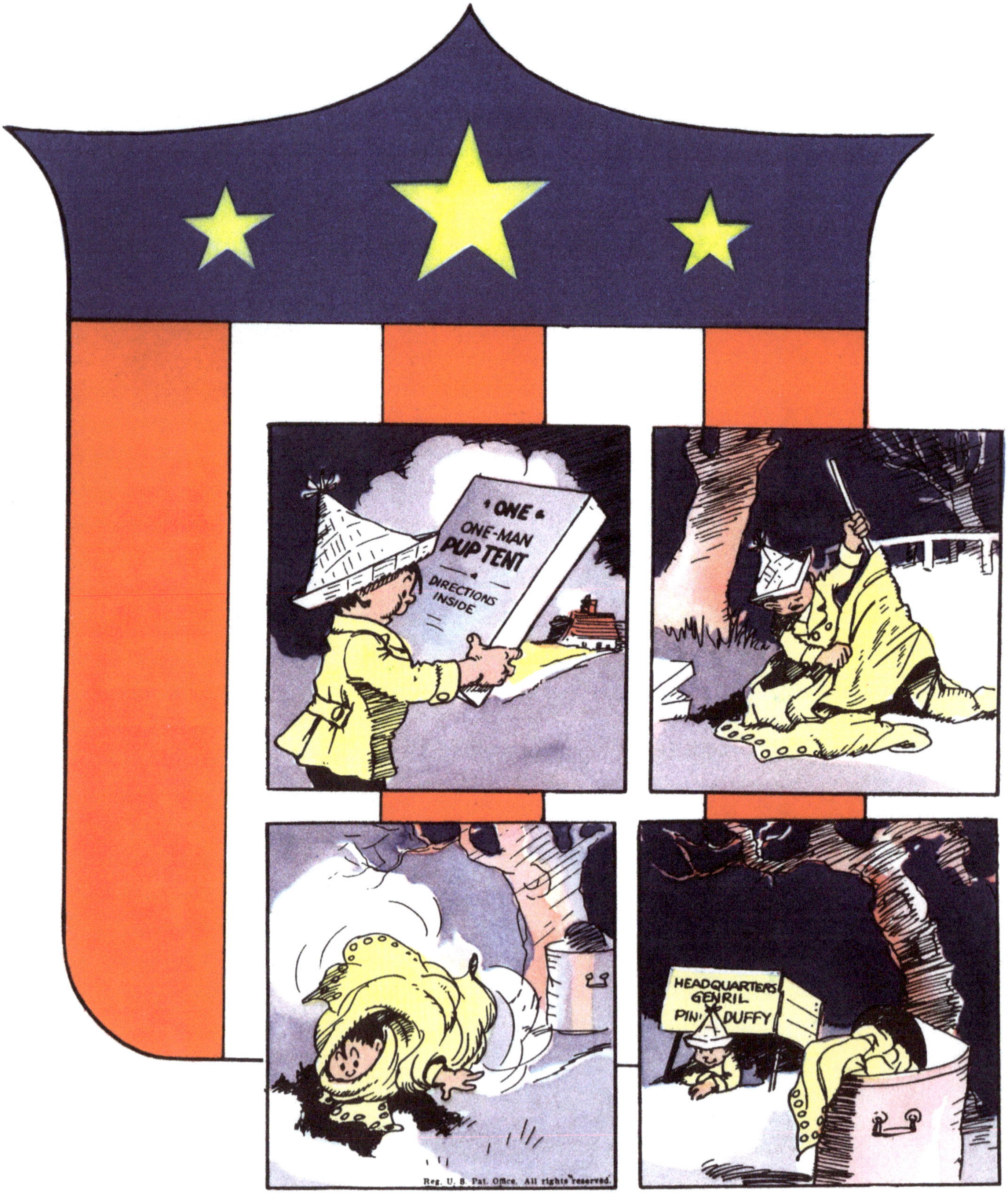
ONE
ONE-MAN PUP TENT
DIRECTIONS INSIDE
HEADQUARTERS GENRIL PIN' DUFFY
Reg. U. S. Pat. Office. All rights reserved.

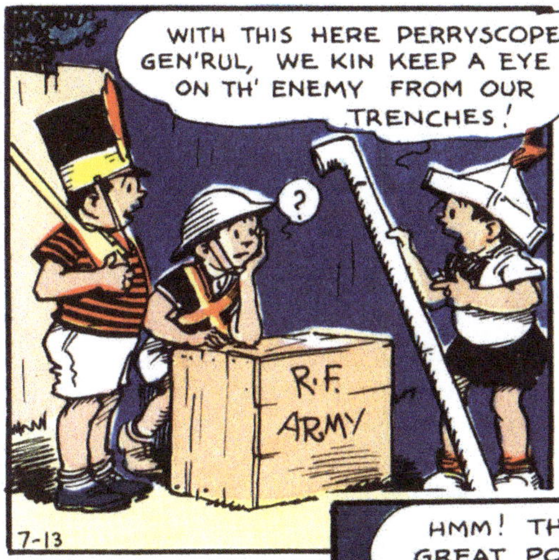
WITH THIS HERE PERRYSCOPE, GEN'RUL, WE KIN KEEP A EYE ON TH' ENEMY FROM OUR TRENCHES!
?
R.F. ARMY
7-13

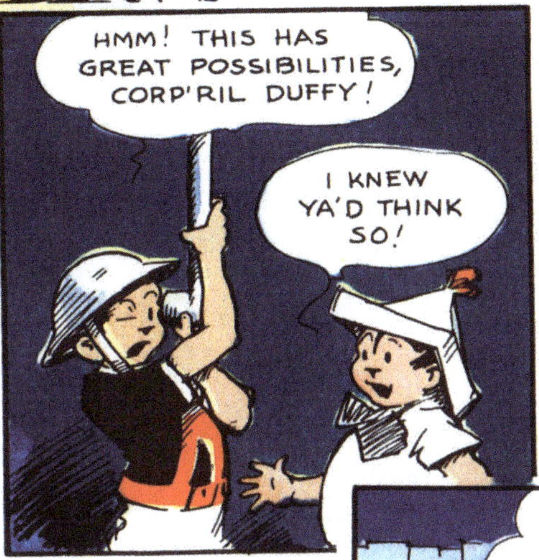
HMM! THIS HAS GREAT POSSIBILITIES, CORP'RIL DUFFY!
I KNEW YA'D THINK SO!

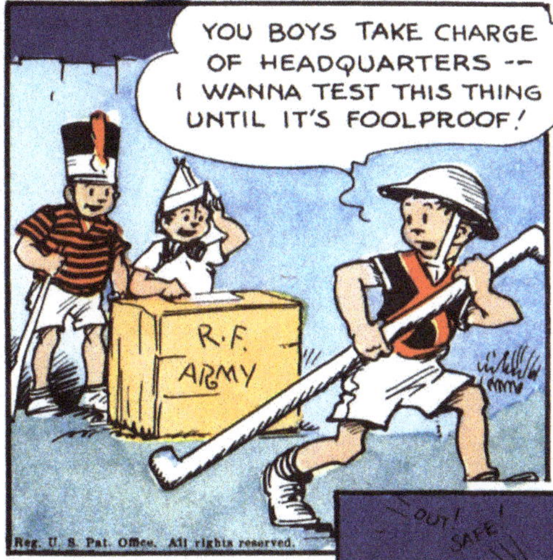
YOU BOYS TAKE CHARGE OF HEADQUARTERS -- I WANNA TEST THIS THING UNTIL IT'S FOOLPROOF!
R.F. ARMY
Reg. U. S. Pat. Office. All rights reserved.

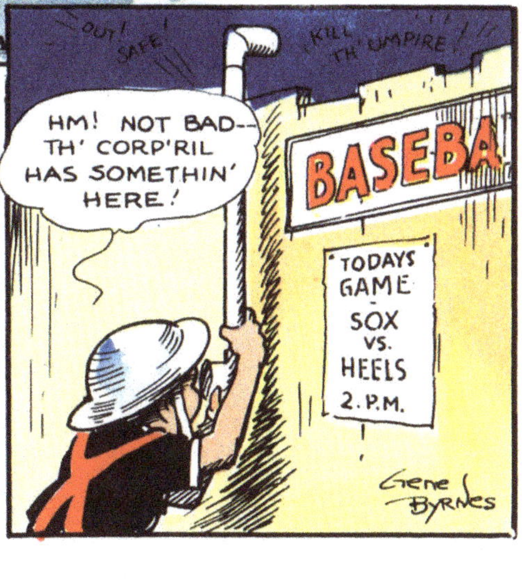
OUT!
SAFE!
KILL TH' UMPIRE!
HM! NOT BAD-- TH' CORP'RIL HAS SOMETHIN' HERE!
BASEBA
TODAYS GAME
SOX VS. HEELS
2. P.M.
Gene Byrnes

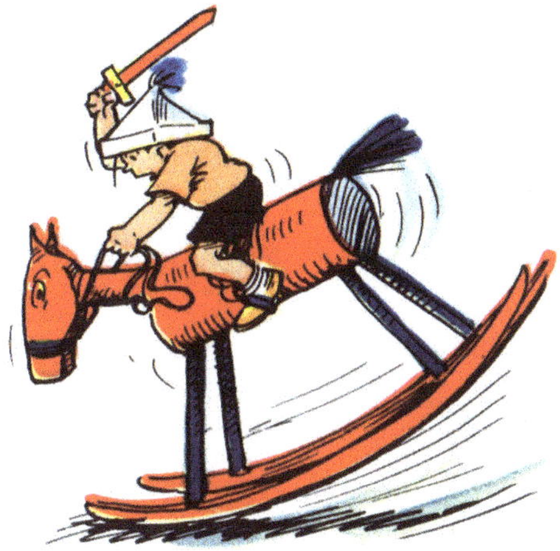

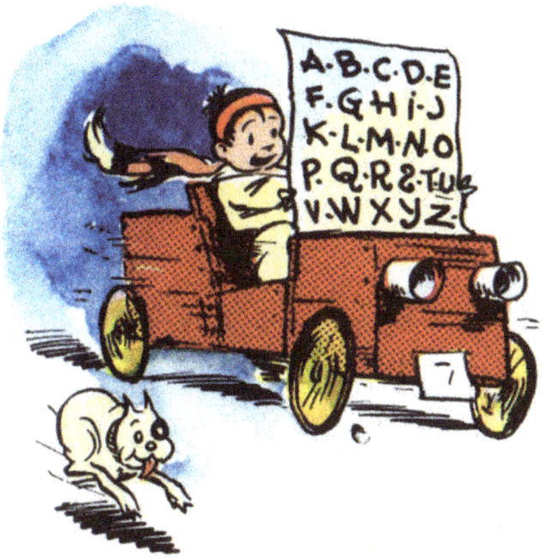
A·B·C·D·E
F·G·H·I·J
K·L·M·N·O
V·W·X·Y·Z

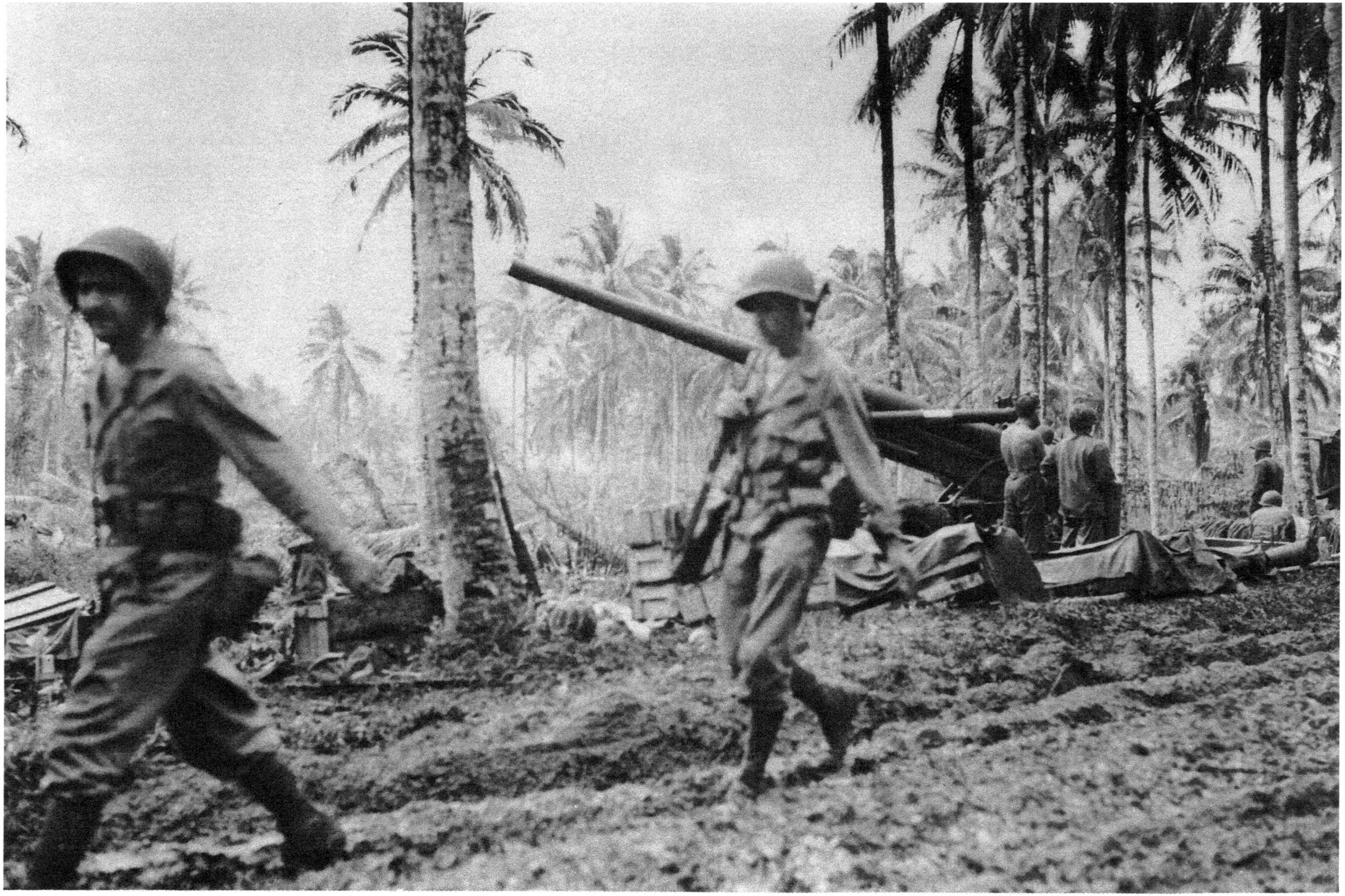

Official Photo: U. S. Army Signal Corps

An American 155 mm. gun blazes away at Japanese positions 11 miles away, somewhere in the South Pacific

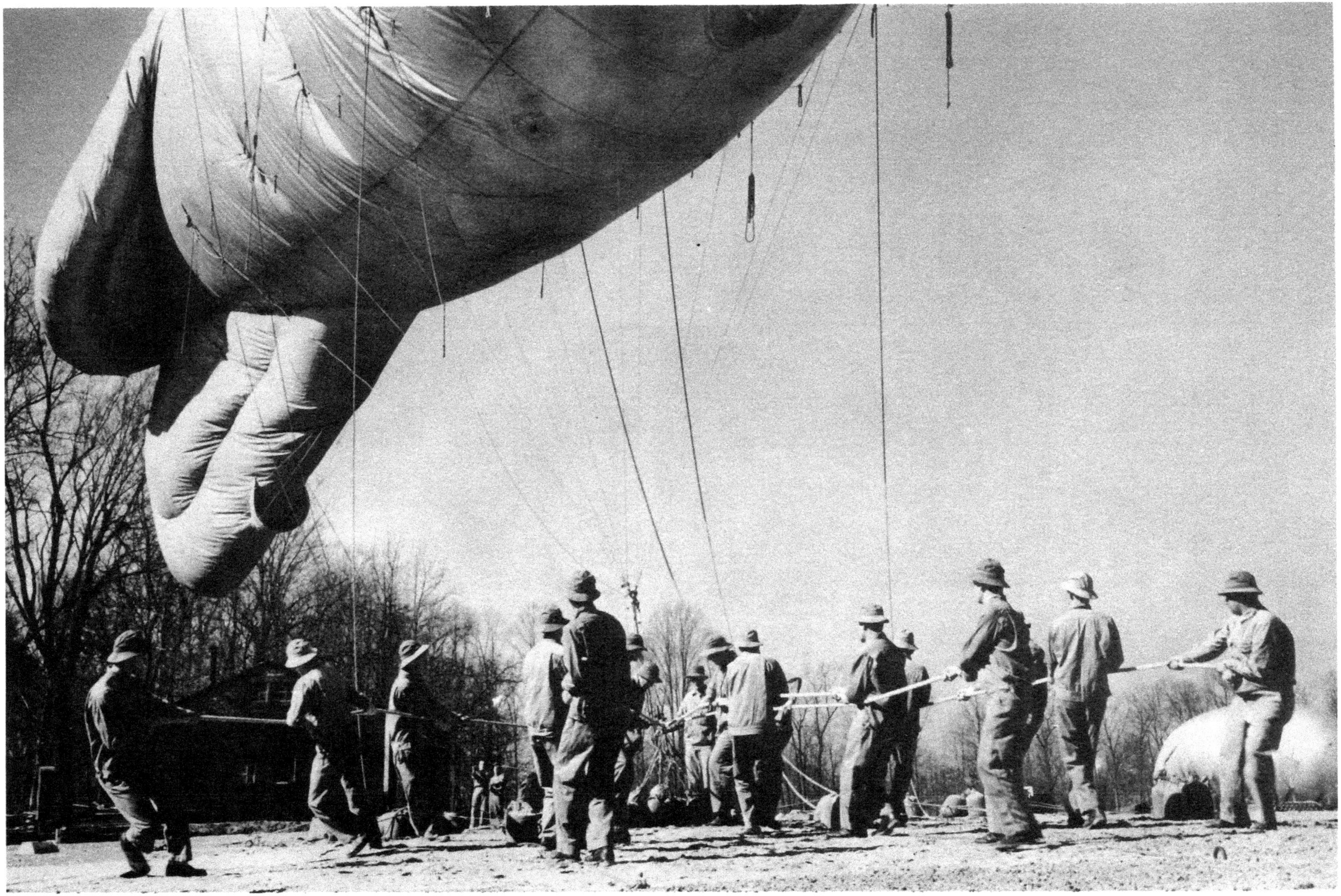

Official Photo: U. S. Army

A barrage balloon and ground crew protecting a vital point in our defense system

REVIEWIN STAND
OFFICERS ONLY

THINK HE'S GOOD ENOUGH FOR OUR ARMY GEN'RUL?
TAKE 'IM AWAY- HE'S TOO GOOD!

I NEED A GUY WITH GOOD EYESIGHT FOR A EXTER-SPECIAL MISSION!
NOT ME, GEN! I'M NEARSIGHTED!
PHOOEY! WE'LL GIVE YOU A EYE TEST-- YOU CAN'T DODGE DUTY WHILE I'M AROUND!
X-Q-J Z-B-F R...
STOP! STOP! THA'S ENOUGH! YOU WON'T DO!
A B C D E F G H I J K L
HEY! LOOKIT THAT SIGN ON TH' TRUCK OVER THERE -- "FREE ICE-CREAM CONES AT FINEBERG'S!"

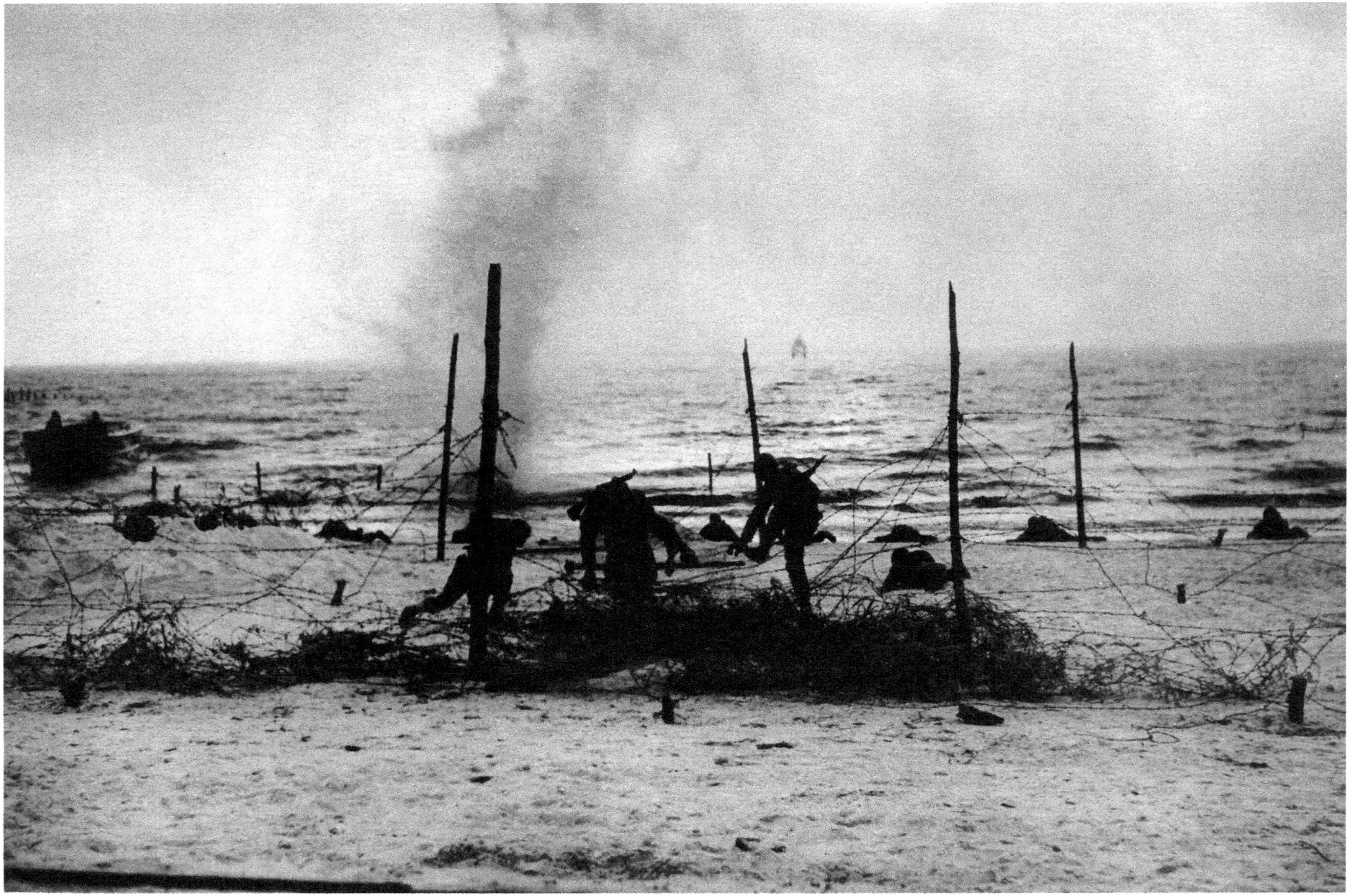

Official Photo: U. S. Army Signal Corps

Engineer Amphibian Command—the Army's newest streamlined combat force, headed by Brigadier General David A. D. Ogden, Camp Gordon Johnston, Fla., . . . Infantry advance thru fire (on stomachs) live ammunition machine firing close above their heads 42

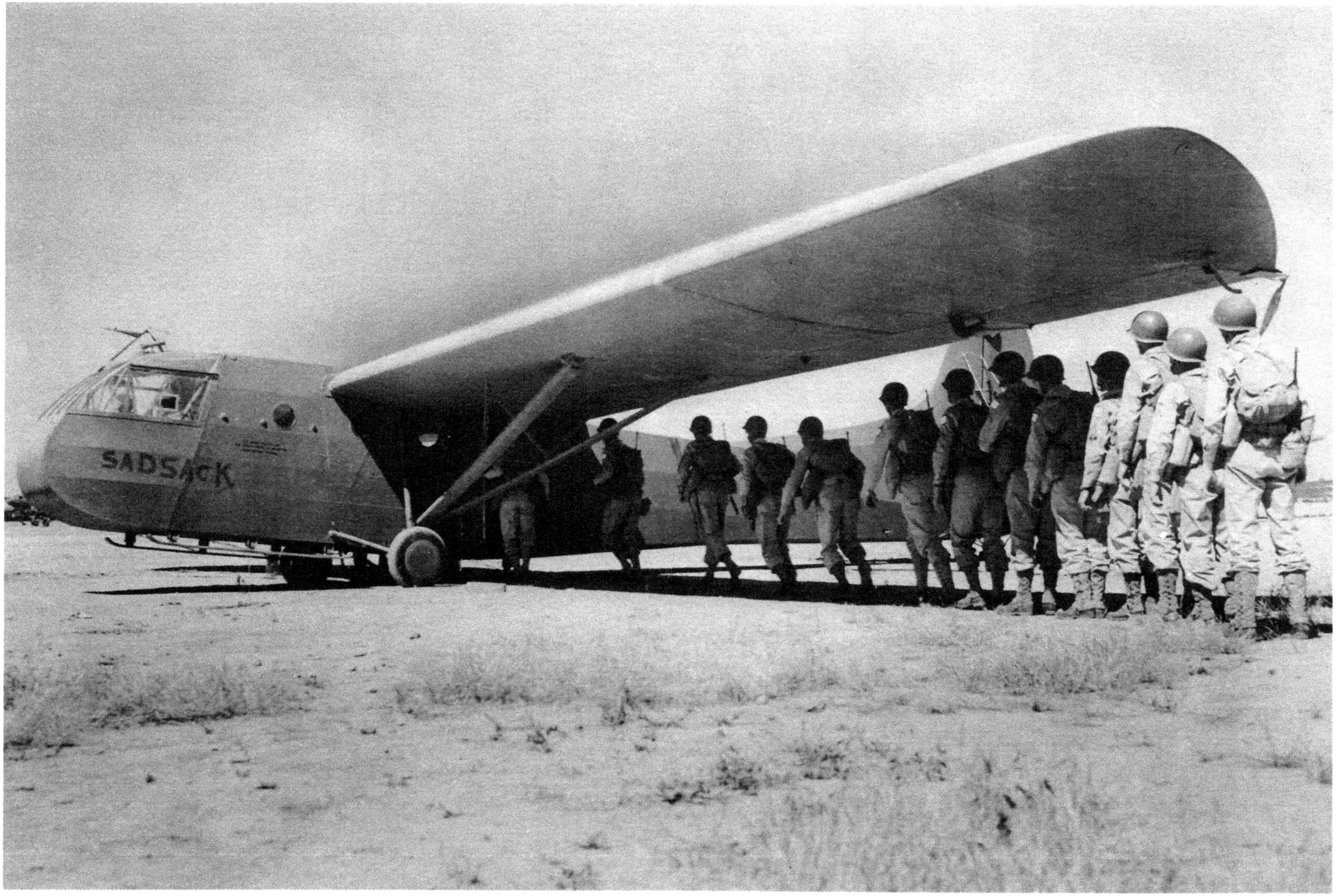
SADSACK

Official Photo: U. S. Army Signal Corps

Airborne infantry boarding a troop carrier for invasion

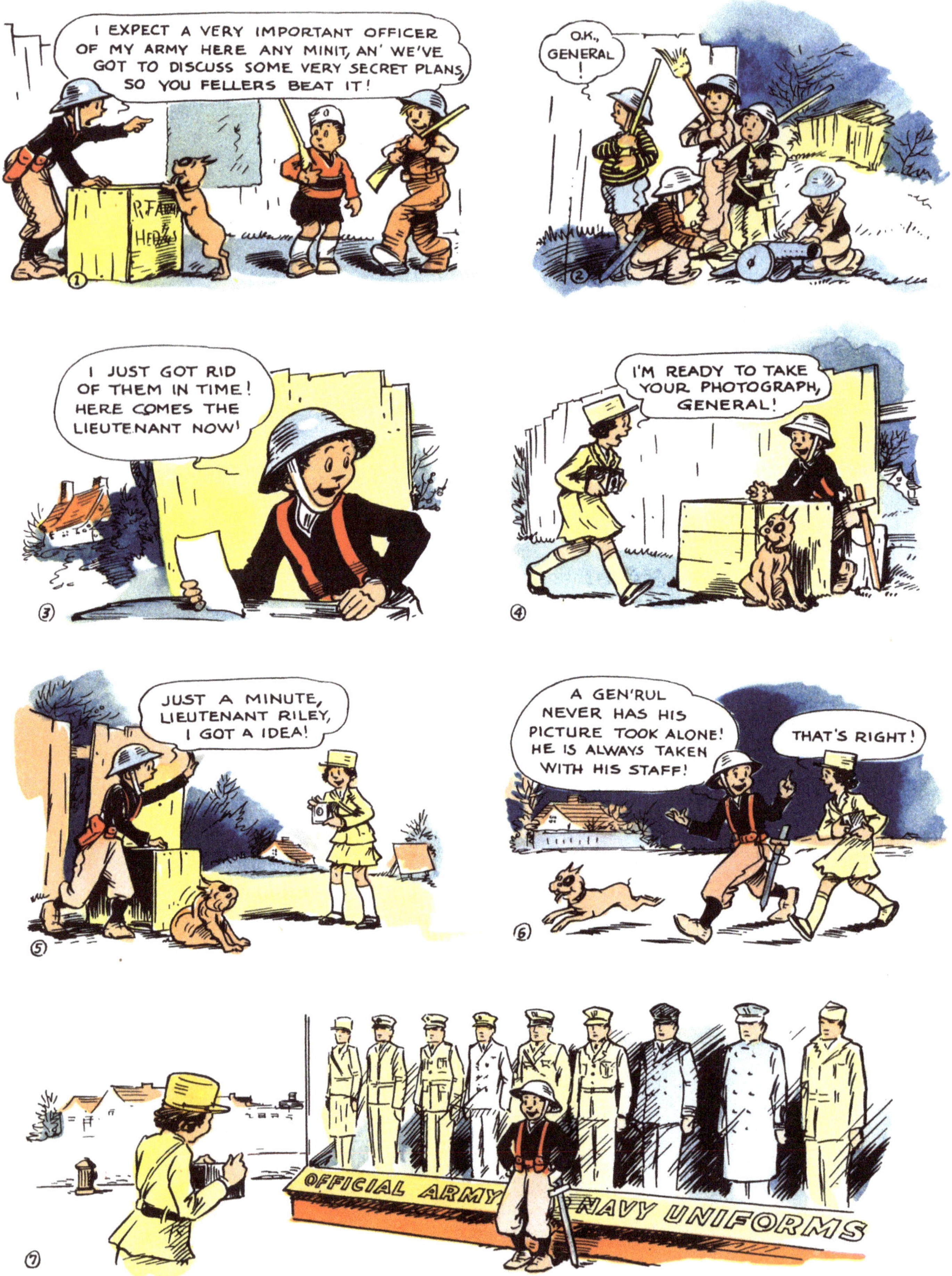
I EXPECT A VERY IMPORTANT OFFICER OF MY ARMY HERE ANY MINIT, AN' WE'VE GOT TO DISCUSS SOME VERY SECRET PLANS, SO YOU FELLERS BEAT IT!
O.K., GENERAL!
I JUST GOT RID OF THEM IN TIME! HERE COMES THE LIEUTENANT NOW!
I'M READY TO TAKE YOUR PHOTOGRAPH, GENERAL!
JUST A MINUTE, LIEUTENANT RILEY, I GOT A IDEA!
A GEN'RUL NEVER HAS HIS PICTURE TOOK ALONE! HE IS ALWAYS TAKEN WITH HIS STAFF!
THAT'S RIGHT!
OFFICIAL ARMY NAVY UNIFORMS

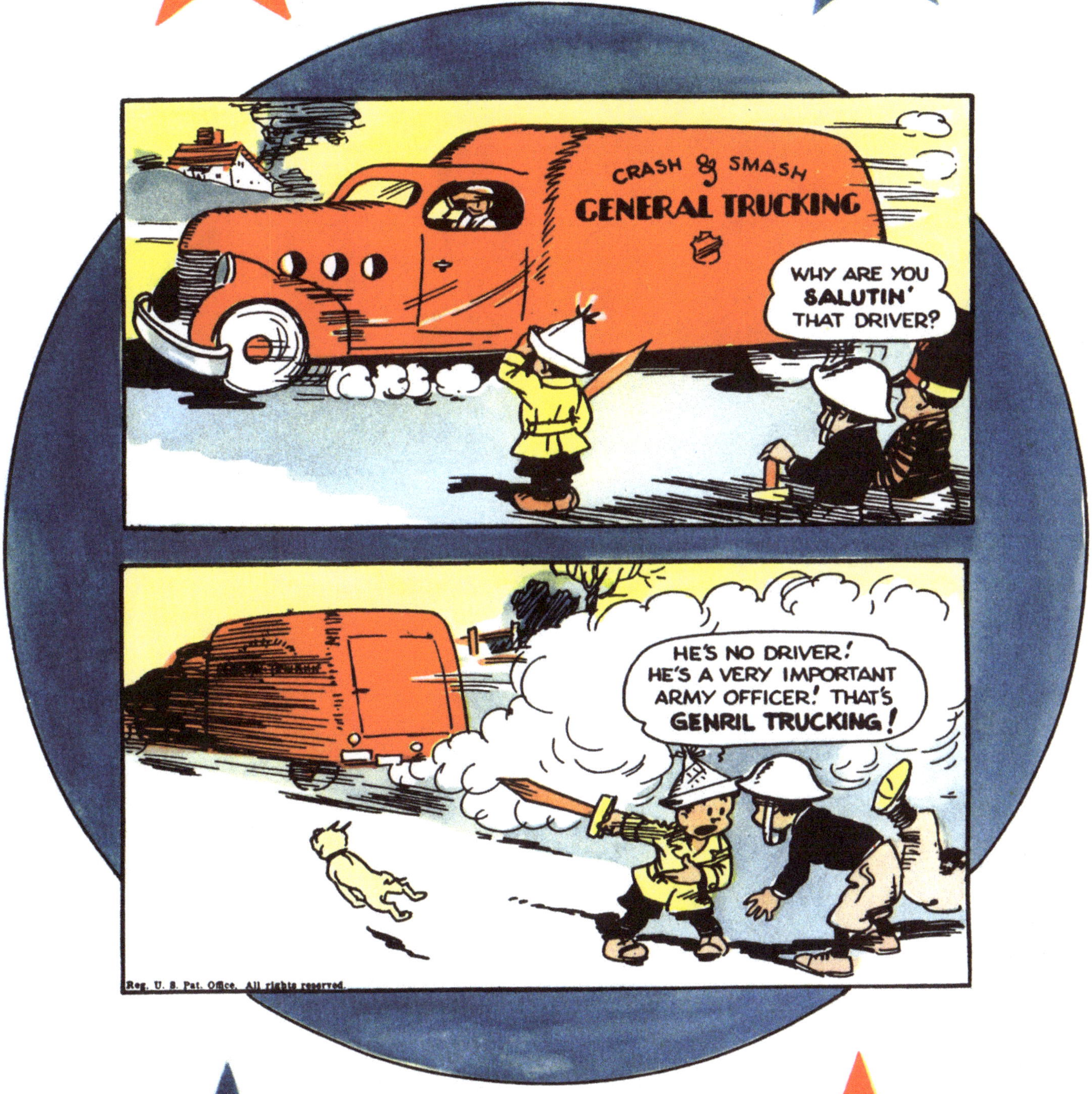
CRASH & SMASH
GENERAL TRUCKING
WHY ARE YOU SALUTIN' THAT DRIVER?
HE'S NO DRIVER! HE'S A VERY IMPORTANT ARMY OFFICER! THAT'S GENRIL TRUCKING!
Reg. U. S. Pat. Office. All rights reserved.

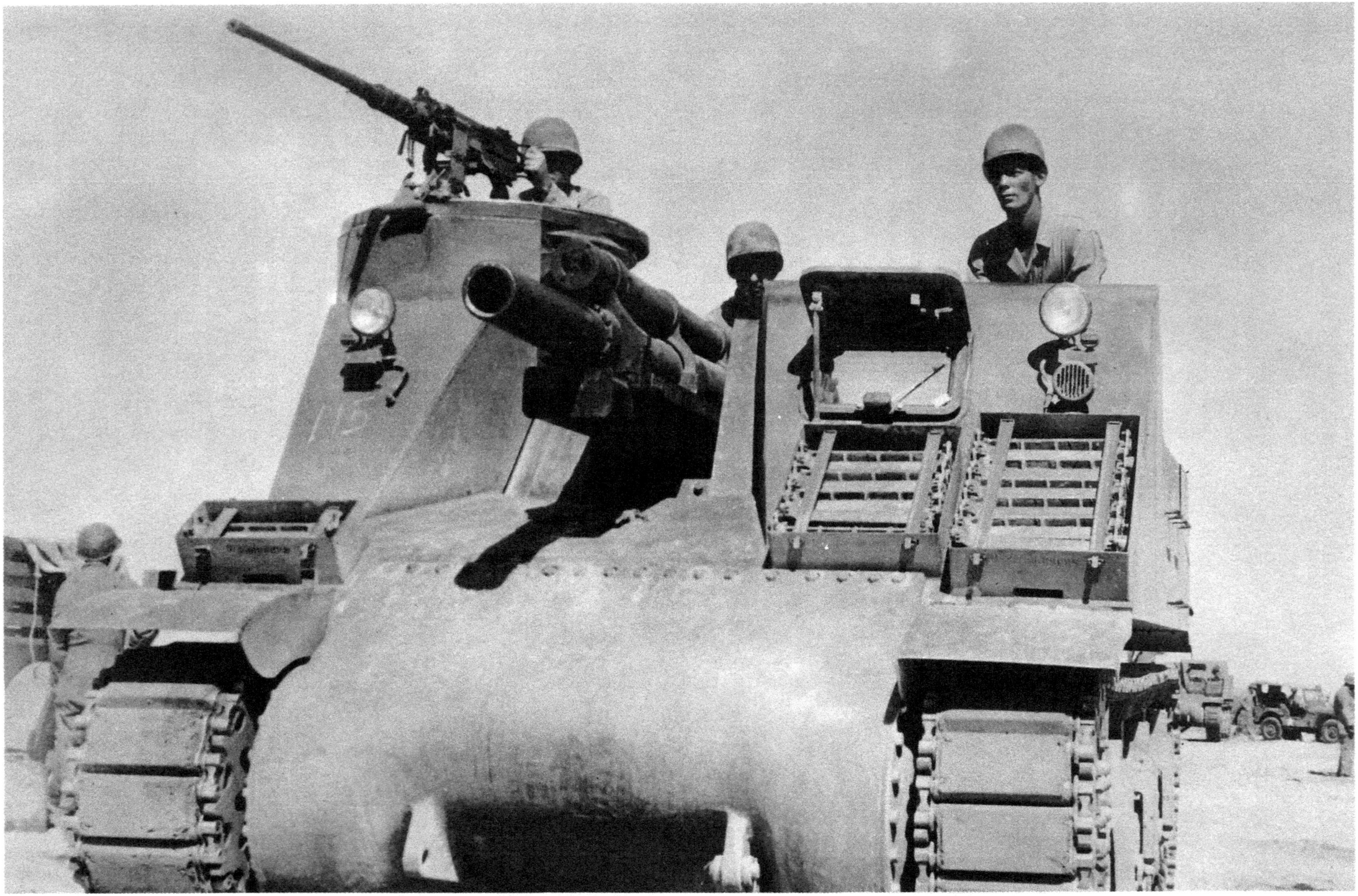

Official Photo: U. S. Army Signal Corps

One of the army's powerful tank destroyers, the M-7, drilling in the desert near the Iron Mountains in California. It is armed with a 105 mm. Howitzer and a .50 caliber automatic gun

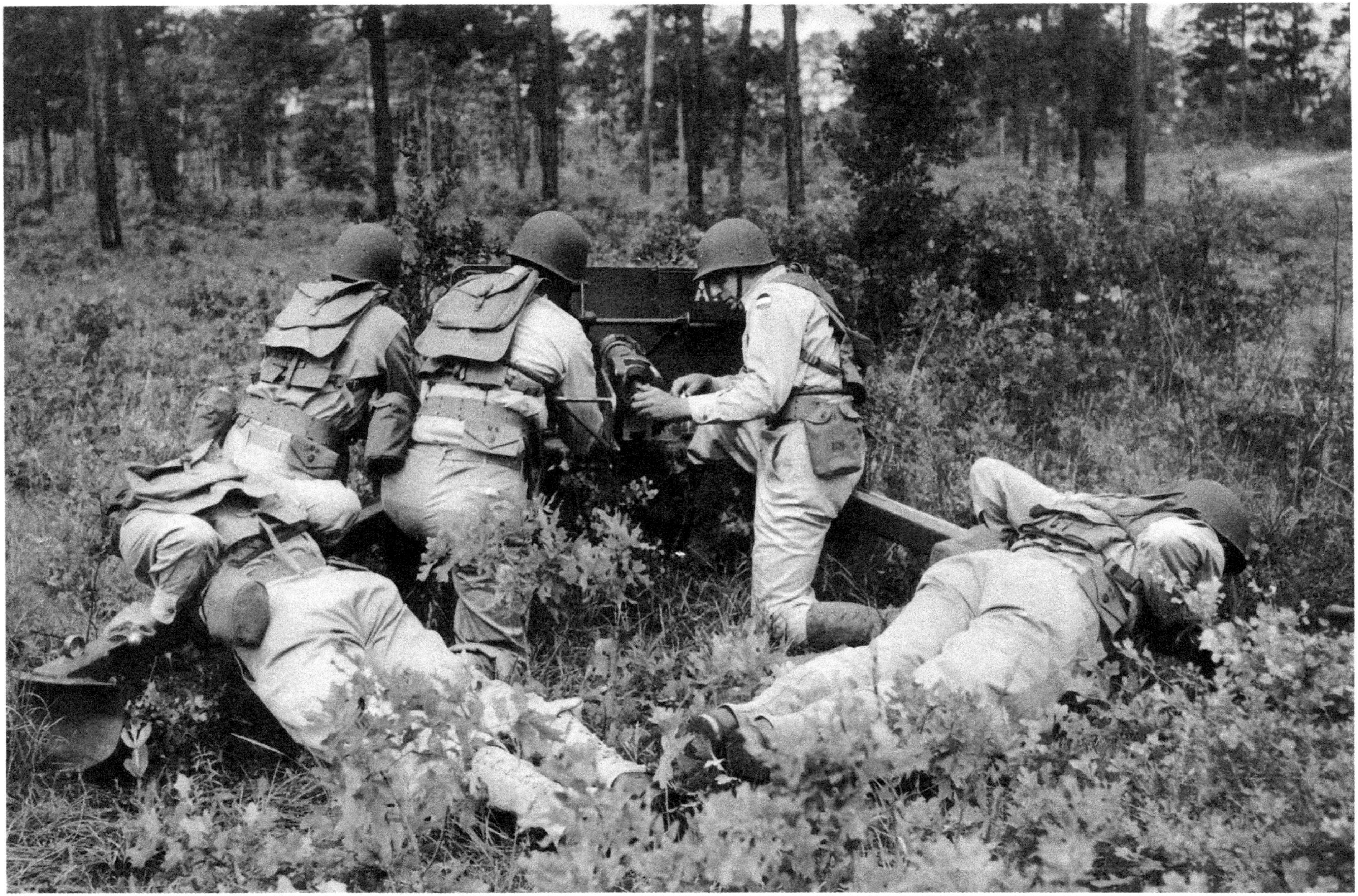

Official Photo: U. S. Army Infantry School

Infantry men operating a 37 mm. anti-tank gun. Two soldiers bear down on the gun trails to force them into the ground

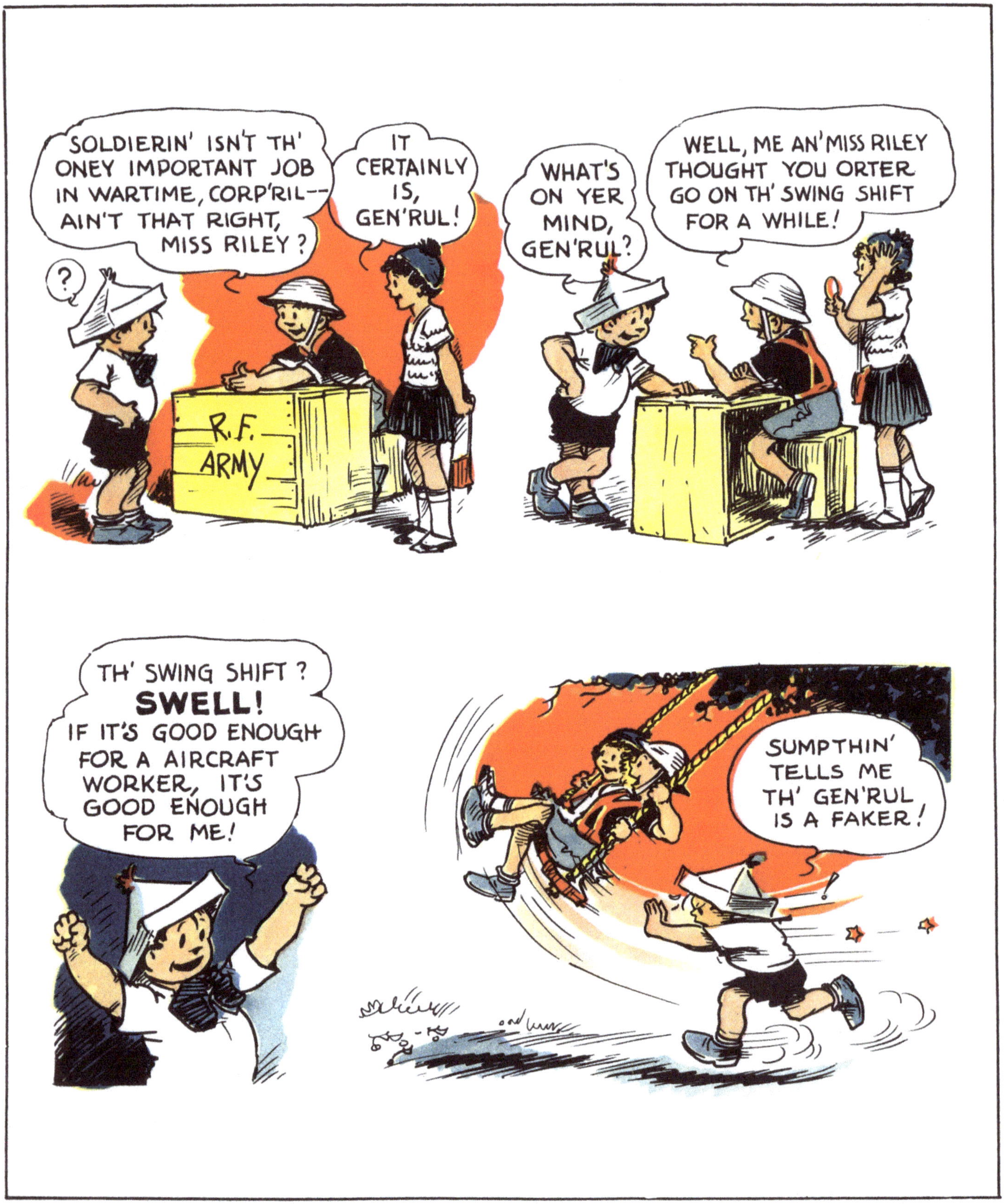

SOLDIERIN' ISN'T TH' ONEY IMPORTANT JOB IN WARTIME, CORP'RIL-- AIN'T THAT RIGHT, MISS RILEY ?
IT CERTAINLY IS, GEN'RUL!
?
R. F. ARMY
WHAT'S ON YER MIND, GEN'RUL?
WELL, ME AN' MISS RILEY THOUGHT YOU ORTER GO ON TH' SWING SHIFT FOR A WHILE!
TH' SWING SHIFT ? **SWELL!** IF IT'S GOOD ENOUGH FOR A AIRCRAFT WORKER, IT'S GOOD ENOUGH FOR ME!
SUMPTHIN' TELLS ME TH' GEN'RUL IS A FAKER!

ICE CREAM
'PSST—! WE'VE HOOKED SOMEONE!
CANDY & SODA
SODA
NoTize US 2 EXPERINSED SoLDiers WiLL ACK AS A CONVOY FOR KIDS KARRYIN CANDY - PRICE CANDY one peece each ice CREAM cones one Lick each.

STAND FIRM BODY GUARD— YOU'VE GOT NOTHIN' T' WORRY ABOUT, - Y'R GEN'RIL'S RIGHT BEHIND YOU!
I RESIGN!
SOCK!
OUCH!

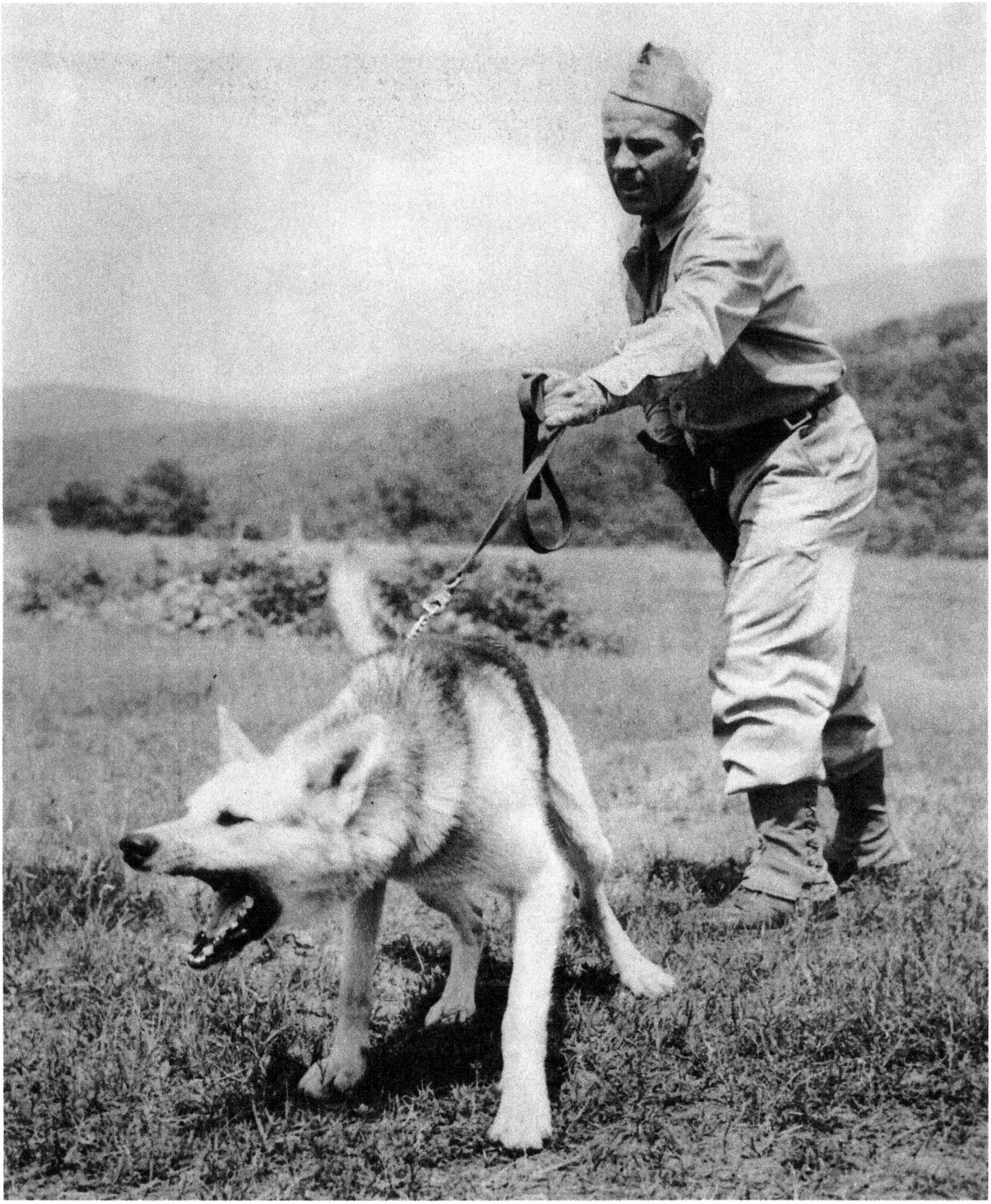

Official Photo: U. S. Army Signal Corps

In vigilance a soldier and a trained war dog together are equal to six men

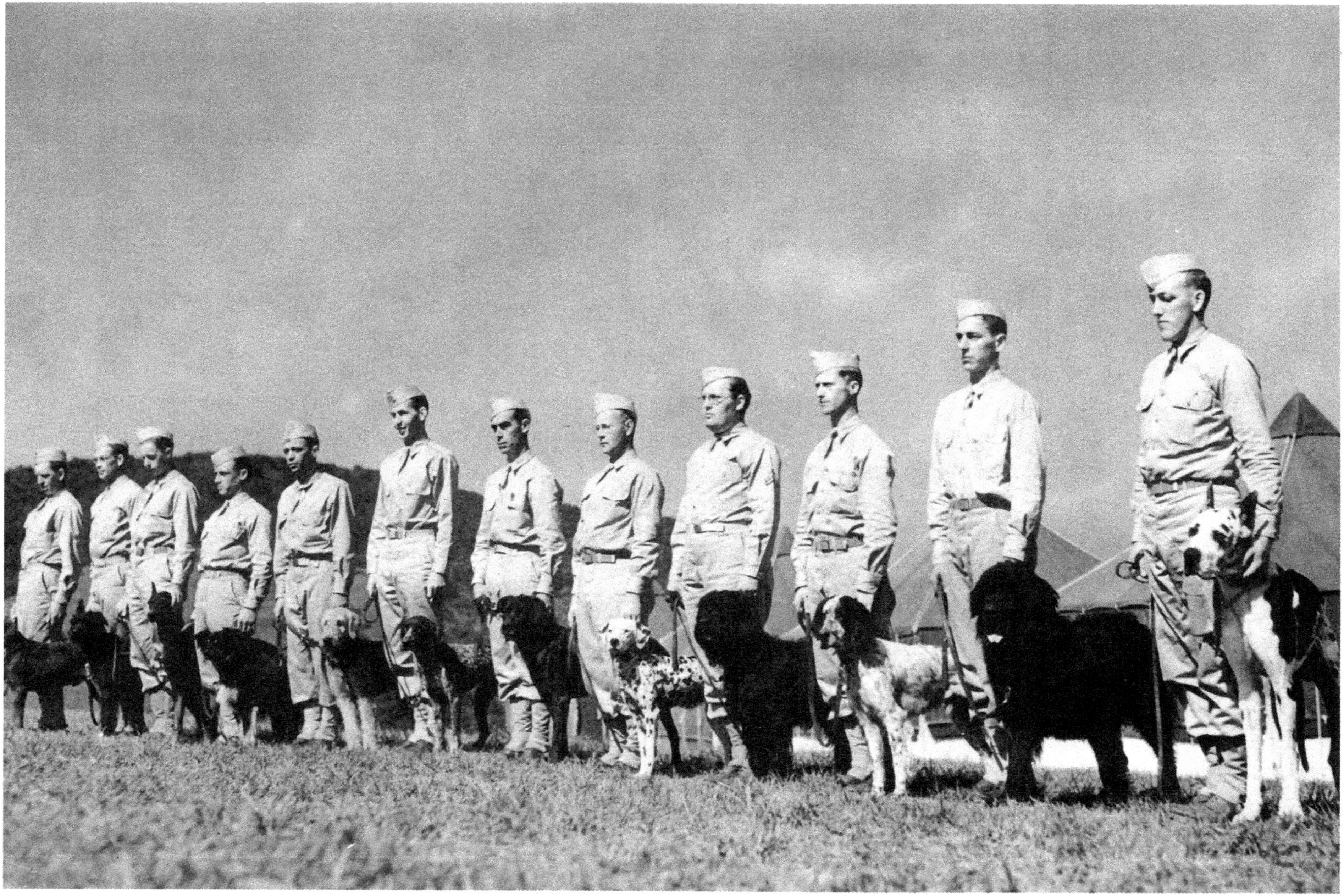

Official Photo: U. S. Army Signal Corps

A demonstration of perfect training. These war dogs stand at attention with their attendants at a K-9 training center

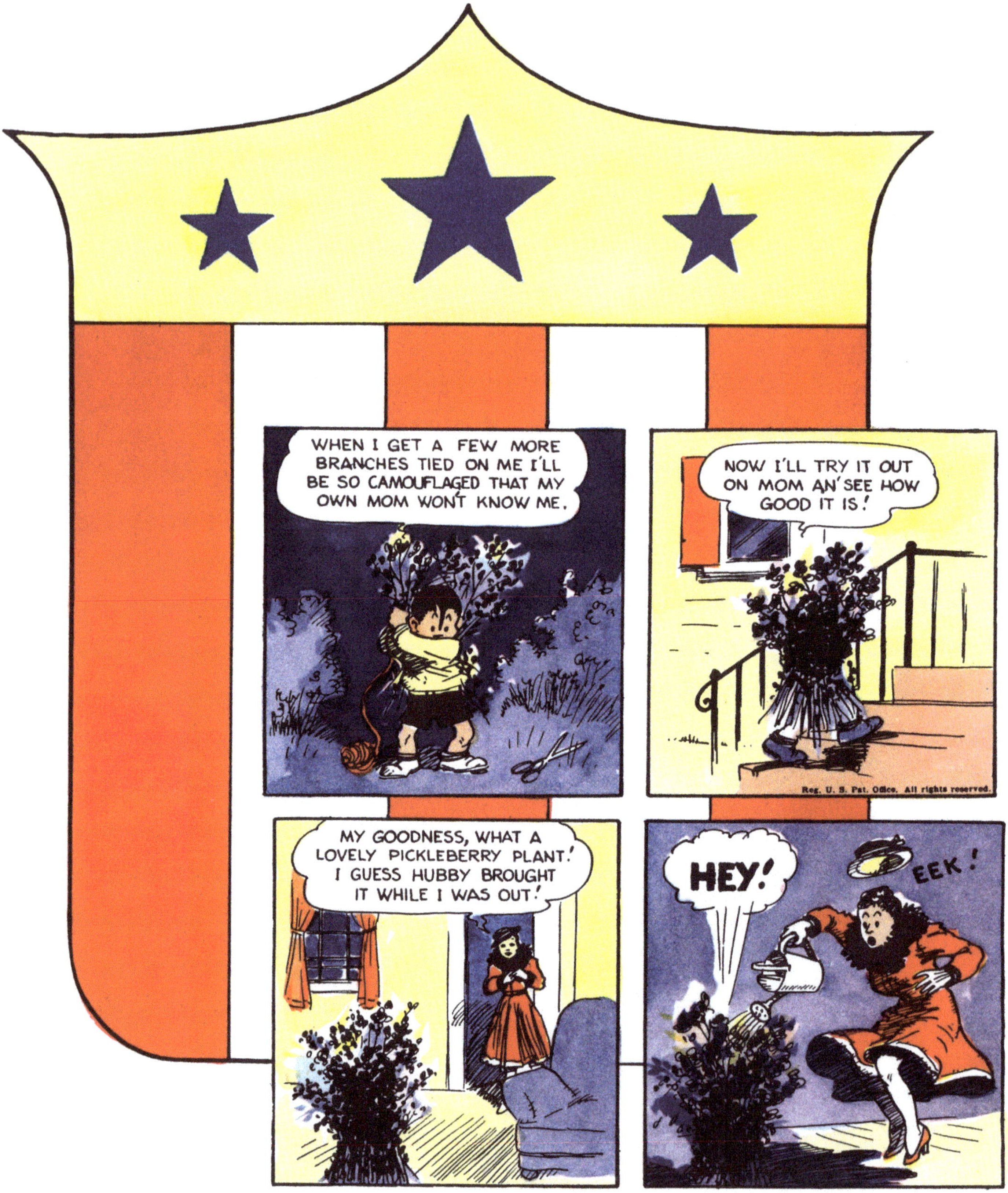
WHEN I GET A FEW MORE BRANCHES TIED ON ME I'LL BE SO CAMOUFLAGED THAT MY OWN MOM WON'T KNOW ME.
NOW I'LL TRY IT OUT ON MOM AN' SEE HOW GOOD IT IS!
Reg. U. S. Pat. Office. All rights reserved.
MY GOODNESS, WHAT A LOVELY PICKLEBERRY PLANT! I GUESS HUBBY BROUGHT IT WHILE I WAS OUT!
HEY!
EEK!

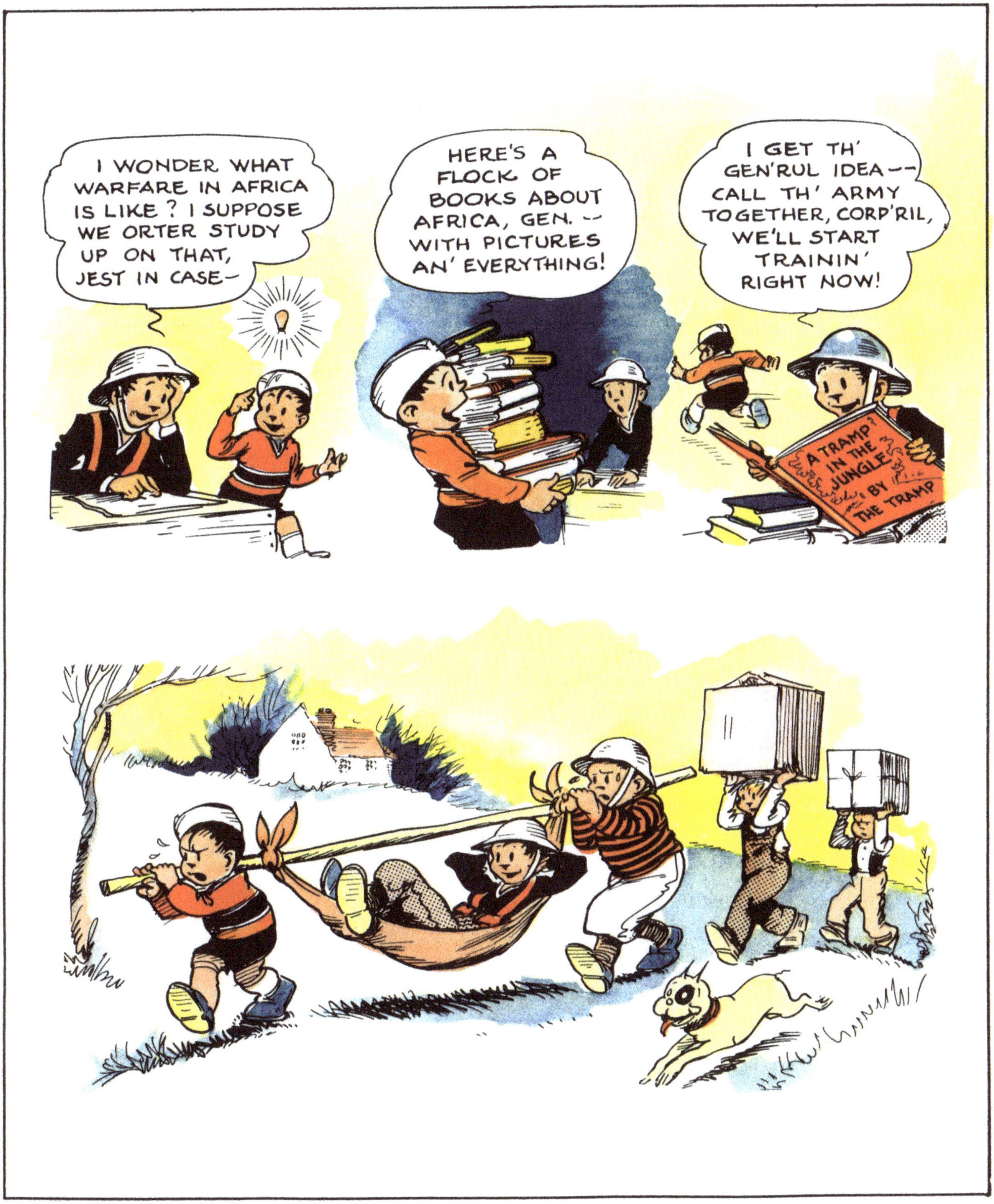
I WONDER WHAT WARFARE IN AFRICA IS LIKE? I SUPPOSE WE ORTER STUDY UP ON THAT, JEST IN CASE—
HERE'S A FLOCK OF BOOKS ABOUT AFRICA, GEN. — WITH PICTURES AN' EVERYTHING!
I GET TH' GEN'RUL IDEA— CALL TH' ARMY TOGETHER, CORP'RIL, WE'LL START TRAININ' RIGHT NOW!
A TRAMP IN THE JUNGLE BY THE TRAMP

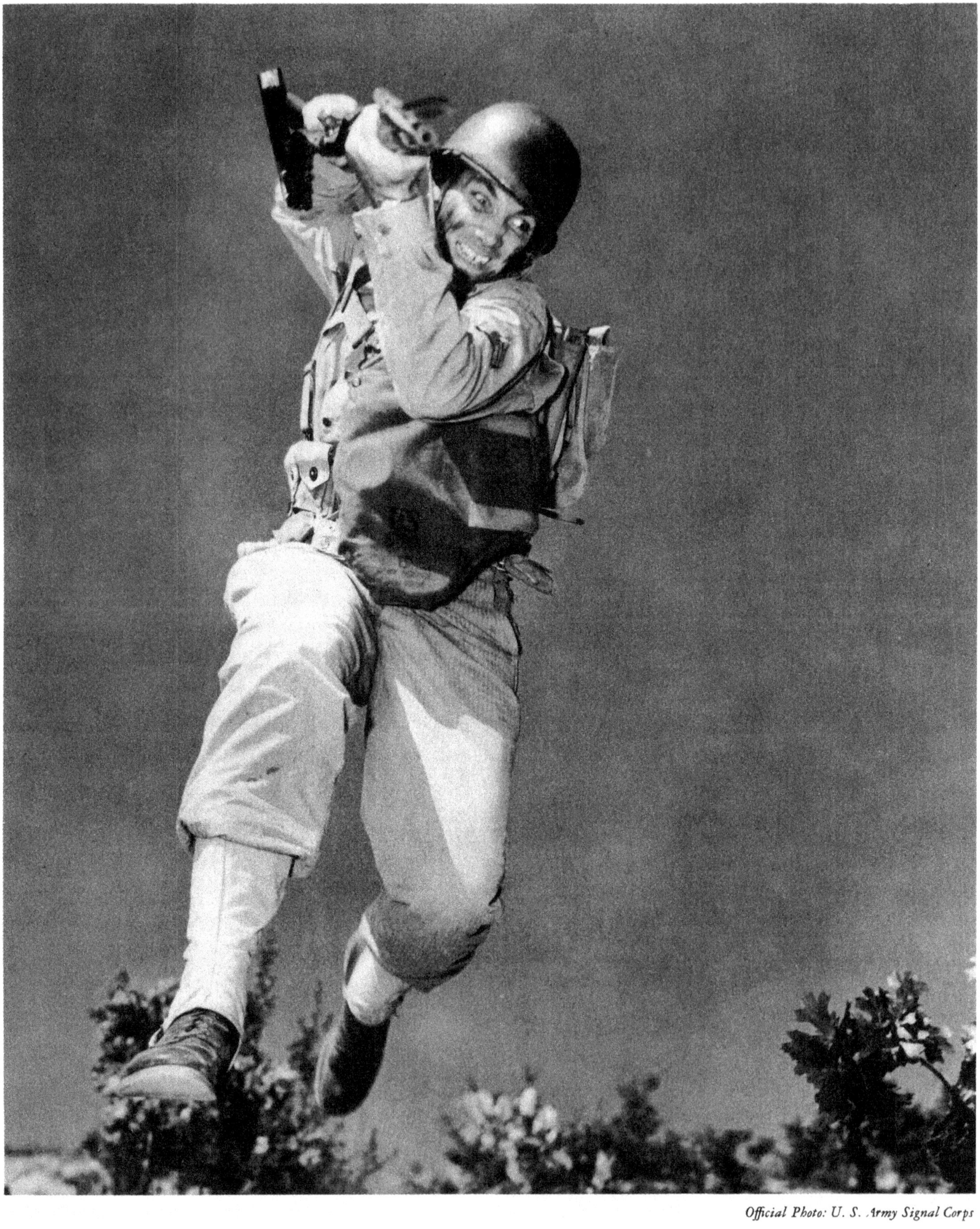

Official Photo: U. S. Army Signal Corps

This American soldier demonstrating a bayonet charge is the type of fighter upholding our finest military traditions

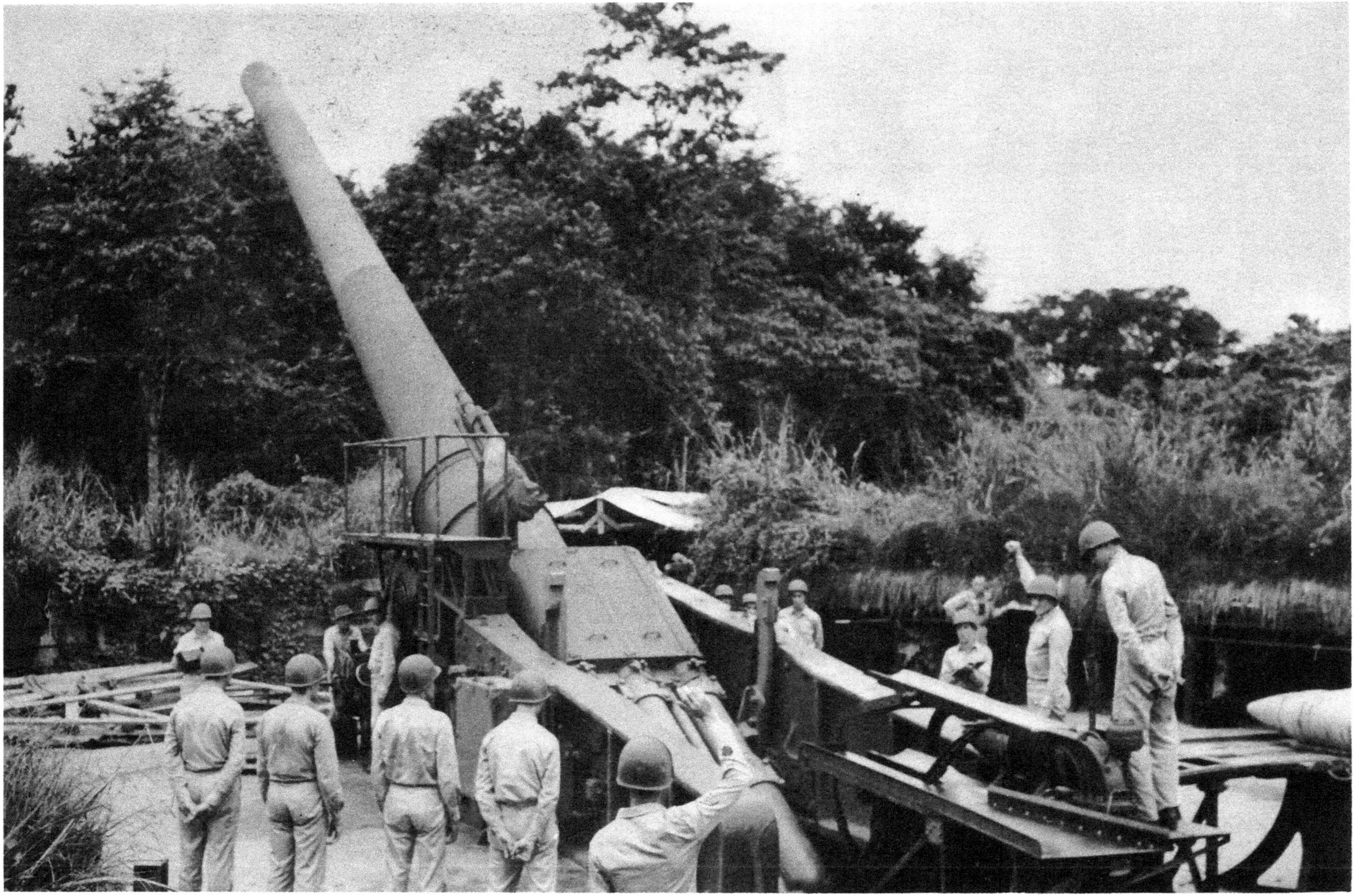

Official Photo: U. S. Army

One of the big coast defense guns at an army base in the Caribbean

HAVE YA GOT ANY MORE BULLETS, GEN'RUL? I'D KINDA LIKE T'DOT THAT "I"!
PINHEAD DUFFY

REMEMBER THAT'S A IMPORTANT DISPATCH, CORP'RIL – IF TH' ENEMY KETCHES YOU, IT'S UP T' YOU T'SWALLER IT!

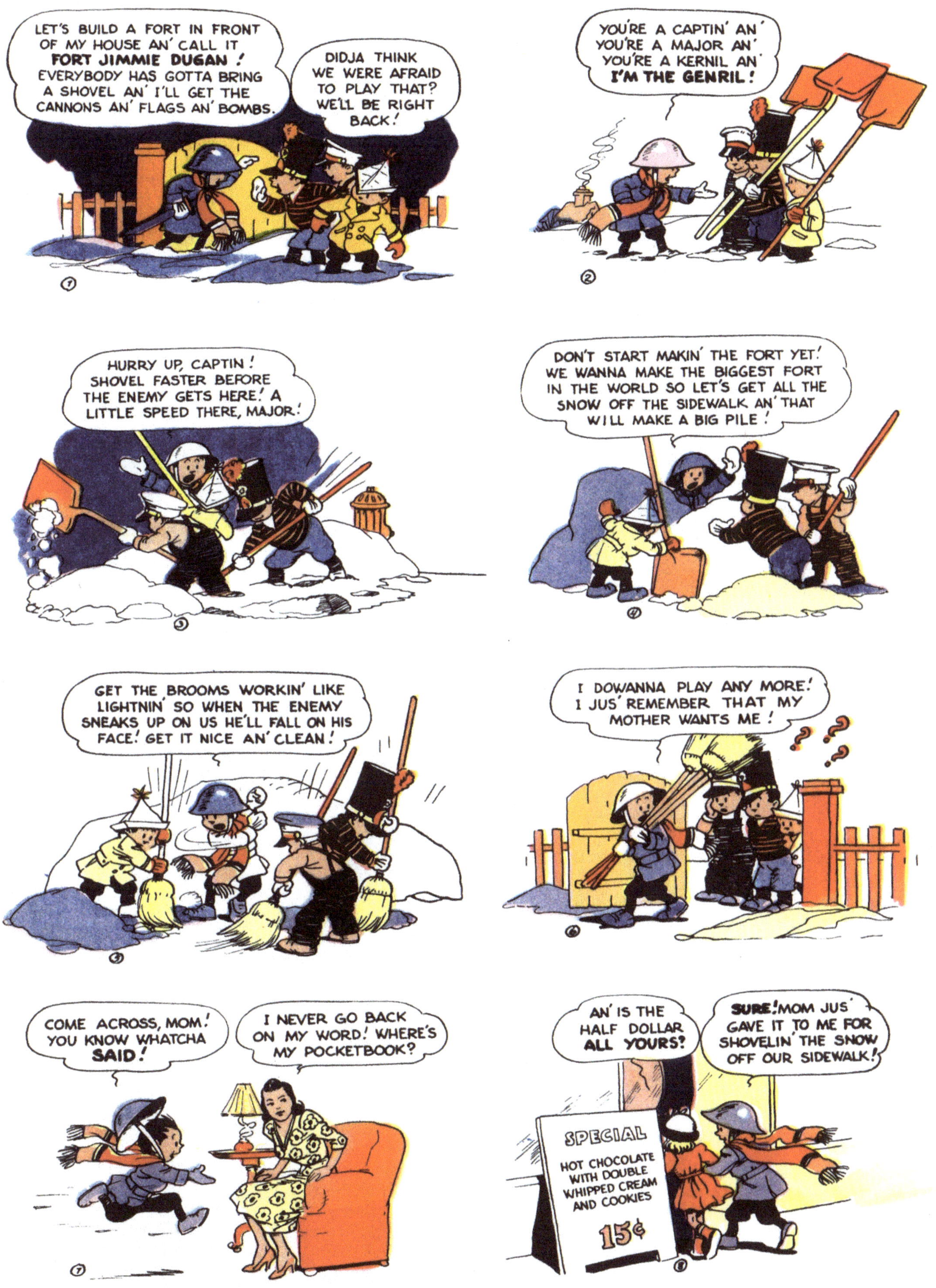
LET'S BUILD A FORT IN FRONT OF MY HOUSE AN' CALL IT **FORT JIMMIE DUGAN!** EVERYBODY HAS GOTTA BRING A SHOVEL AN' I'LL GET THE CANNONS AN' FLAGS AN' BOMBS.
DIDJA THINK WE WERE AFRAID TO PLAY THAT? WE'LL BE RIGHT BACK!
YOU'RE A CAPTIN' AN' YOU'RE A MAJOR AN' YOU'RE A KERNIL AN' **I'M THE GENRIL!**
HURRY UP, CAPTIN! SHOVEL FASTER BEFORE THE ENEMY GETS HERE! A LITTLE SPEED THERE, MAJOR!
DON'T START MAKIN' THE FORT YET! WE WANNA MAKE THE BIGGEST FORT IN THE WORLD SO LET'S GET ALL THE SNOW OFF THE SIDEWALK AN' THAT WILL MAKE A BIG PILE!
GET THE BROOMS WORKIN' LIKE LIGHTNIN' SO WHEN THE ENEMY SNEAKS UP ON US HE'LL FALL ON HIS FACE! GET IT NICE AN' CLEAN!
I DOWANNA PLAY ANY MORE! I JUS' REMEMBER THAT MY MOTHER WANTS ME!
COME ACROSS, MOM! YOU KNOW WHATCHA **SAID!**
I NEVER GO BACK ON MY WORD! WHERE'S MY POCKETBOOK?
AN' IS THE HALF DOLLAR **ALL YOURS?**
SURE! MOM JUS' GAVE IT TO ME FOR SHOVELIN' THE SNOW OFF OUR SIDEWALK!
SPECIAL
HOT CHOCOLATE WITH DOUBLE WHIPPED CREAM AND COOKIES
15¢

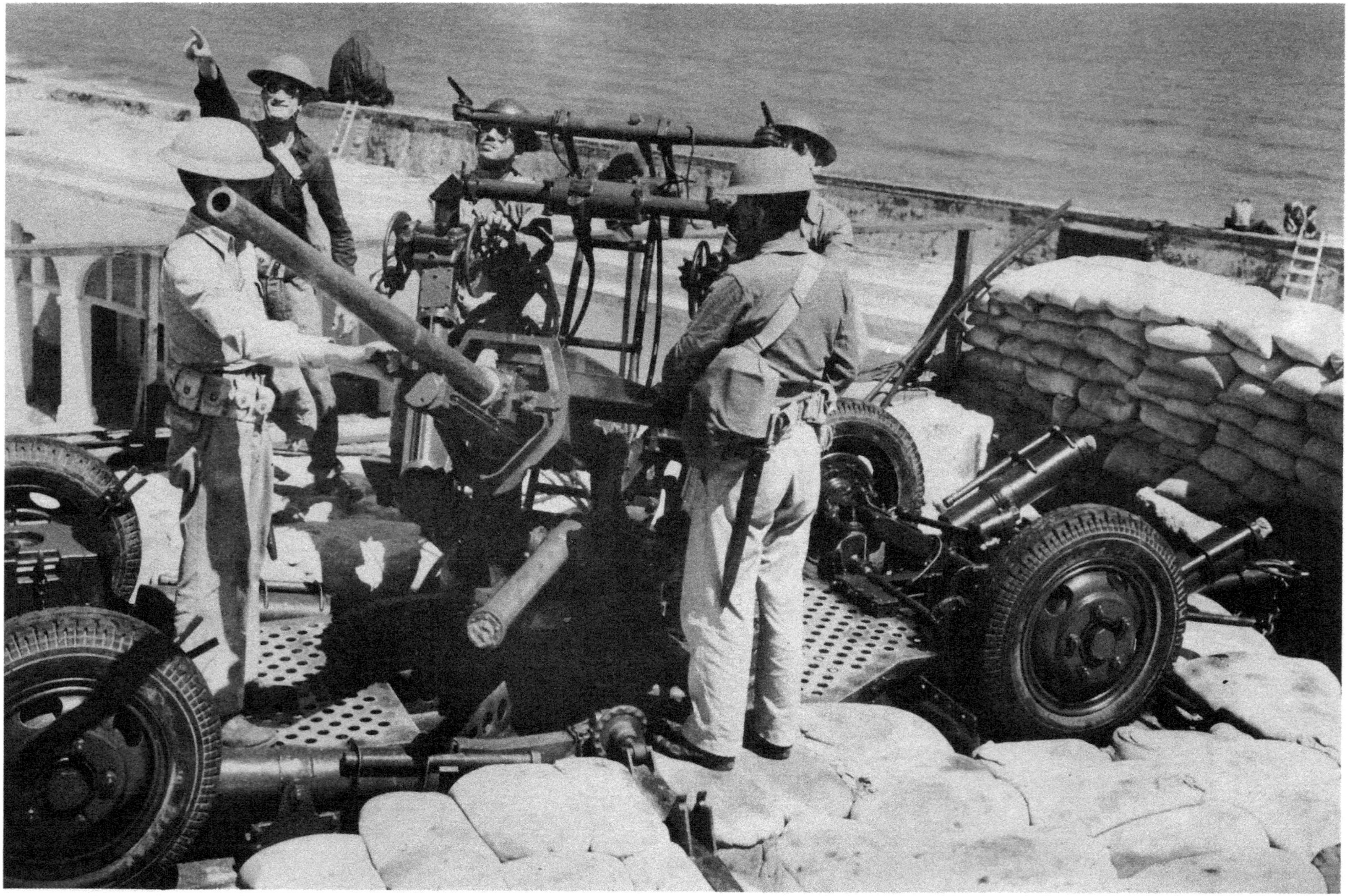

Official Photo: U. S. Army Signal Corps

A gun crew tracking planes at a Caribbean outpost. They spend hours daily tracking all planes in sight. This gives them excellent practice so that they may be able to get the guns into instant action in case of an air attack

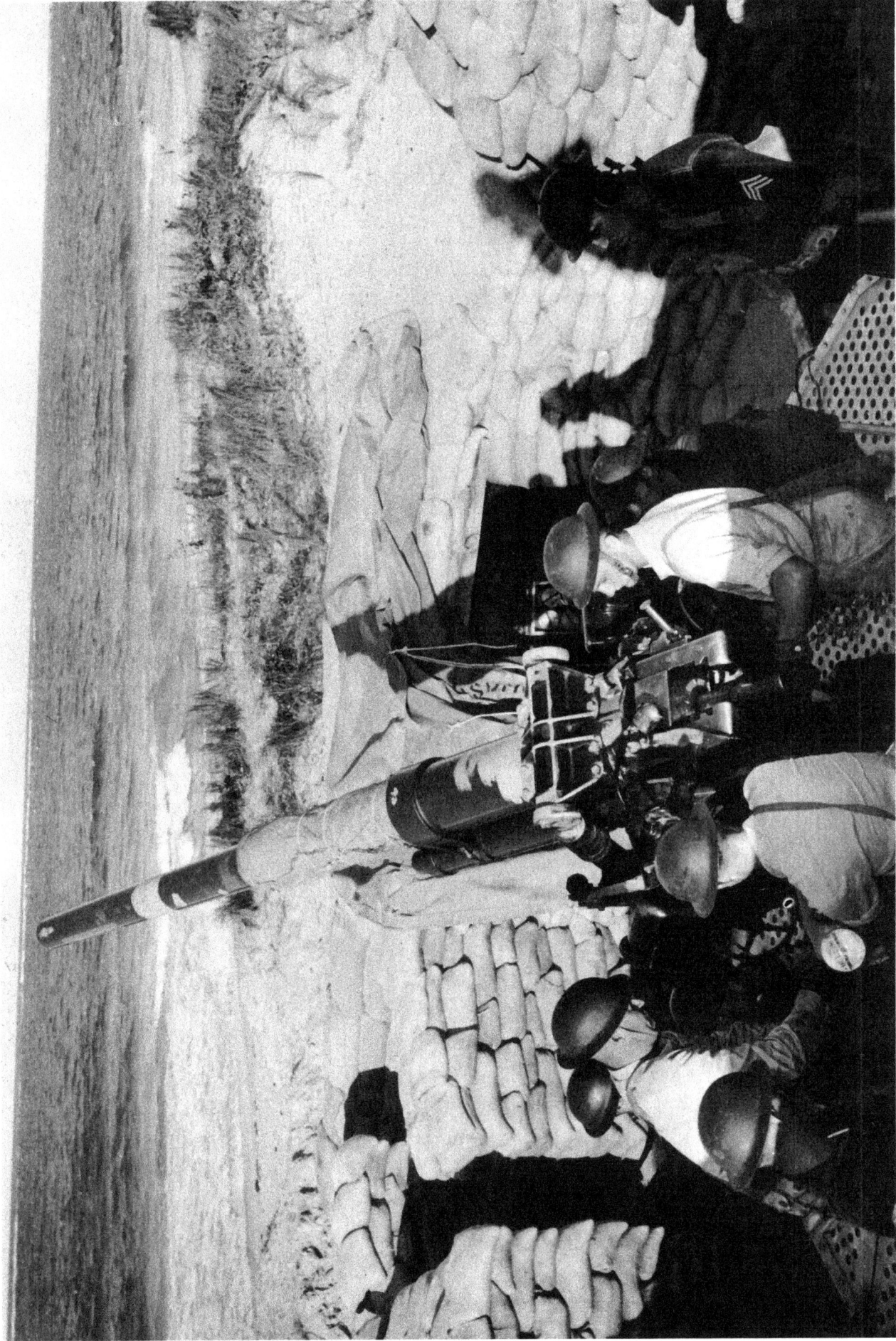

Official Photo: U. S. Army Signal Corps

These soldiers after receiving gun elevation shoot a dummy shell at imagined aircraft during a drill in Puerto Rico

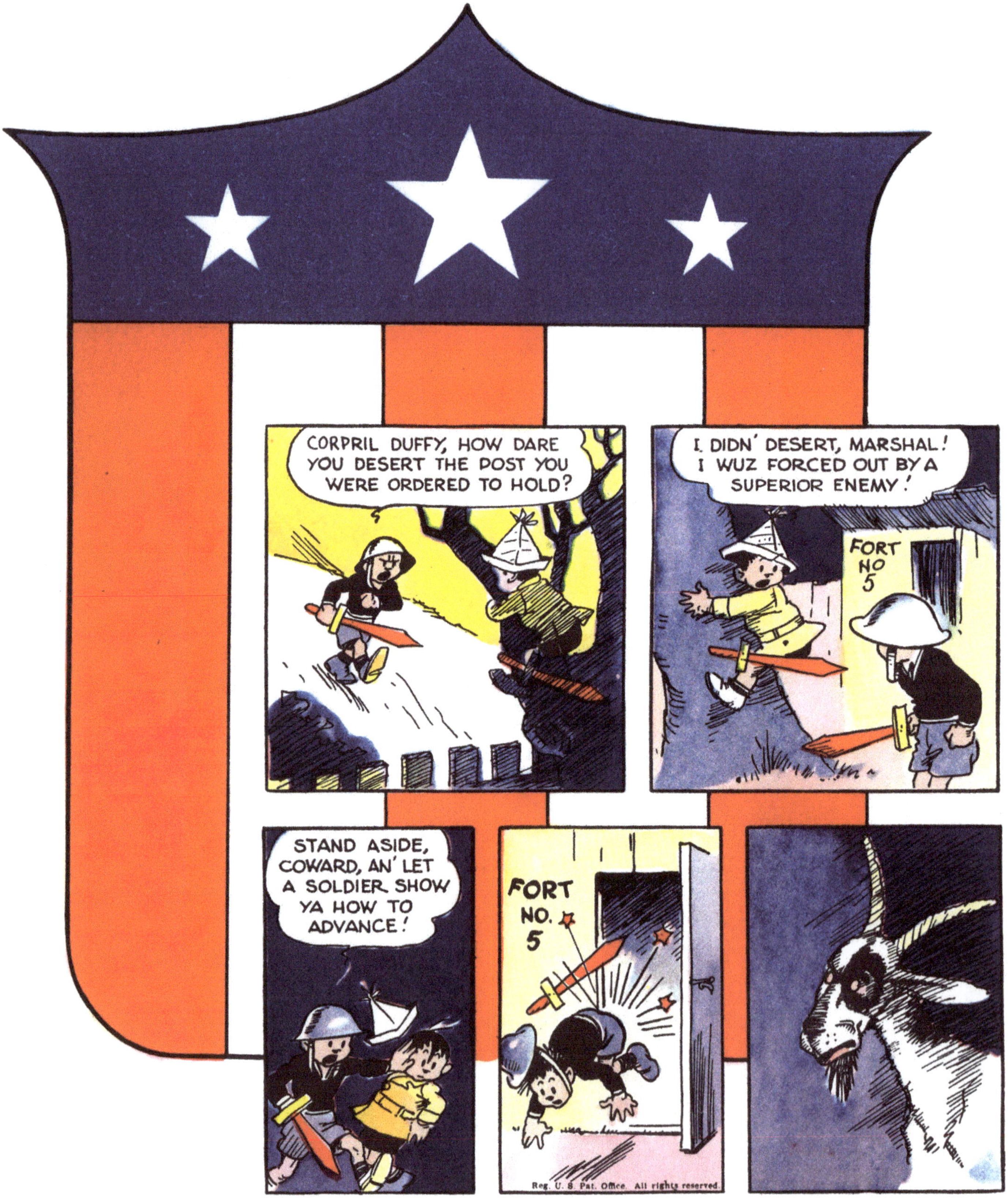
CORPRIL DUFFY, HOW DARE YOU DESERT THE POST YOU WERE ORDERED TO HOLD?
I DIDN' DESERT, MARSHAL! I WUZ FORCED OUT BY A SUPERIOR ENEMY!
FORT NO 5
STAND ASIDE, COWARD, AN' LET A SOLDIER SHOW YA HOW TO ADVANCE!
FORT NO. 5
Reg. U. S. Pat. Office. All rights reserved.

OUR POSITION IS PRETTY TOUGH! IT LOOKS LIKE WE'RE GONNA HAFTA RETREAT!
RETREAT TRIPLE-QUICK, MEN! FOLLOW ME--I GOT A GREAT IDEA! I'LL MAKE THE ENEMY PUT A STOP TO THEIR FIRING!
CRYSTAL PLATE GLASS CO.
Reg. U. S. Pat. Office. All rights reserved.

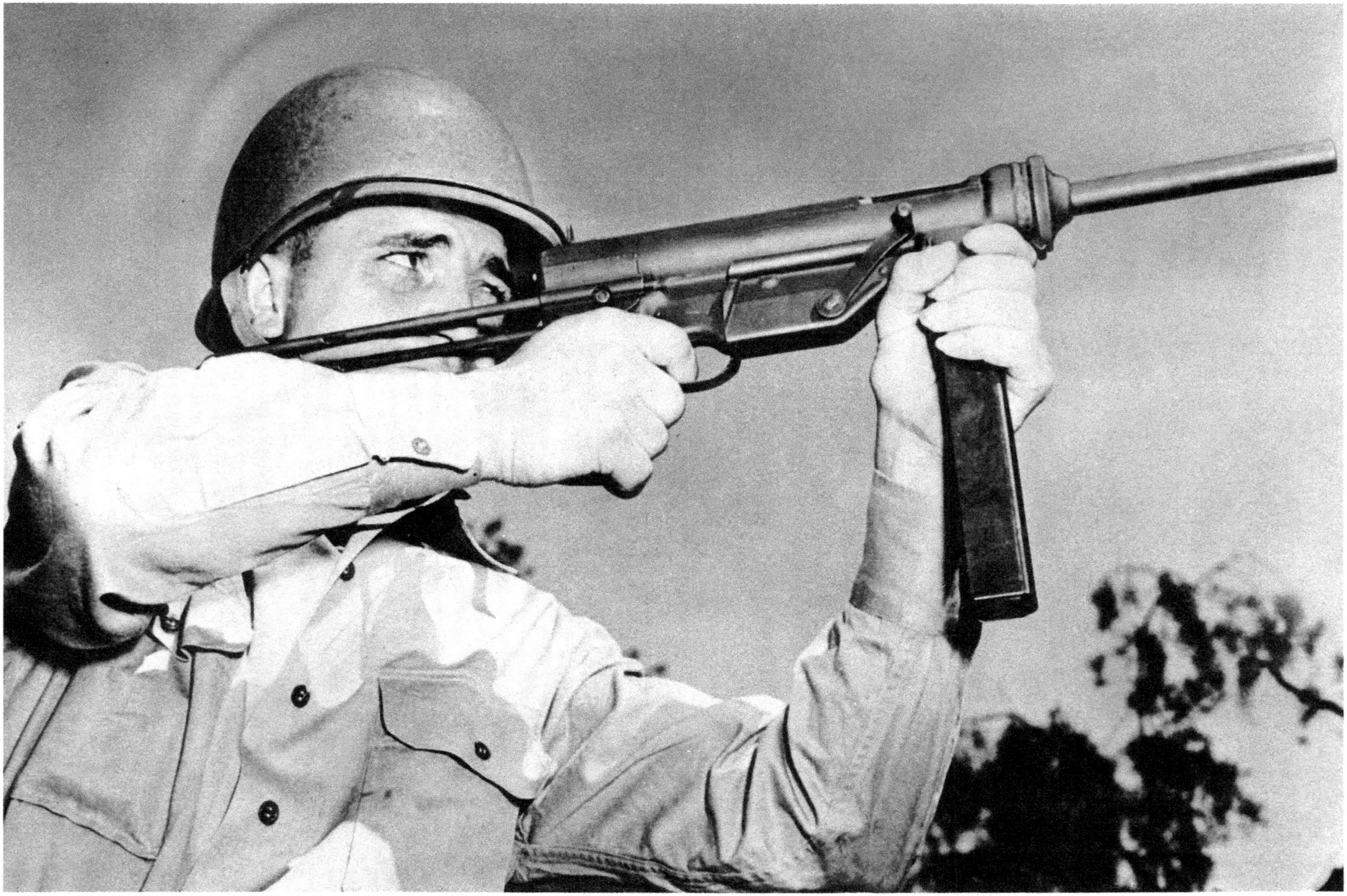

Official Photo: U. S. Army

Soldier operating .45 caliber sub-machine gun. Because of its compactness, lightness and effectiveness it is an excellent weapon for guerrilla fighting

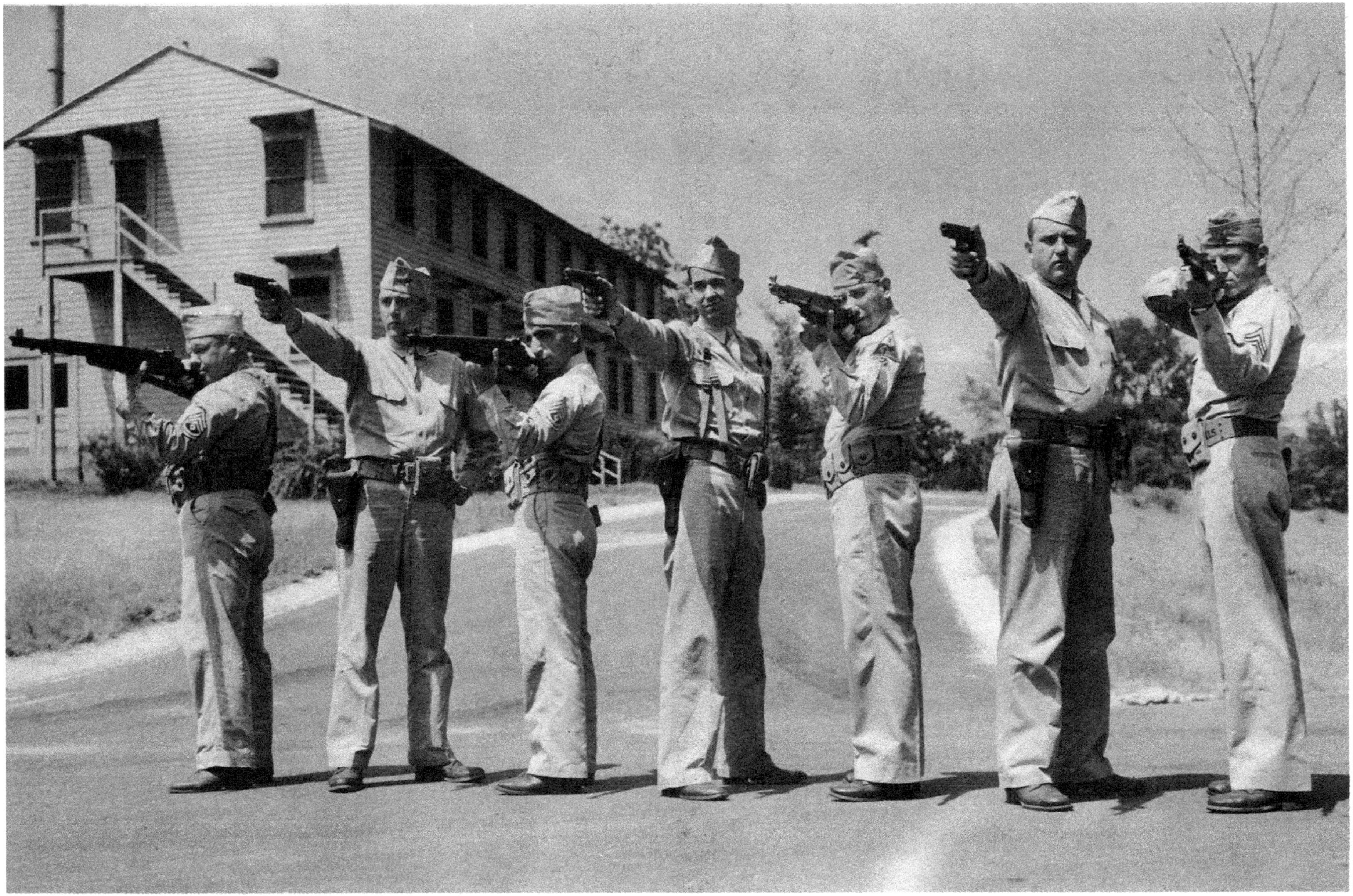

Official Photo: U. S. Army Signal Corps

Champions all—pictured above are a few of the expert rifle and pistol shots of the 10th Arm'd Division. L. to R. 1st Sgt. Adam J. Gutowski, S/Sgt. Perry E. Lawrence, 1st Sgt. Albert Martina, M/Sgt. Virgil E. Pecor, M/Sgt. Frank Rossio, T/Sgt. John J. Little, Sgt. George R. Lee

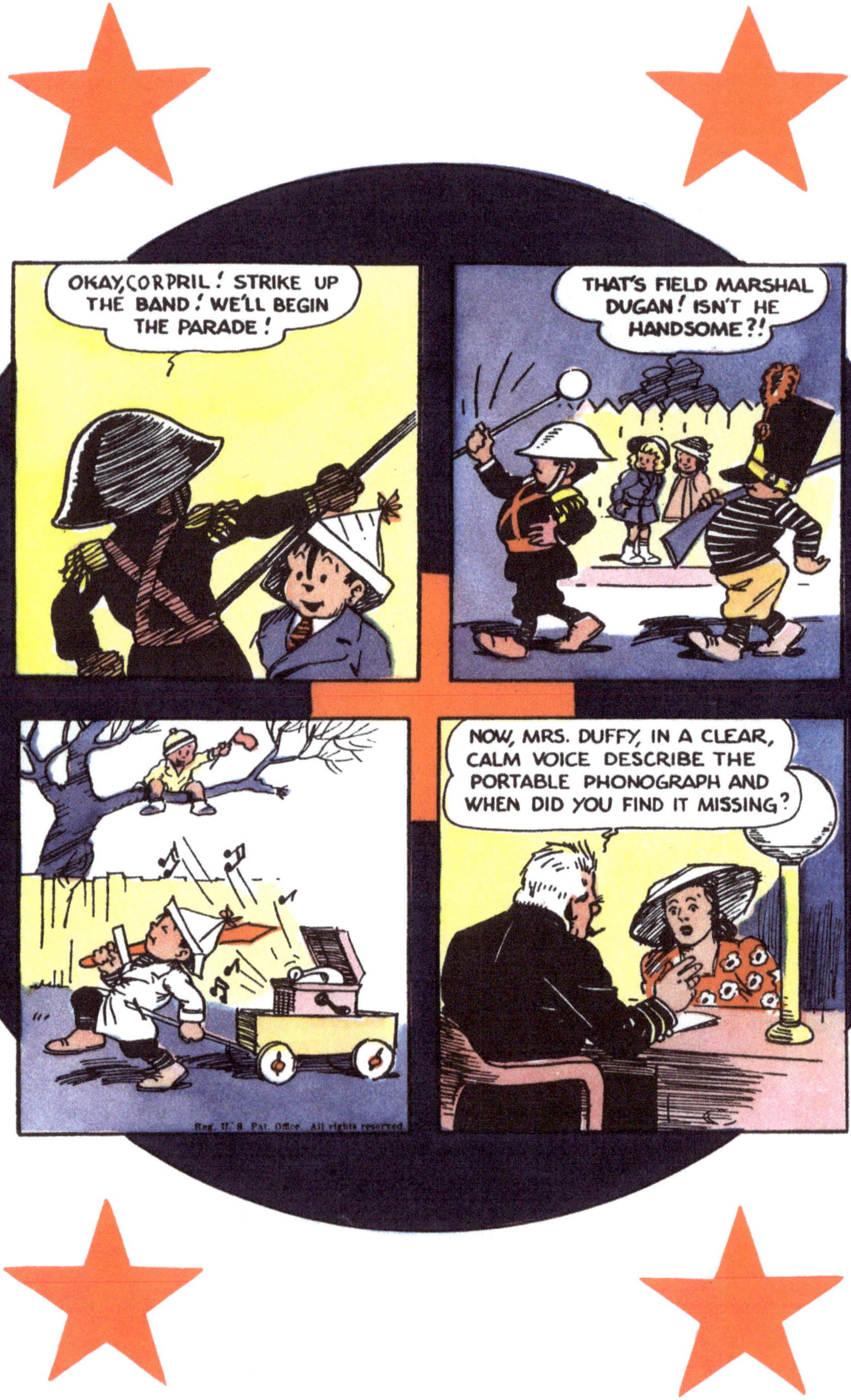

OKAY, CORPRIL! STRIKE UP THE BAND! WE'LL BEGIN THE PARADE!
THAT'S FIELD MARSHAL DUGAN! ISN'T HE HANDSOME?!
Reg. U. S. Pat. Office. All rights reserved.
NOW, MRS. DUFFY, IN A CLEAR, CALM VOICE DESCRIBE THE PORTABLE PHONOGRAPH AND WHEN DID YOU FIND IT MISSING?

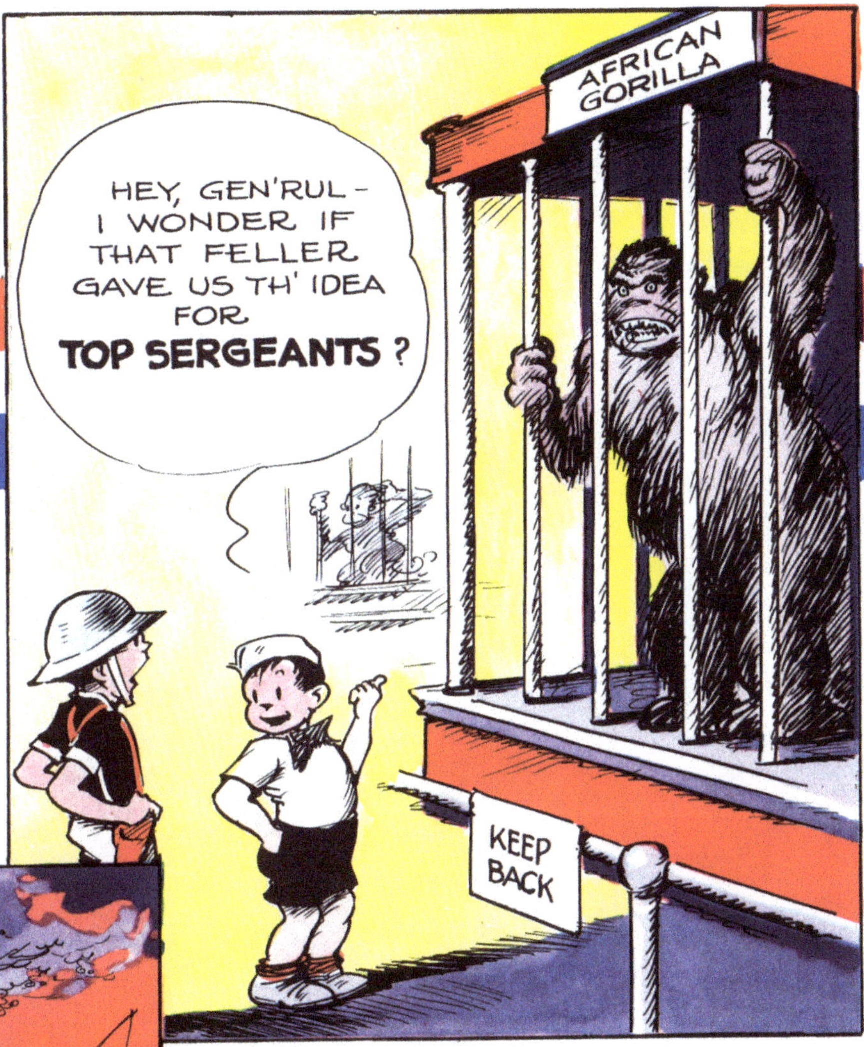
AFRICAN GORILLA
HEY, GEN'RUL - I WONDER IF THAT FELLER GAVE US TH' IDEA FOR **TOP SERGEANTS** ?
KEEP BACK

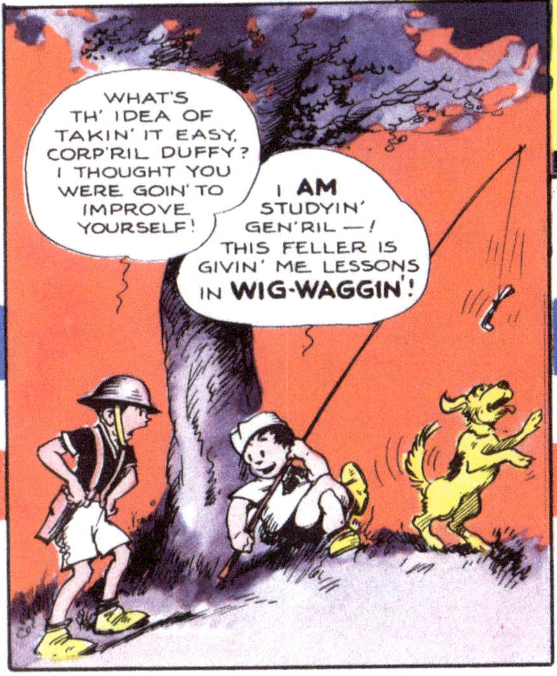
WHAT'S TH' IDEA OF TAKIN' IT EASY, CORP'RIL DUFFY? I THOUGHT YOU WERE GOIN' TO IMPROVE YOURSELF!
I **AM** STUDYIN' GEN'RIL—! THIS FELLER IS GIVIN' ME LESSONS IN **WIG-WAGGIN'**!

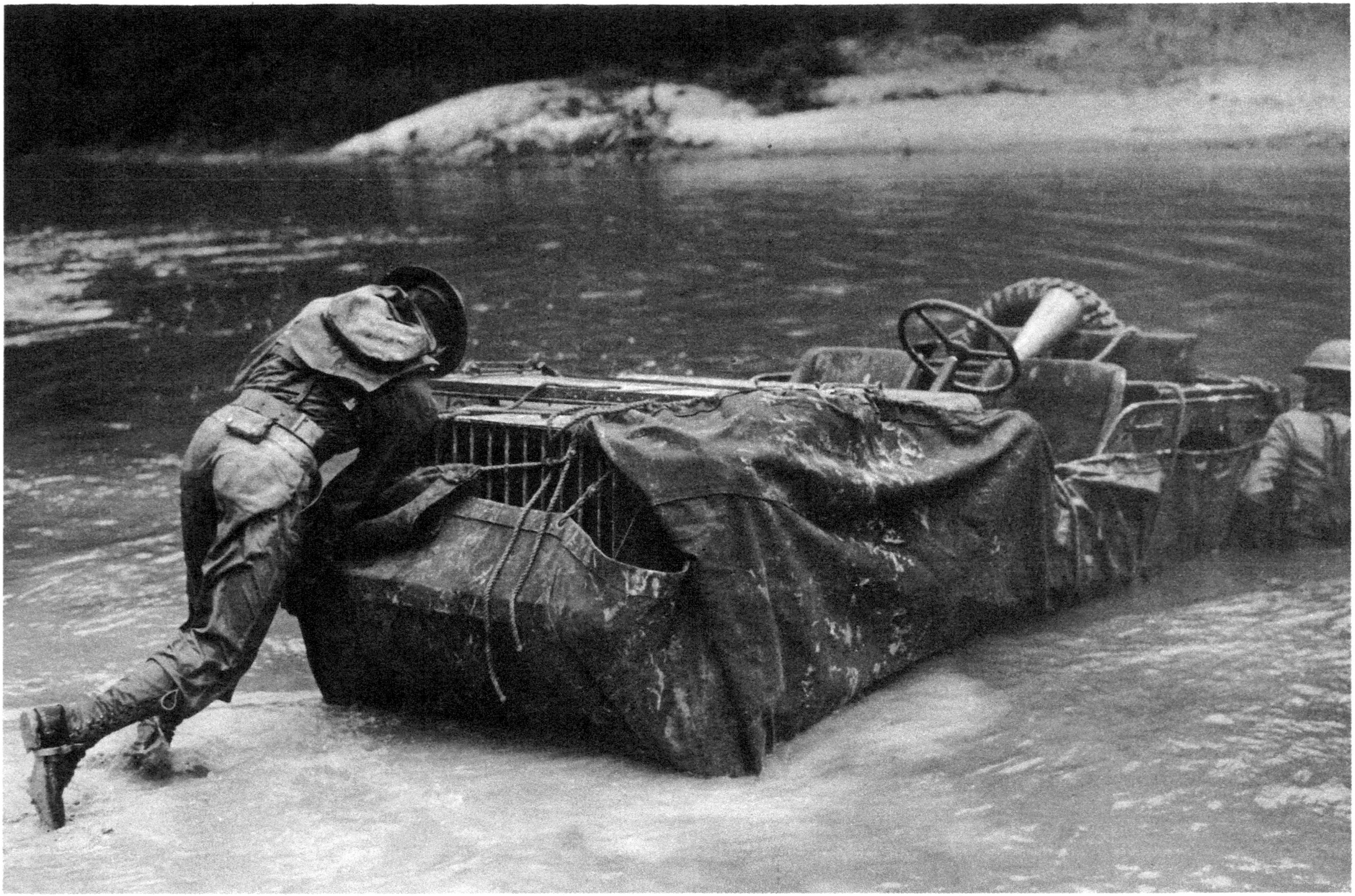

Official Photo: U. S. Army Signal Corps

Soldiers ford their jeep across a stream. A water-tight cover is wrapped around the under part of the jeep enabling the machine to float with ease.

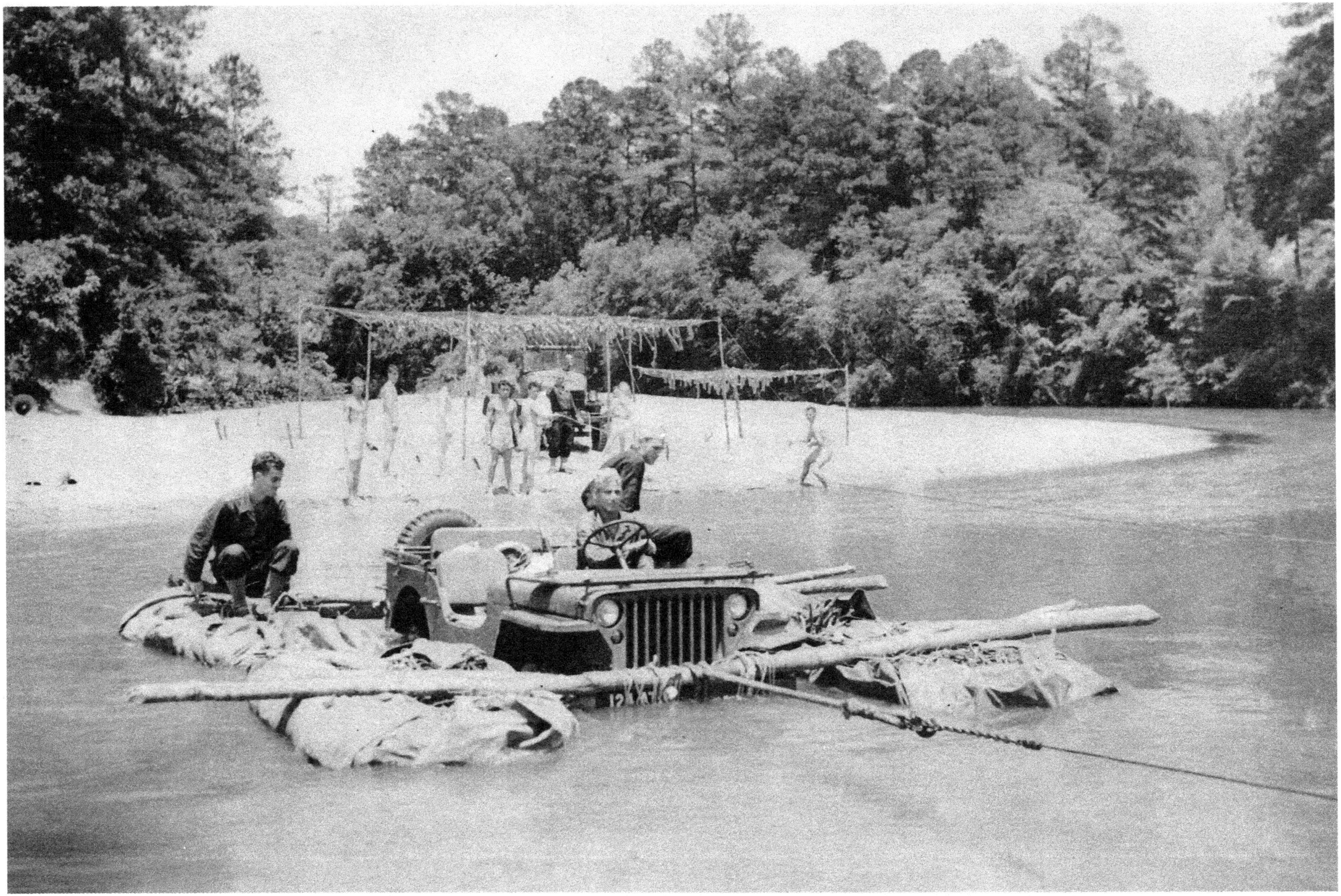

Official Photo: U. S. Army Signal Corps

Another method of floating a jeep across a river. Tarpaulins filled with straw are used as pontoons to support the car and its crew during passage

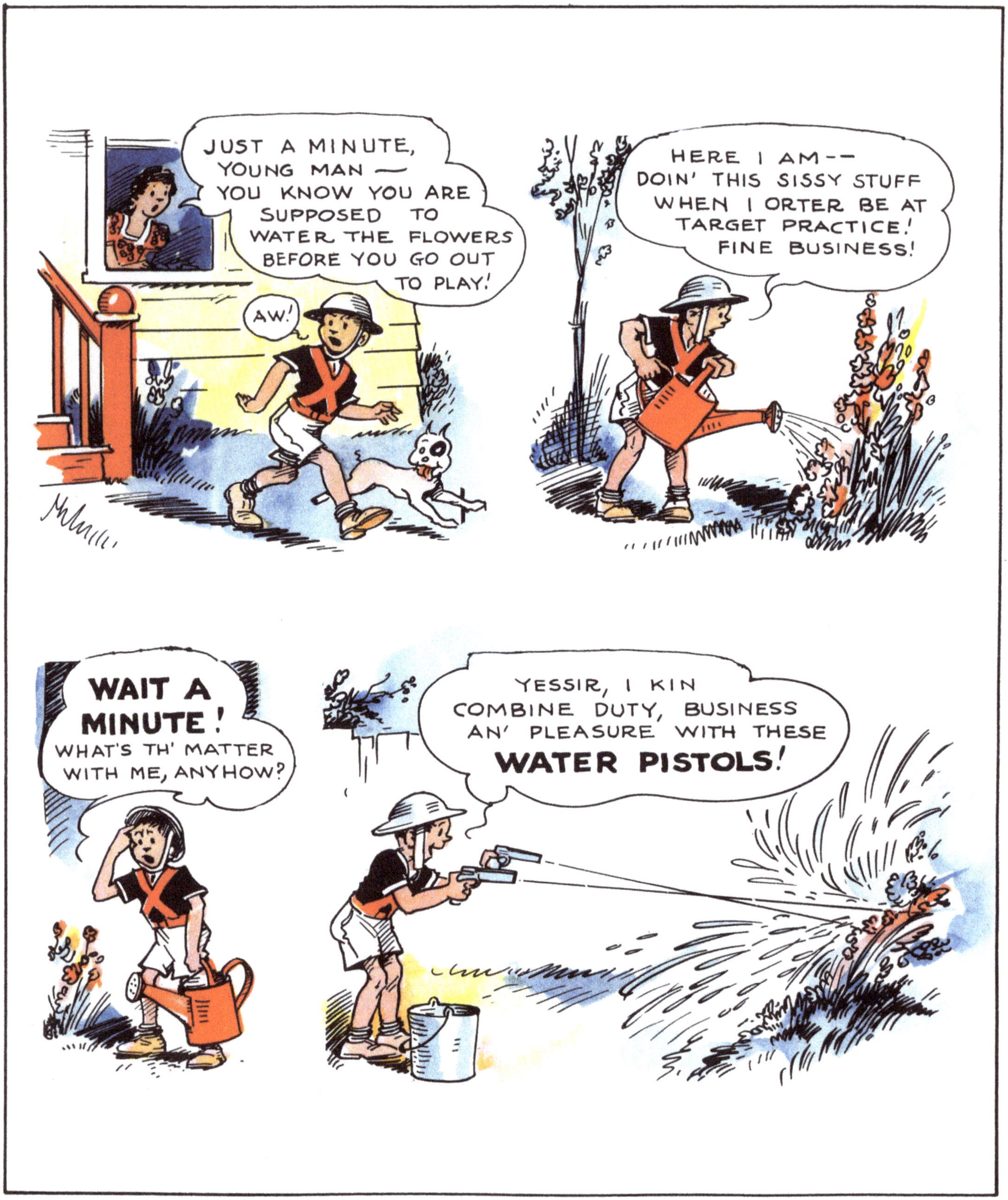
JUST A MINUTE, YOUNG MAN — YOU KNOW YOU ARE SUPPOSED TO WATER THE FLOWERS BEFORE YOU GO OUT TO PLAY!
AW!
HERE I AM -- DOIN' THIS SISSY STUFF WHEN I ORTER BE AT TARGET PRACTICE! FINE BUSINESS!
WAIT A MINUTE! WHAT'S TH' MATTER WITH ME, ANYHOW?
YESSIR, I KIN COMBINE DUTY, BUSINESS AN' PLEASURE WITH THESE WATER PISTOLS!

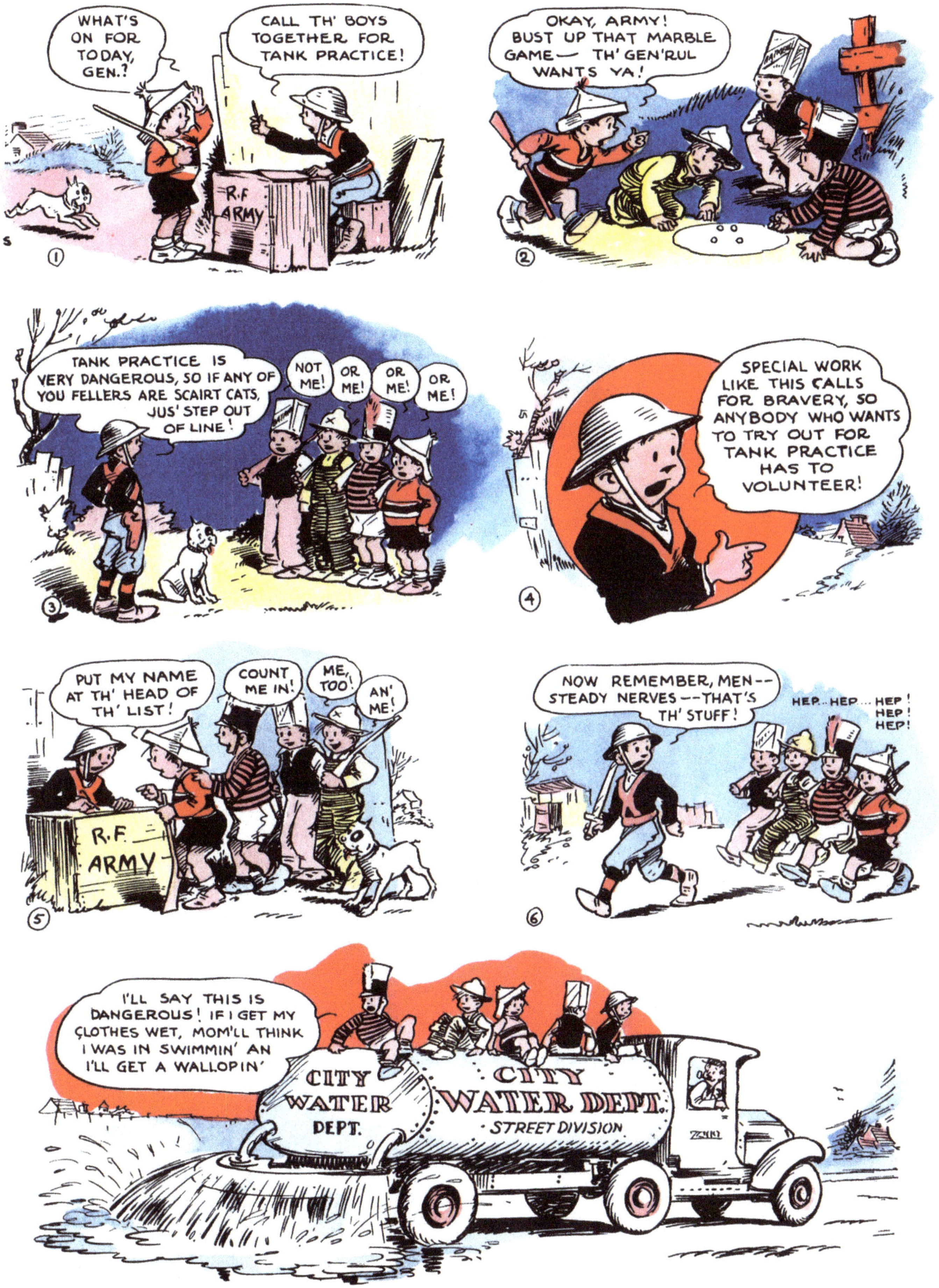
WHAT'S ON FOR TODAY, GEN.?
CALL TH' BOYS TOGETHER FOR TANK PRACTICE!
R.F. ARMY
OKAY, ARMY! BUST UP THAT MARBLE GAME— TH' GEN'RUL WANTS YA!
TANK PRACTICE IS VERY DANGEROUS, SO IF ANY OF YOU FELLERS ARE SCAIRT CATS, JUS' STEP OUT OF LINE!
NOT ME!
OR ME!
OR ME!
OR ME!
SPECIAL WORK LIKE THIS CALLS FOR BRAVERY, SO ANYBODY WHO WANTS TO TRY OUT FOR TANK PRACTICE HAS TO VOLUNTEER!
PUT MY NAME AT TH' HEAD OF TH' LIST!
COUNT ME IN!
ME, TOO!
AN' ME!
R.F. ARMY
NOW REMEMBER, MEN-- STEADY NERVES--THAT'S TH' STUFF!
HEP...HEP...HEP! HEP! HEP!
I'LL SAY THIS IS DANGEROUS! IF I GET MY CLOTHES WET, MOM'LL THINK I WAS IN SWIMMIN' AN I'LL GET A WALLOPIN'
CITY WATER DEPT.
CITY WATER DEPT.
STREET DIVISION

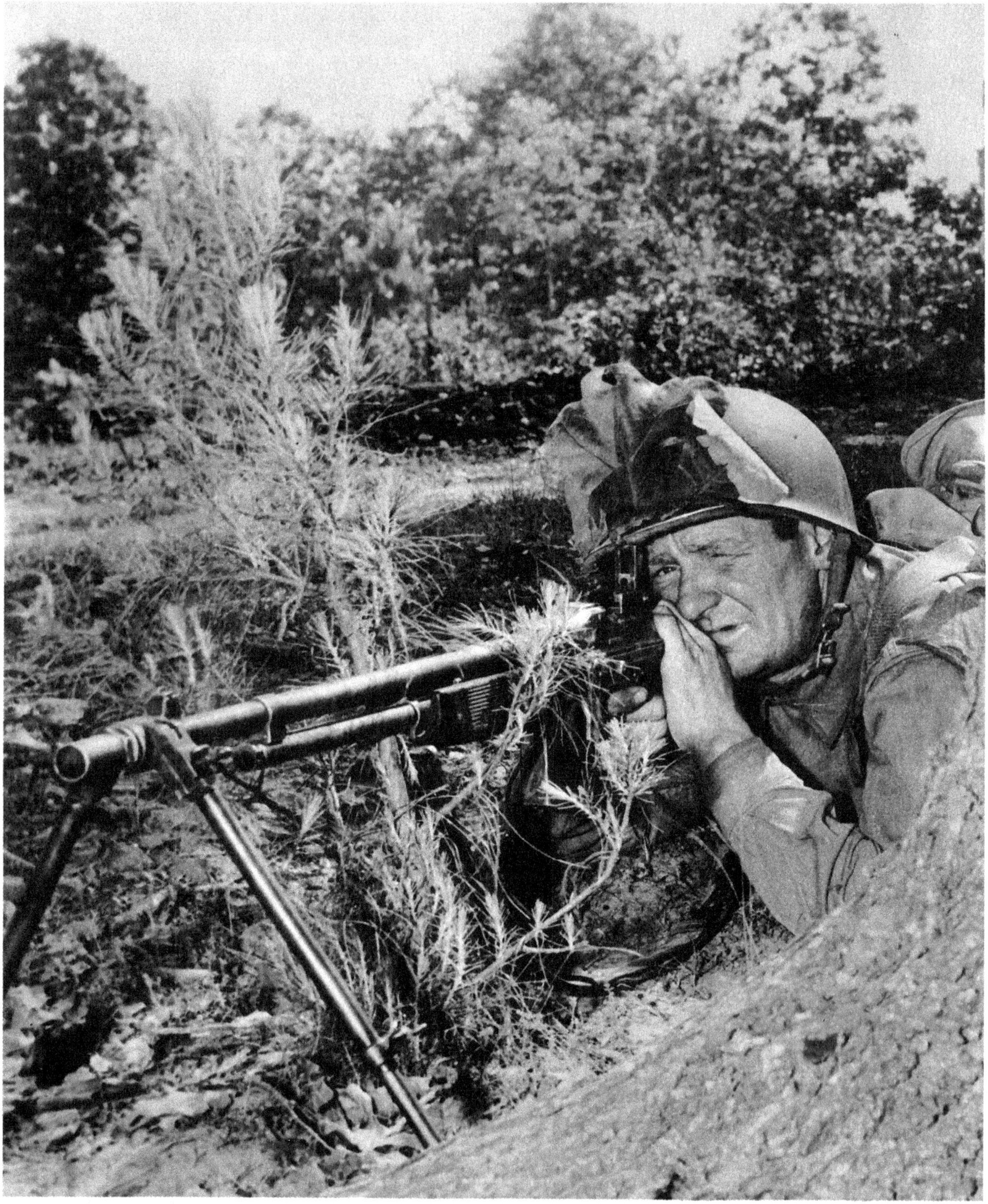

Official Photo: U. S. Army

The Browning Automatic Rifle can be used either for semi-automatic fire or to deliver a burst of 20 shots. The .30 calibre weapon weighs approximately 21 pounds with a bipod and is operated by a three-man team: gunner, assistant gunner and ammunition carrier.

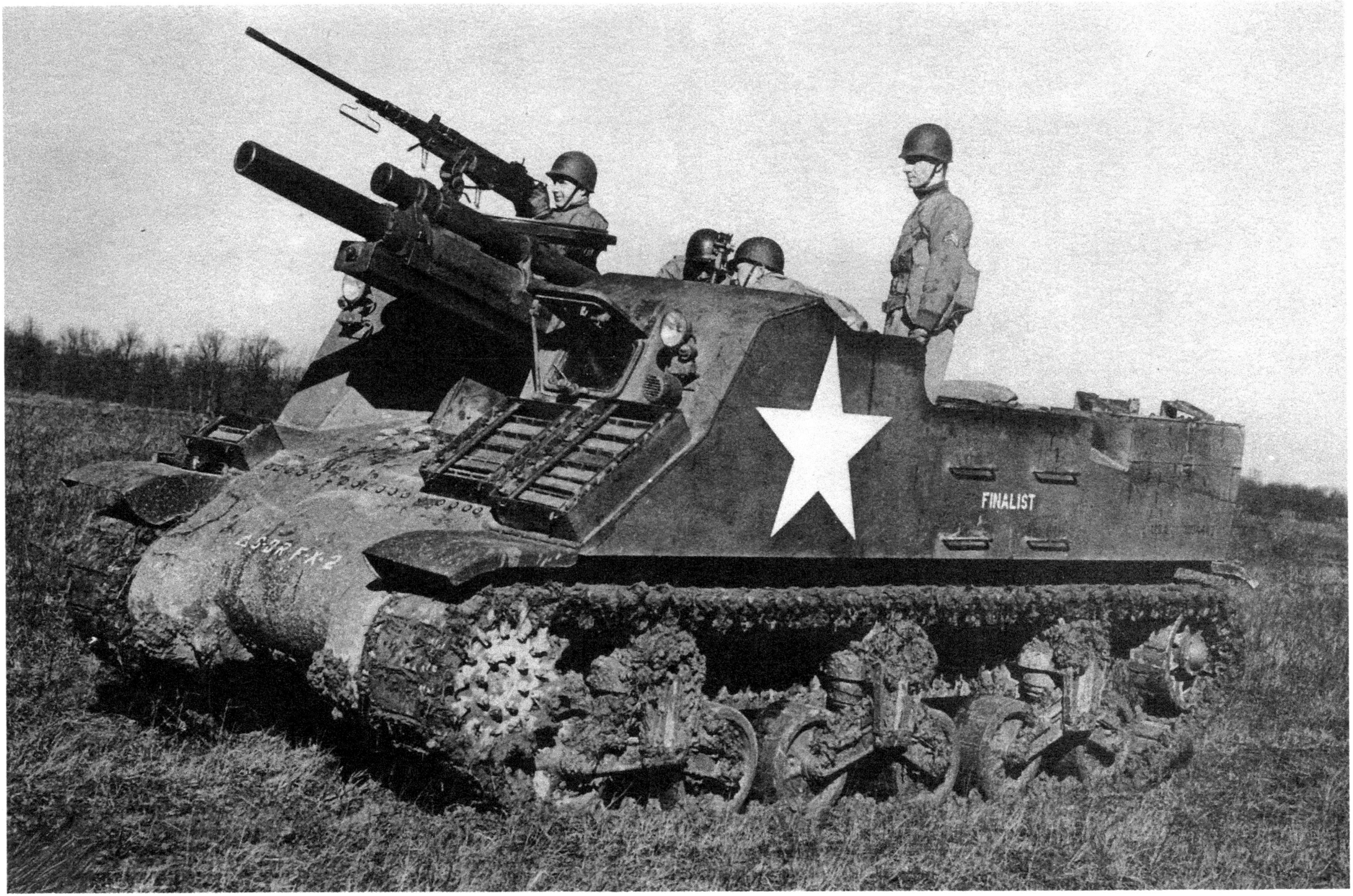
FINALIST

Official Photo: U. S. Army Signal Corps

M-7-105 mm. Howitzer Anti-tank Artillery Piece at Armored Force, in Fort Knox, Kentucky

CORPRIL DUFFY! A GOOD SOLDIER HASTA OBEY ORDERS NO MATTER HOW TOUGH THEY ARE!
YESSIR!
I HAVE A VERY IMPORTANT MISSION TO OOMLAUF'S BAKERY AN' I'M PICKIN' YOU TO VOLUNTEER!
NEVER FEAR, MARSHAL! I SHALL CARRY OUT YOUR ORDERS OR PERISH IN THE ATTEMPT!
Reg. U. S. Pat. Office. All rights reserved.
PROCEED TO OOMLAUF'S BAKERY AT ONCET AN' PICK UP A LOAF OF SLICED RYE BREAD WHICH YOU WILL DELIVER TO MRS. DUGAN'S HOUSE!
POP

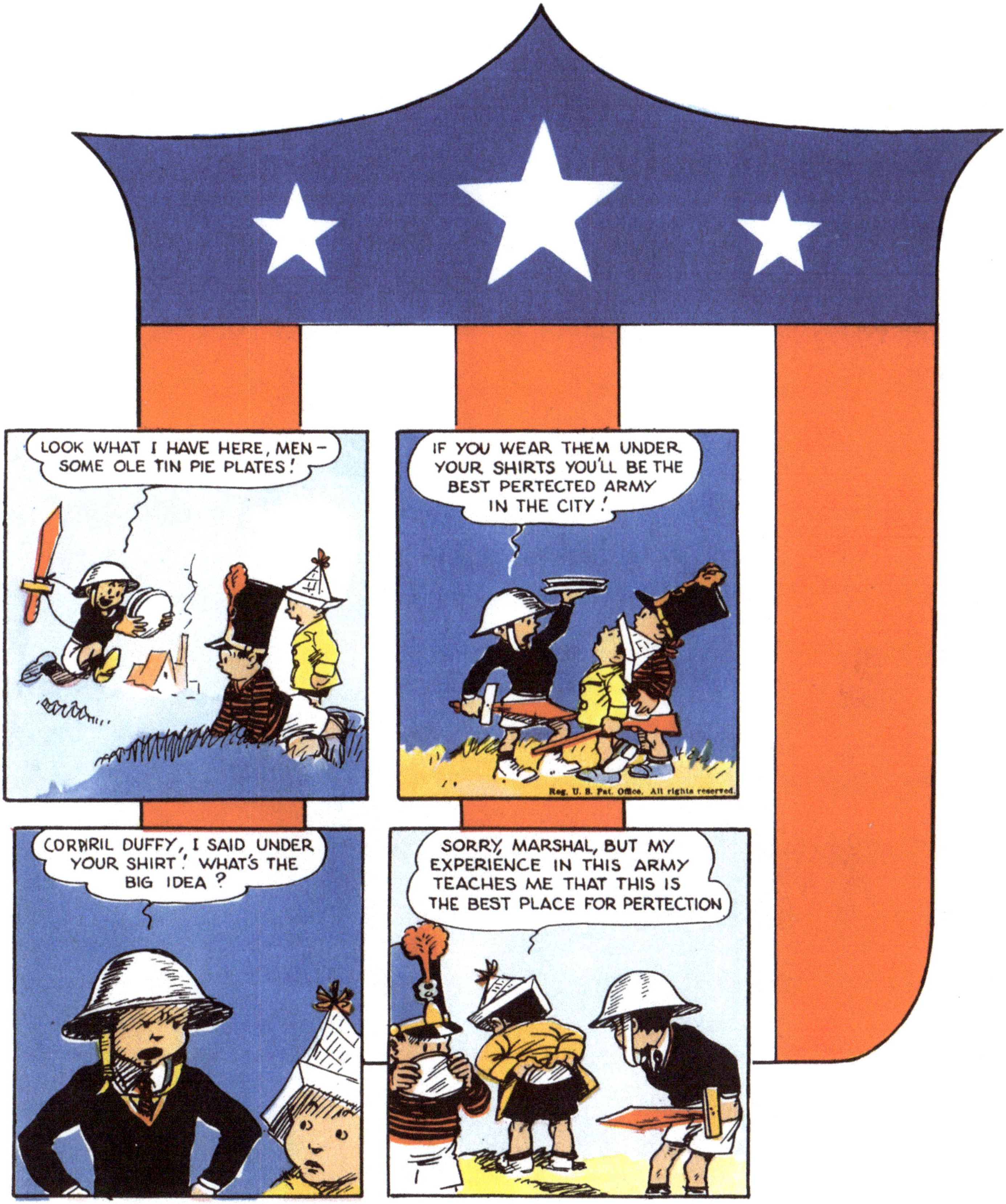

LOOK WHAT I HAVE HERE, MEN— SOME OLE TIN PIE PLATES!
IF YOU WEAR THEM UNDER YOUR SHIRTS YOU'LL BE THE BEST PERTECTED ARMY IN THE CITY!
Reg. U. S. Pat. Office. All rights reserved.
CORPIRIL DUFFY, I SAID UNDER YOUR SHIRT! WHAT'S THE BIG IDEA?
SORRY, MARSHAL, BUT MY EXPERIENCE IN THIS ARMY TEACHES ME THAT THIS IS THE BEST PLACE FOR PERTECTION

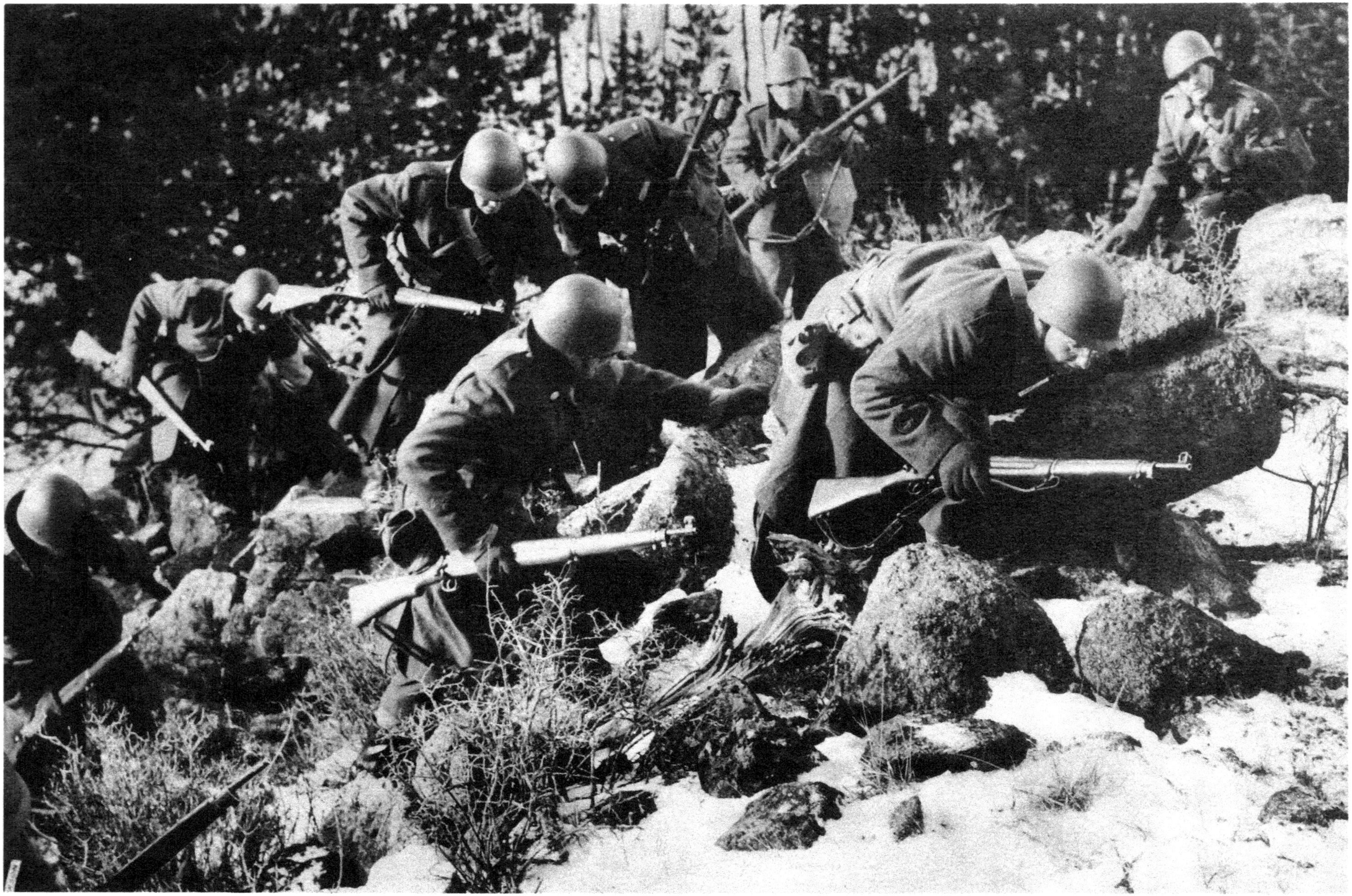

Official Photo: U. S. Army

An O.C.S. class on maneuvers advancing up the icy slopes of a Wyoming mountain. A picked squad from the advance guard crawls around the "enemy" and is ready to continue the attack

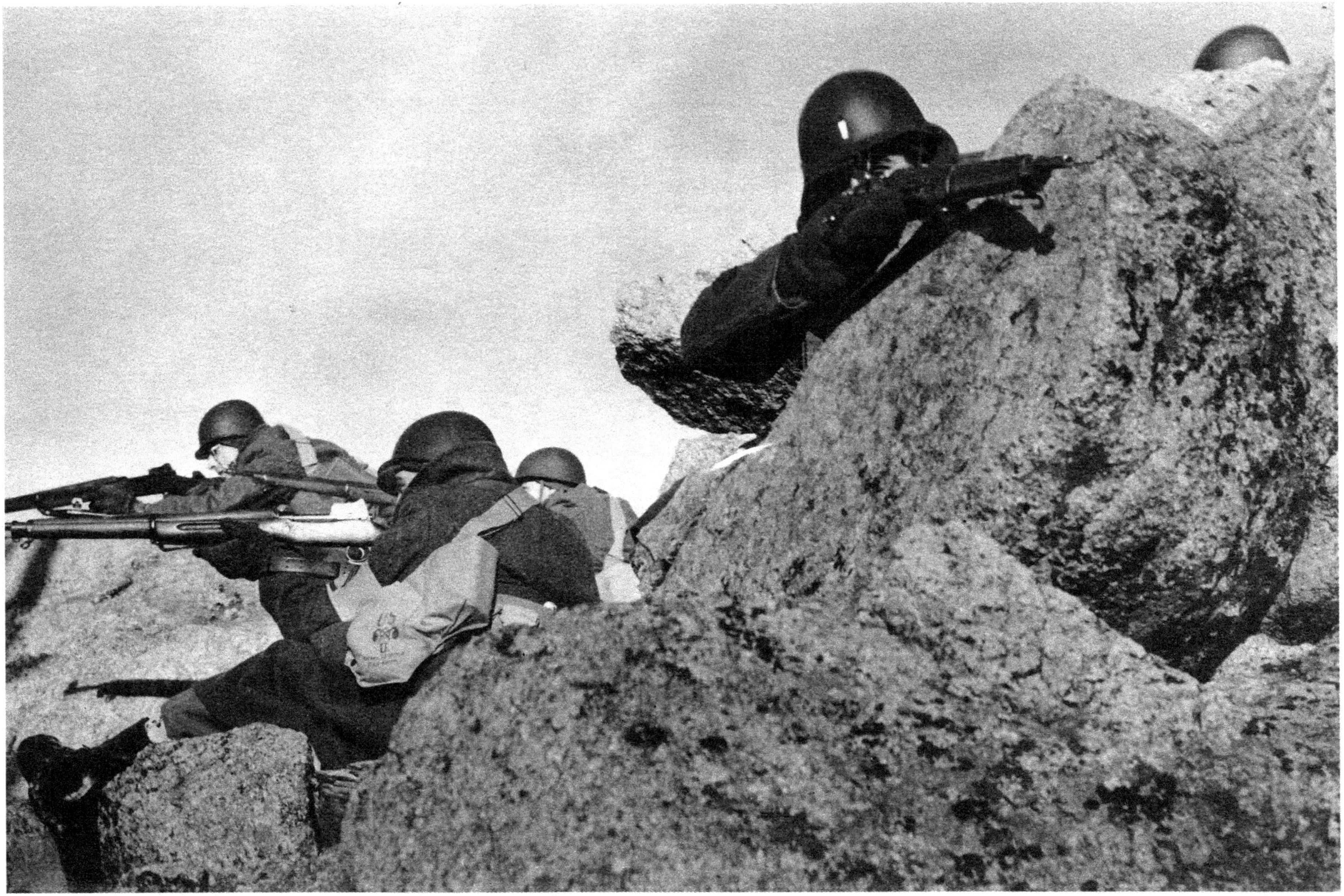

Official Photo: U. S. Army Signal Corps

Fort Frances E. Warren's O.C.S. class on maneuvers, in which they were to plan and execute the movement of supplies up the icy slopes of Pole Mt., Wyoming, 1943. . . . The enemy is discovered and its limited strength noted; the advance guard moves forward and takes up battle positions behind huge boulders.

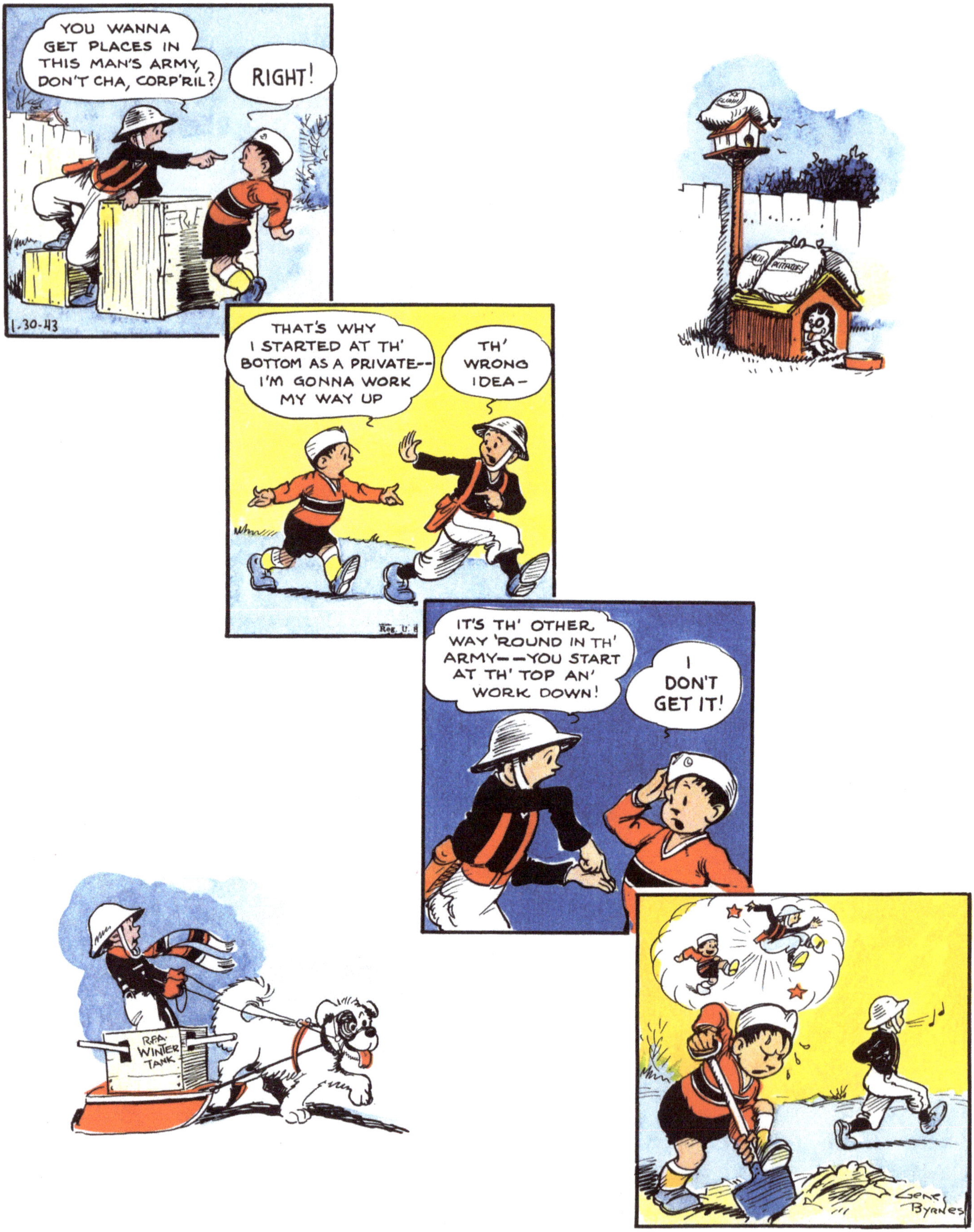
YOU WANNA GET PLACES IN THIS MAN'S ARMY, DON'T CHA, CORP'RIL?
RIGHT!
1-30-43
THAT'S WHY I STARTED AT TH' BOTTOM AS A PRIVATE-- I'M GONNA WORK MY WAY UP
TH' WRONG IDEA-
IT'S TH' OTHER WAY 'ROUND IN TH' ARMY--YOU START AT TH' TOP AN' WORK DOWN!
I DON'T GET IT!
GENE BYRNES
R.F.A. WINTER TANK

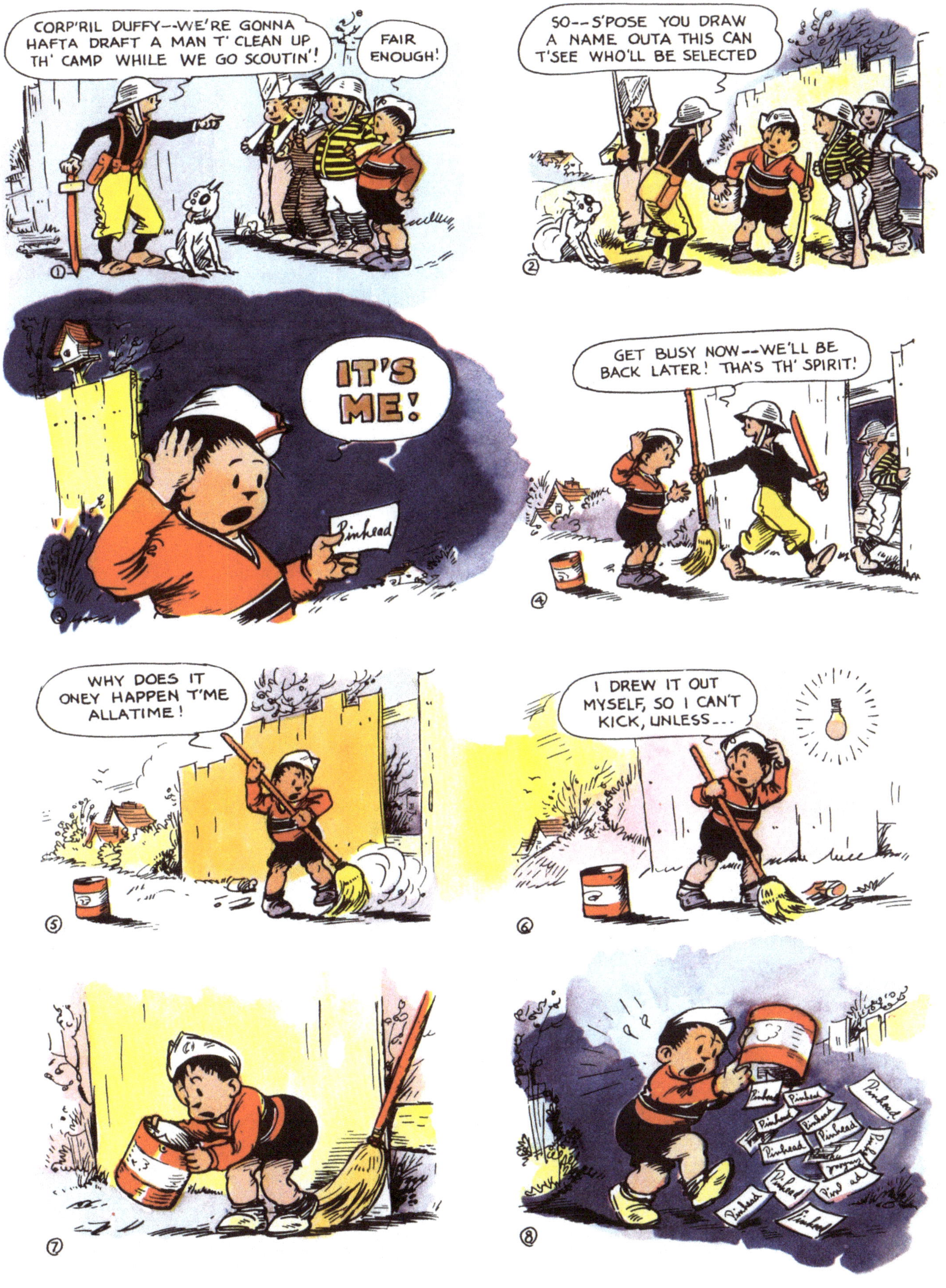
CORP'RIL DUFFY--WE'RE GONNA HAFTA DRAFT A MAN T' CLEAN UP TH' CAMP WHILE WE GO SCOUTIN'!
FAIR ENOUGH!
SO--S'POSE YOU DRAW A NAME OUTA THIS CAN T'SEE WHO'LL BE SELECTED
IT'S ME!
Pinhead
GET BUSY NOW--WE'LL BE BACK LATER! THA'S TH' SPIRIT!
WHY DOES IT ONEY HAPPEN T'ME ALLATIME!
I DREW IT OUT MYSELF, SO I CAN'T KICK, UNLESS...
Pinhead
Pinhead
Pinhead
Pinhead

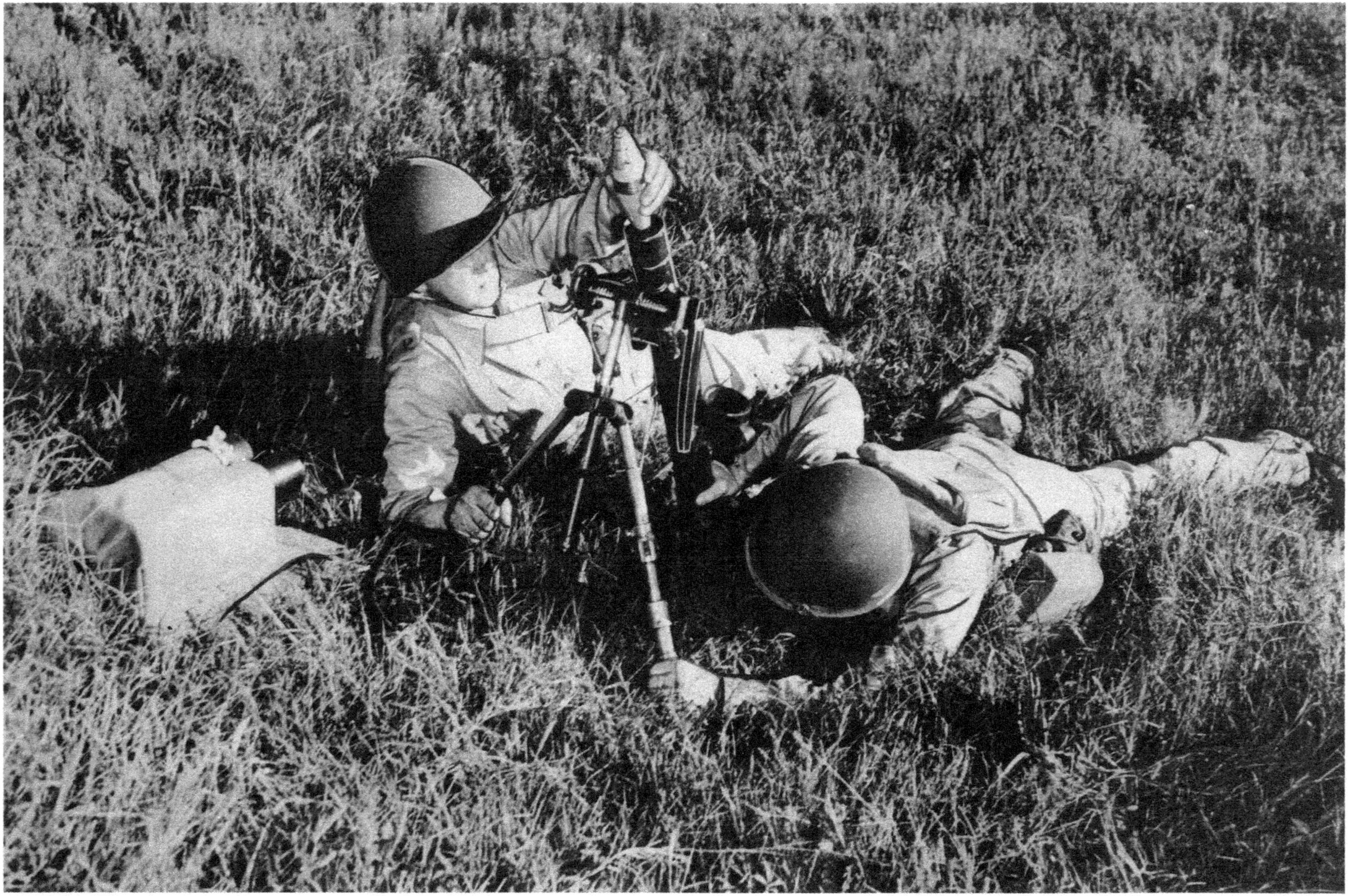

Official Photo: U. S. Army Infantry School

Two soldiers operating a 60 mm. trench mortar. These small guns do terrific damage to the enemy at short range

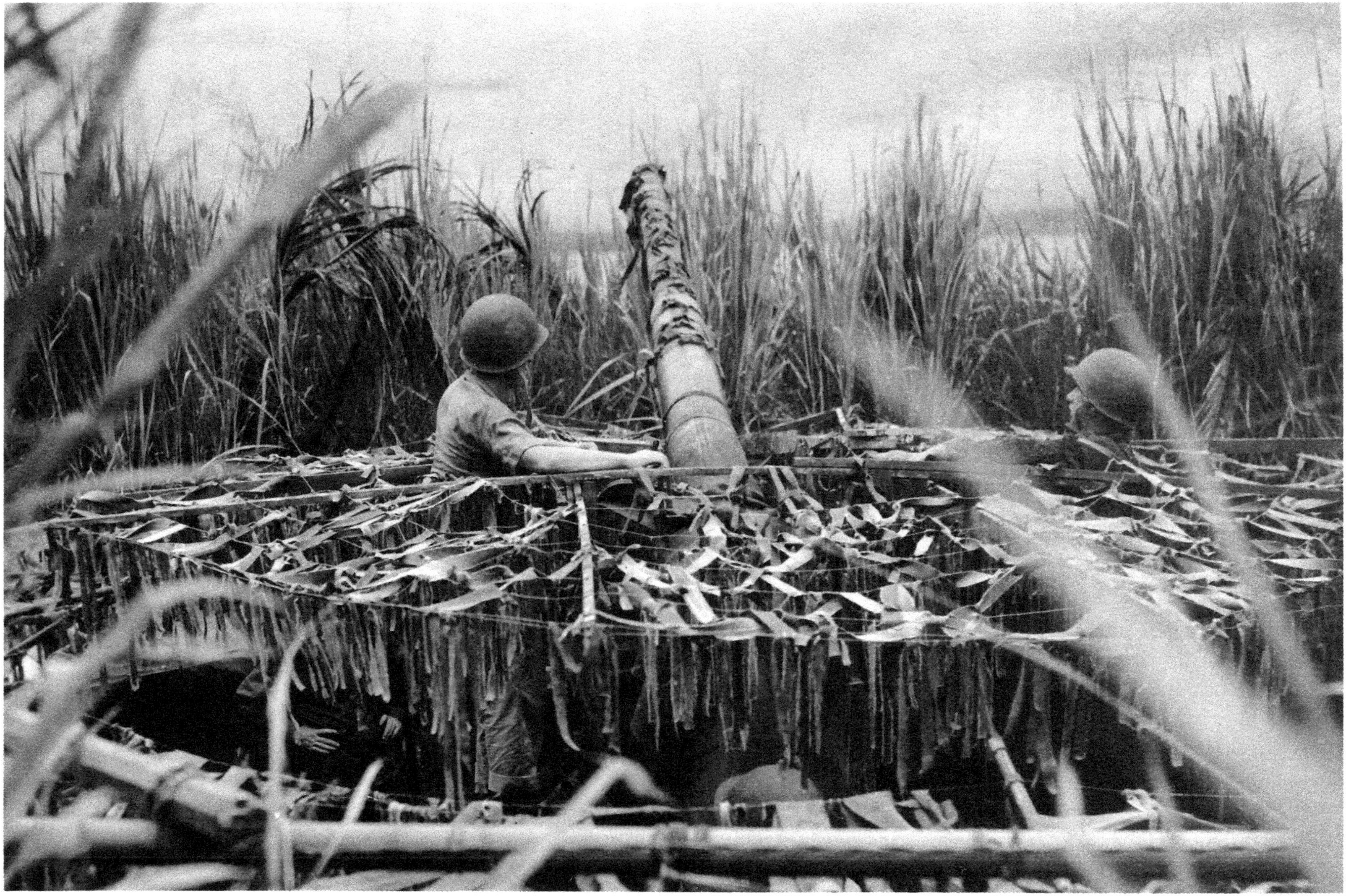

Official Photo: U. S. Army

A camouflaged coast defense gun at one of our bases in the Caribbean

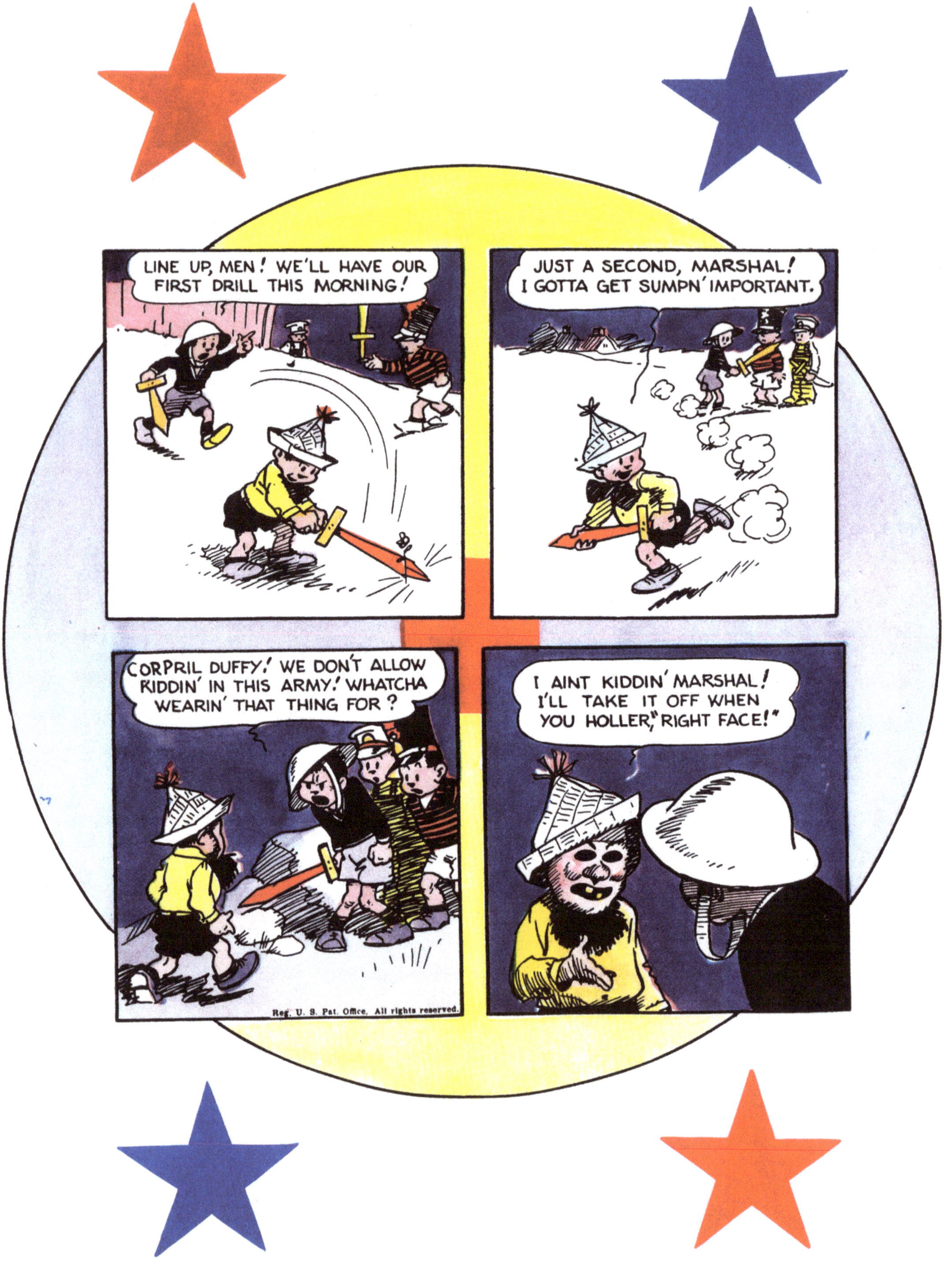
LINE UP, MEN! WE'LL HAVE OUR FIRST DRILL THIS MORNING!
JUST A SECOND, MARSHAL! I GOTTA GET SUMPN' IMPORTANT.
CORPRIL DUFFY! WE DON'T ALLOW KIDDIN' IN THIS ARMY! WHATCHA WEARIN' THAT THING FOR?
I AINT KIDDIN' MARSHAL! I'LL TAKE IT OFF WHEN YOU HOLLER, "RIGHT FACE!"
Reg. U. S. Pat. Office. All rights reserved.

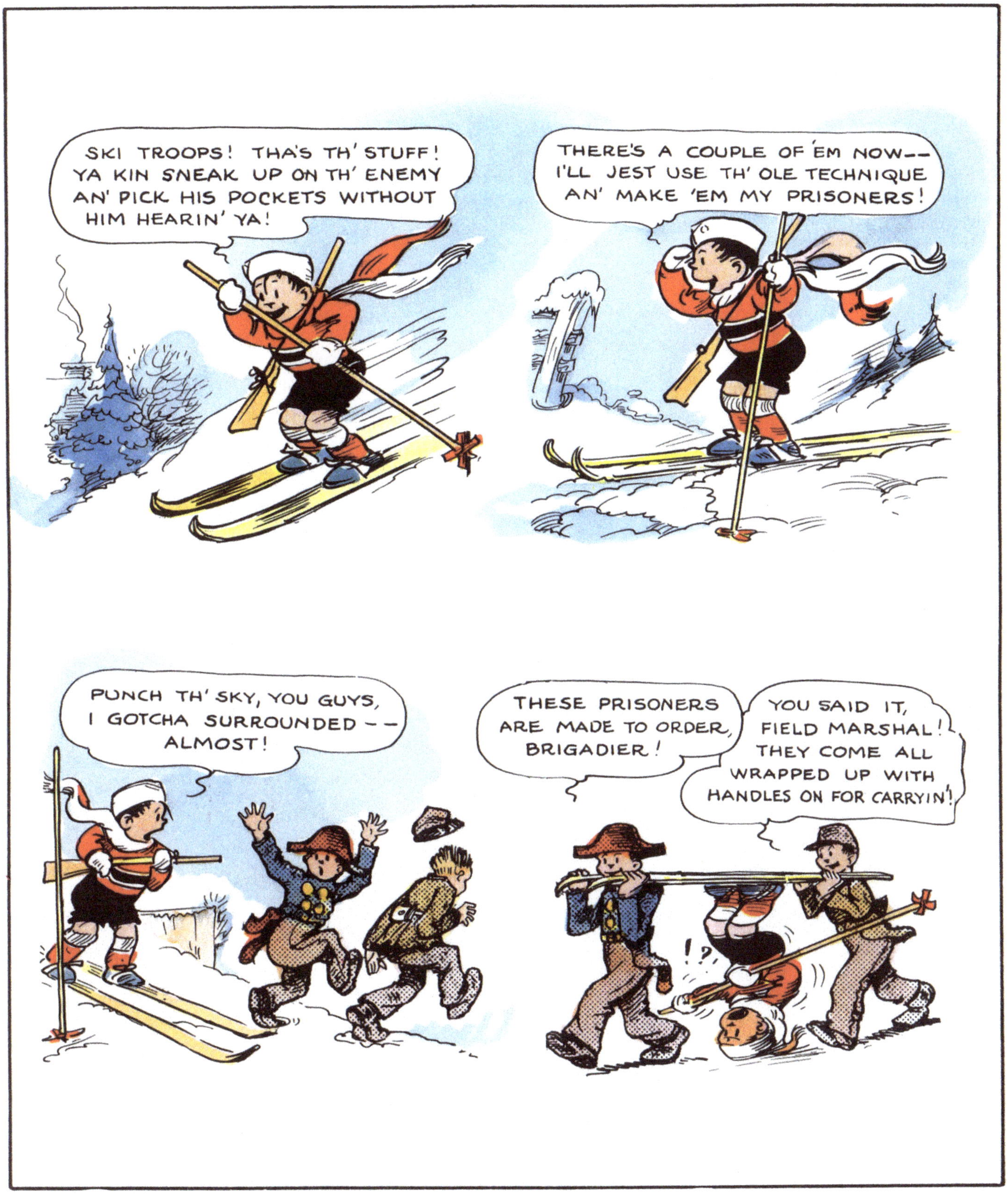
SKI TROOPS! THA'S TH' STUFF! YA KIN SNEAK UP ON TH' ENEMY AN' PICK HIS POCKETS WITHOUT HIM HEARIN' YA!
THERE'S A COUPLE OF 'EM NOW-- I'LL JEST USE TH' OLE TECHNIQUE AN' MAKE 'EM MY PRISONERS!
PUNCH TH' SKY, YOU GUYS, I GOTCHA SURROUNDED-- ALMOST!
THESE PRISONERS ARE MADE TO ORDER, BRIGADIER!
YOU SAID IT, FIELD MARSHAL! THEY COME ALL WRAPPED UP WITH HANDLES ON FOR CARRYIN'!
!?

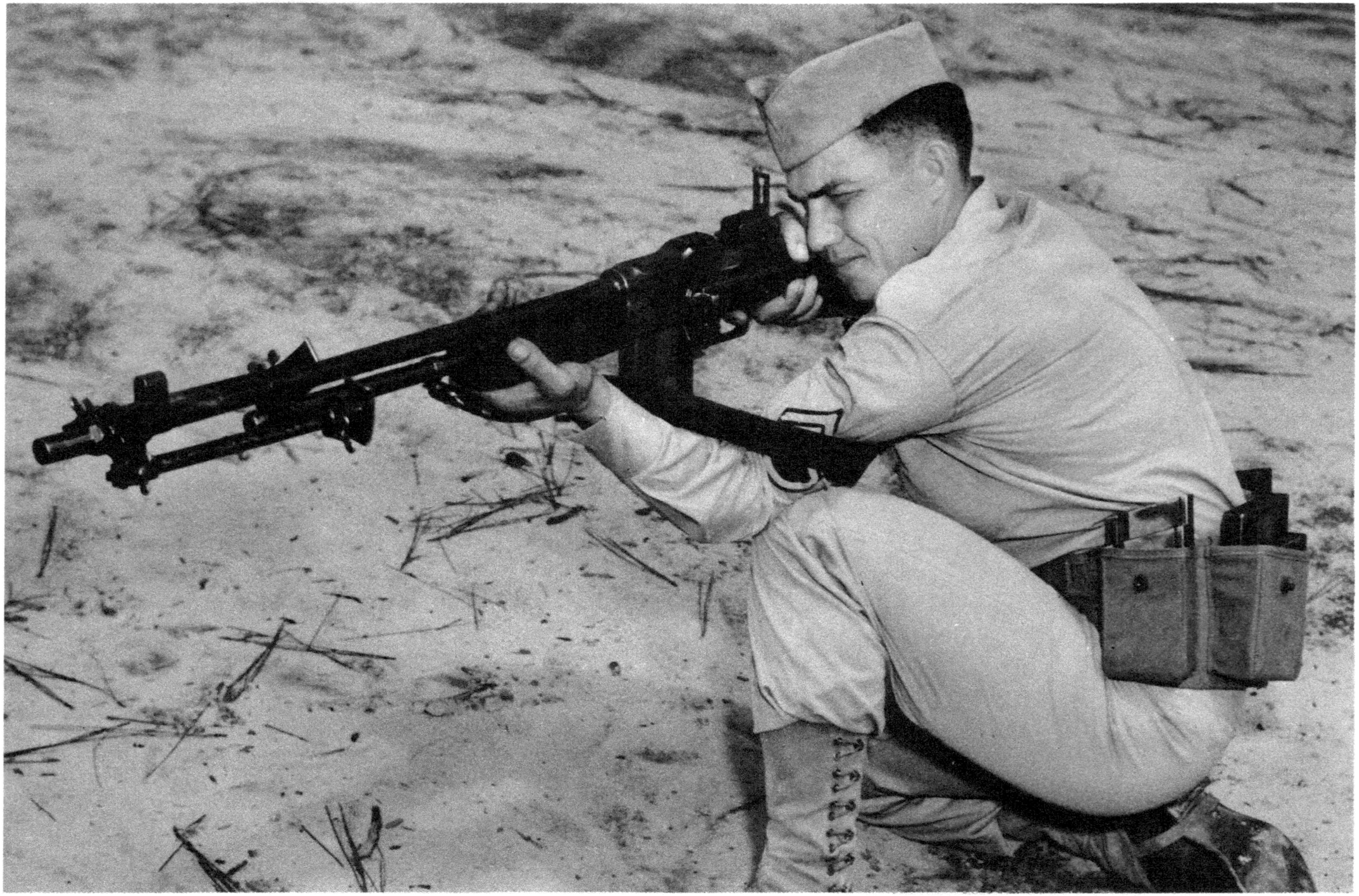

Official Photo: U. S. Army Signal Corps

Fort Benning, Ga., July — Staff Sgt. John J. Lehner of Dolomite near Birmingham, Ala., an enlisted instructor in The Infantry School, Fort Benning, has been credited with one of the most amazing rifle scores in the history of the United States Army. Sgt. Lehner scored 209 out of a possible 210 in all positions with a Browning Automatic Rifle, amazing because of its high rate of fire — 350 to 550 shots per minute

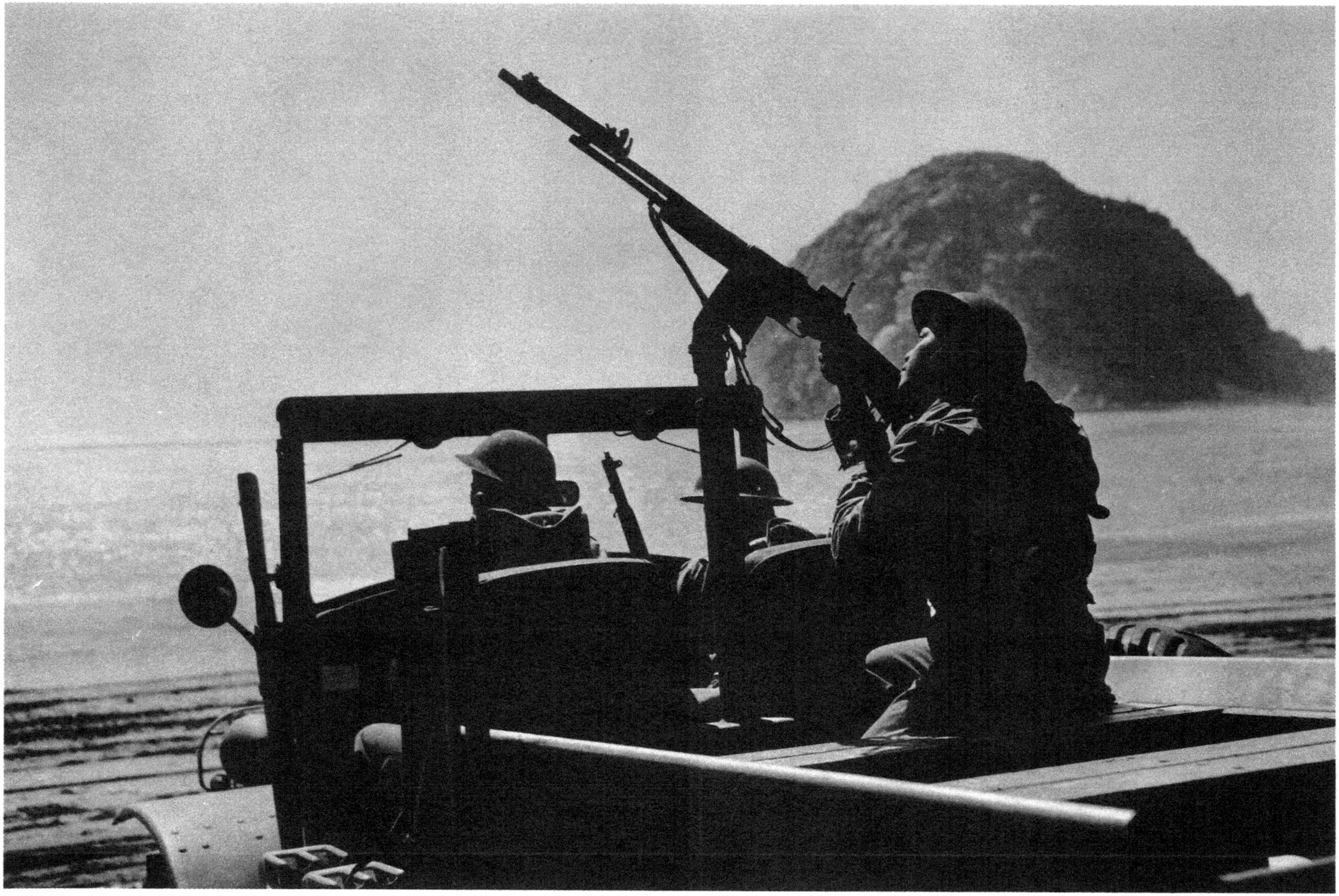

Official Photo: U. S. Army Signal Corps

Filipino soldiers training in the United States for the struggle to liberate their homeland. A soldier uses his automatic rifle as an anti-aircraft gun

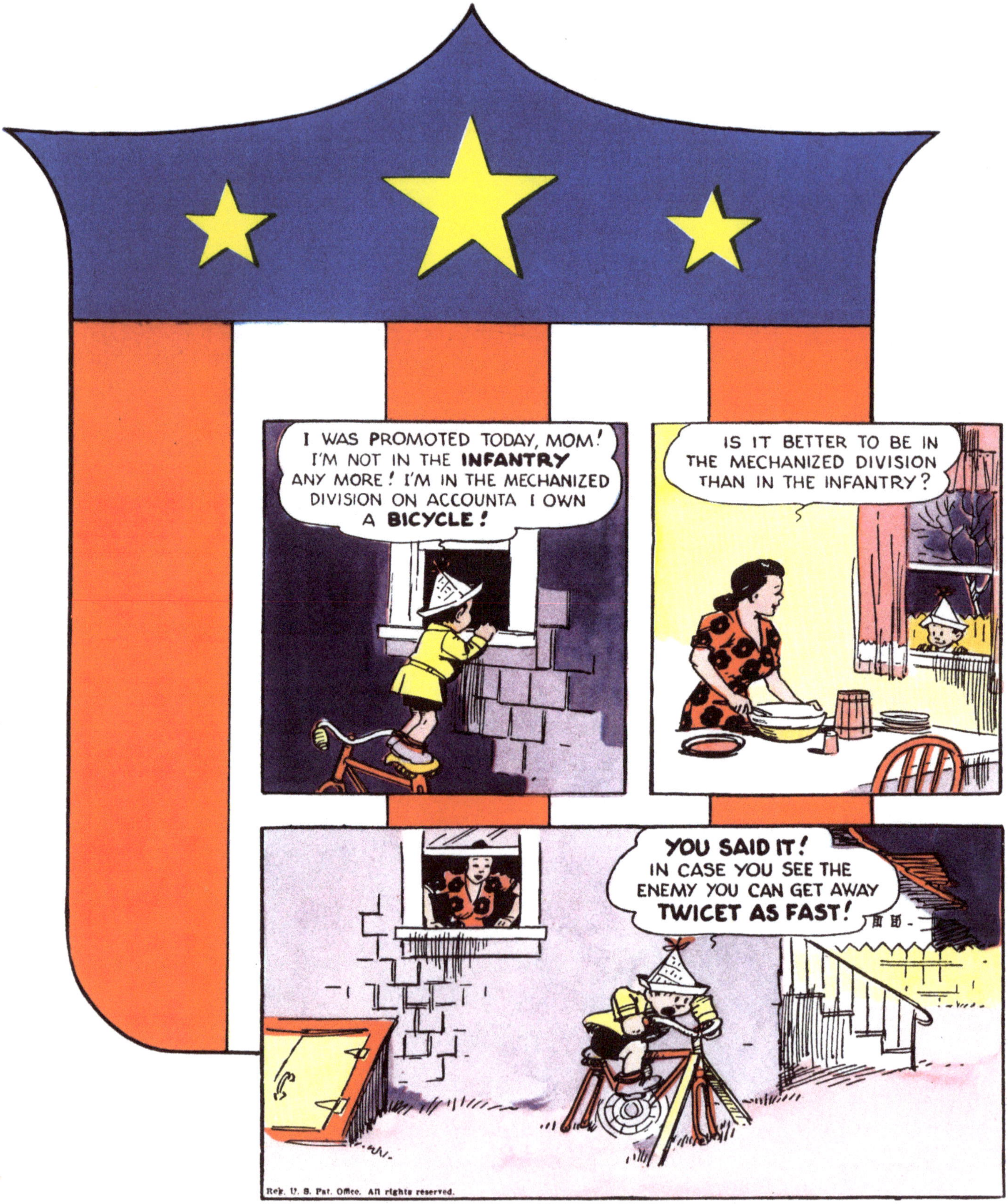
I WAS PROMOTED TODAY, MOM! I'M NOT IN THE **INFANTRY** ANY MORE! I'M IN THE MECHANIZED DIVISION ON ACCOUNTA I OWN A **BICYCLE!**
IS IT BETTER TO BE IN THE MECHANIZED DIVISION THAN IN THE INFANTRY?
YOU SAID IT! IN CASE YOU SEE THE ENEMY YOU CAN GET AWAY **TWICET AS FAST!**
Reg. U. S. Pat. Office. All rights reserved.

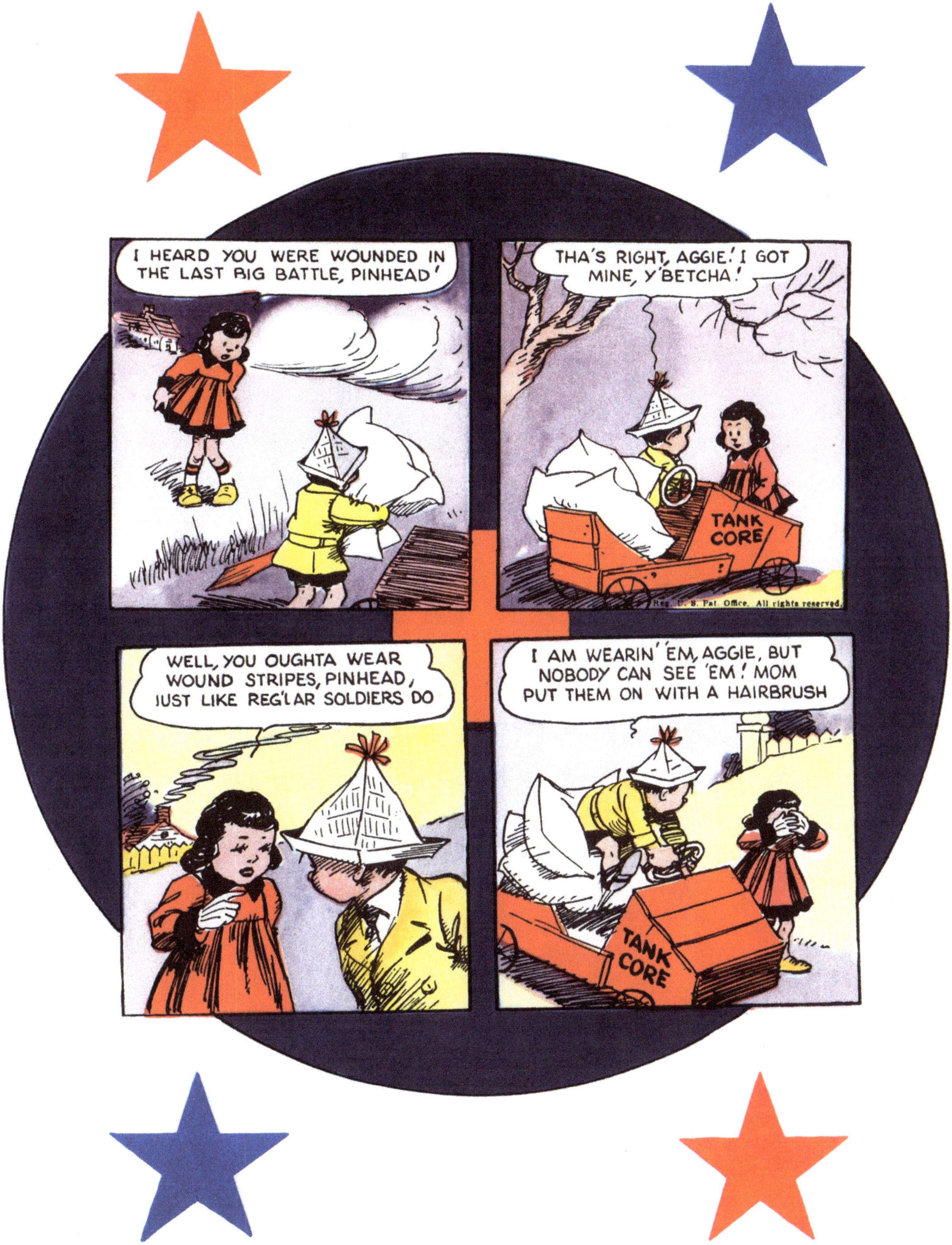
I HEARD YOU WERE WOUNDED IN THE LAST BIG BATTLE, PINHEAD!
THA'S RIGHT, AGGIE! I GOT MINE, Y'BETCHA!
TANK CORE
Reg. U. S. Pat. Office. All rights reserved.
WELL, YOU OUGHTA WEAR WOUND STRIPES, PINHEAD, JUST LIKE REG'LAR SOLDIERS DO
I AM WEARIN' 'EM, AGGIE, BUT NOBODY CAN SEE 'EM! MOM PUT THEM ON WITH A HAIRBRUSH
TANK CORE

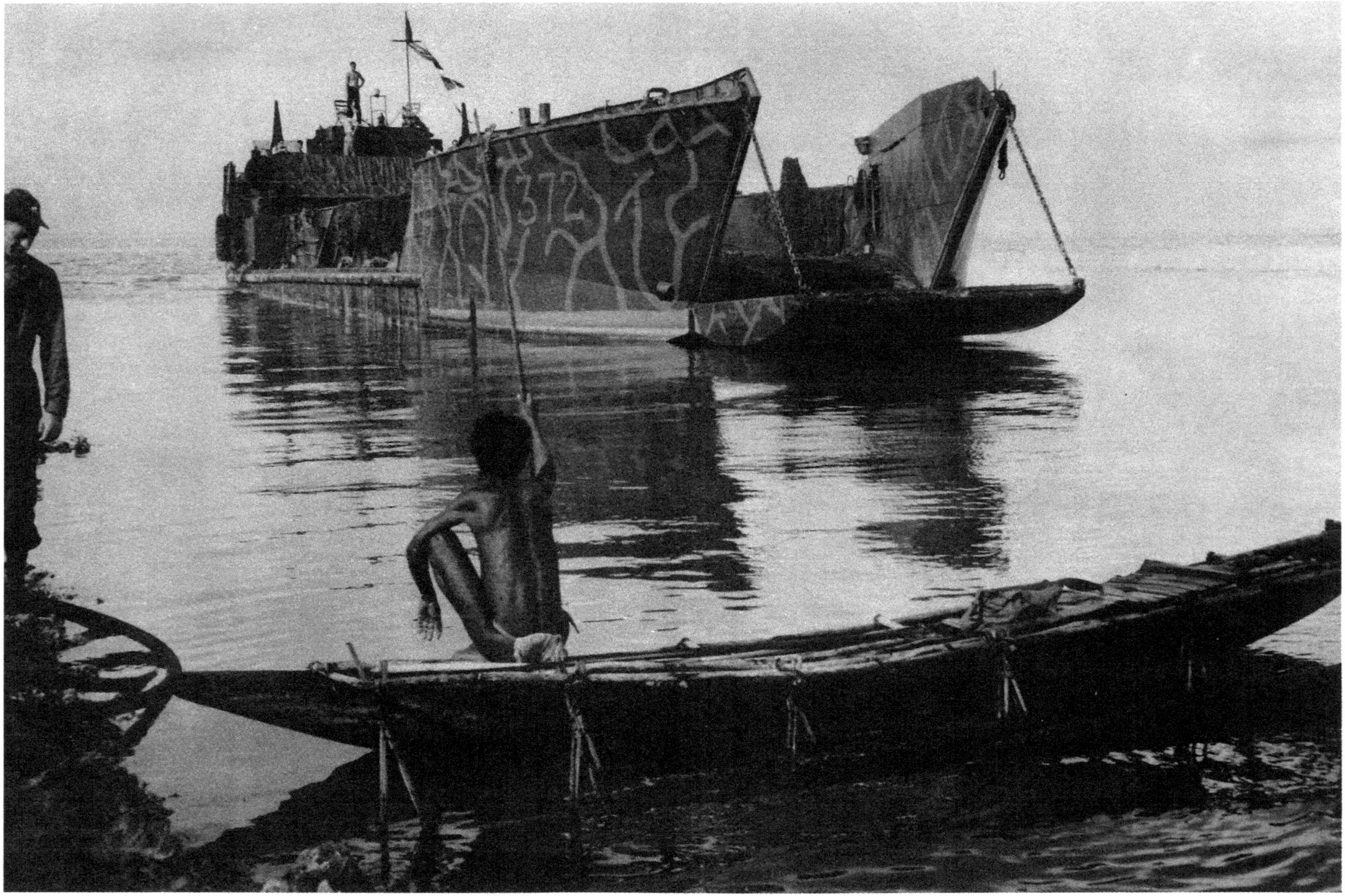
372

Official Photo: U. S. Army Signal Corps

A South Sea Island native inspects an American landing barge which was used in the invasion of his island which had been captured by Japs

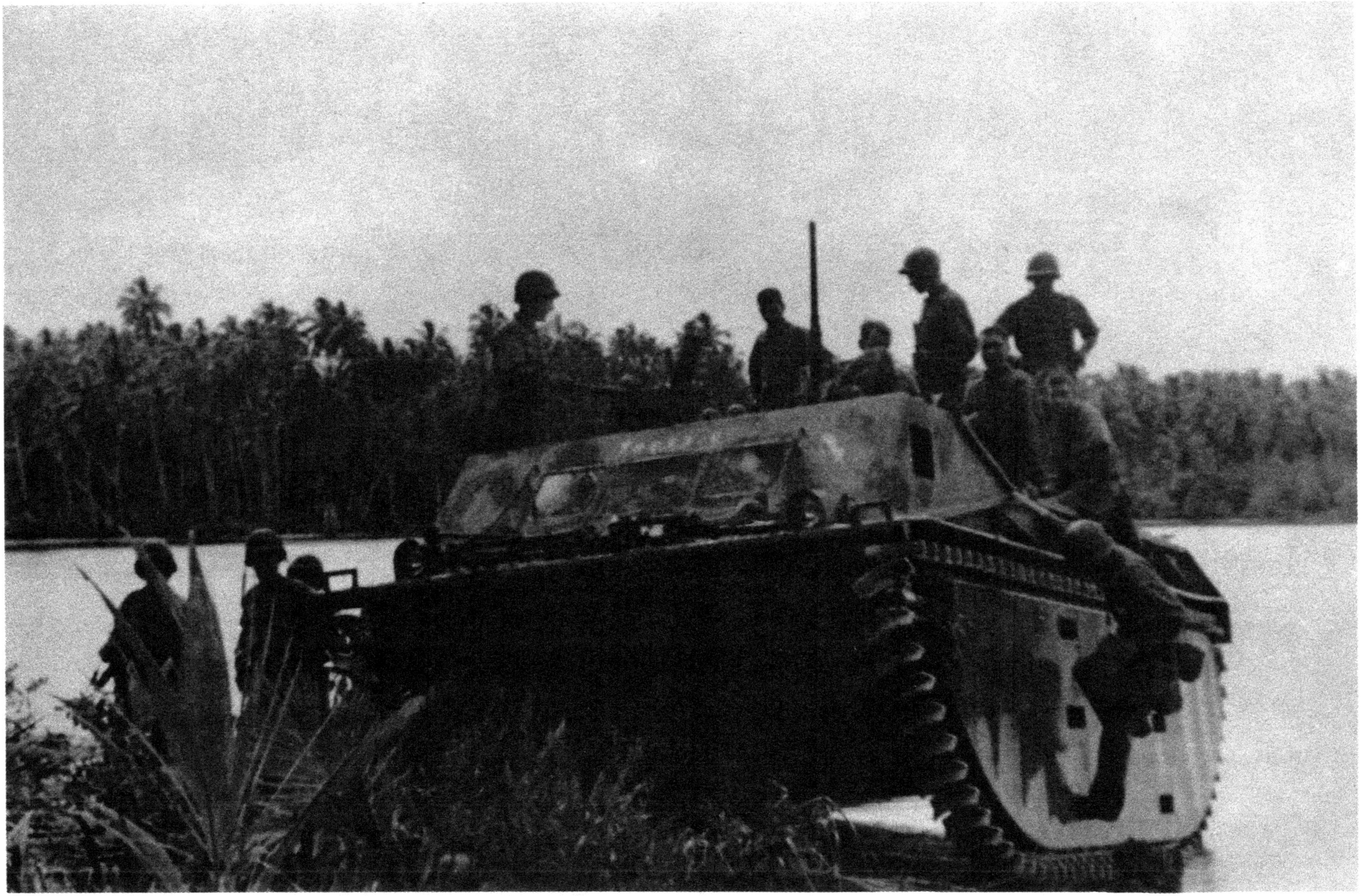

Official Photo: U. S. Army Signal Corps

Tractor men prepare to dismount during landing operations on a South Sea island by American troops

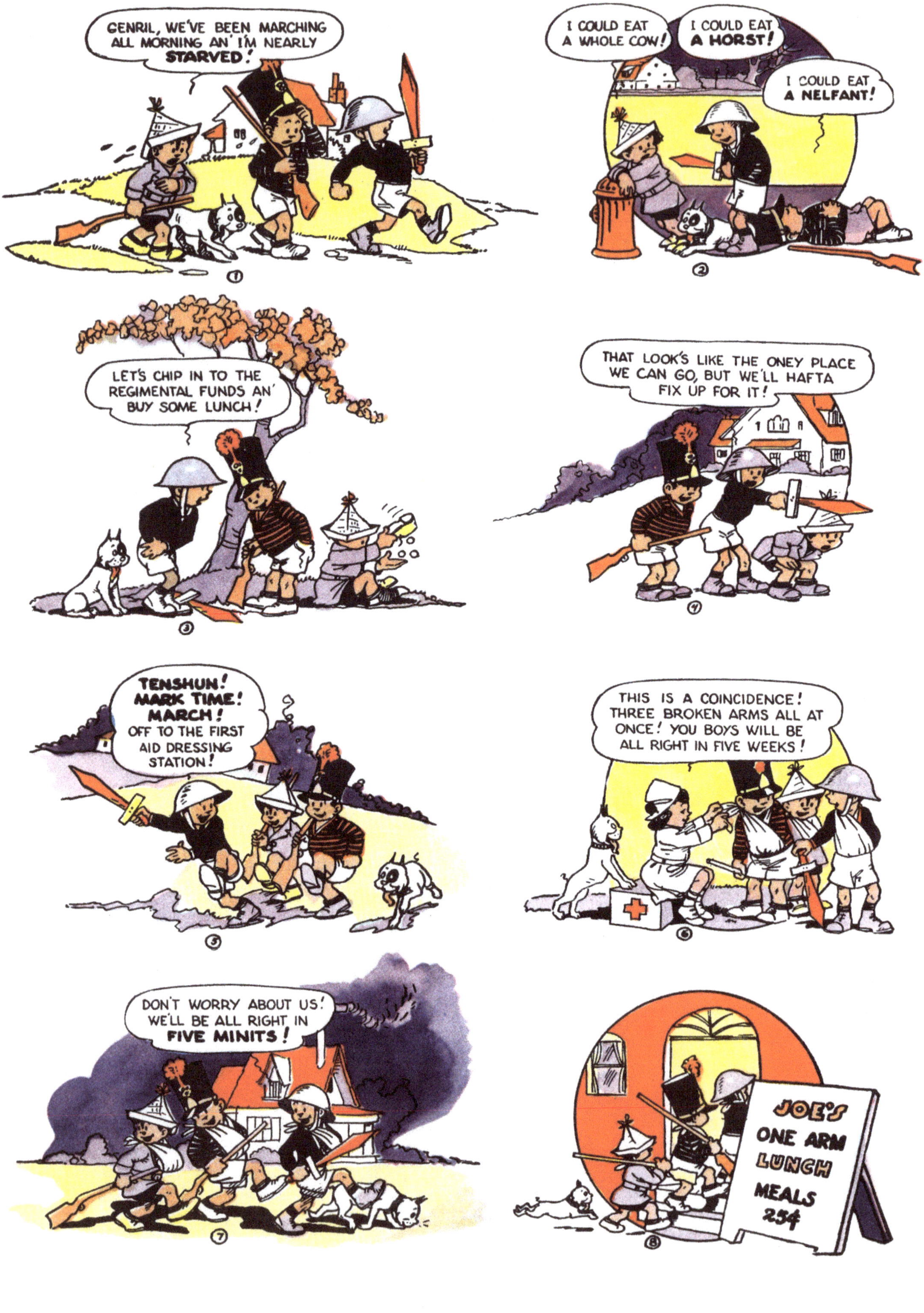
GENRIL, WE'VE BEEN MARCHING ALL MORNING AN' I'M NEARLY STARVED!
I COULD EAT A WHOLE COW!
I COULD EAT A HORST!
I COULD EAT A NELFANT!
LET'S CHIP IN TO THE REGIMENTAL FUNDS AN' BUY SOME LUNCH!
THAT LOOK'S LIKE THE ONEY PLACE WE CAN GO, BUT WE'LL HAFTA FIX UP FOR IT!
TENSHUN! MARK TIME! MARCH! OFF TO THE FIRST AID DRESSING STATION!
THIS IS A COINCIDENCE! THREE BROKEN ARMS ALL AT ONCE! YOU BOYS WILL BE ALL RIGHT IN FIVE WEEKS!
DON'T WORRY ABOUT US! WE'LL BE ALL RIGHT IN FIVE MINITS!
JOE'S ONE ARM LUNCH MEALS 25¢

AS MEMBER OF TH' SUICIDE SQUAD, YOUR FIRST JOB IS T' GO DOWN AN' TELL MY MOM I WANT A DIME AN' DON'T TAKE NO FOR AN ANSWER!
I RESIGN!
R.F. ARMY

YOU TOLE ME TO FALL IN DIDN'TCHA? SO I DID!

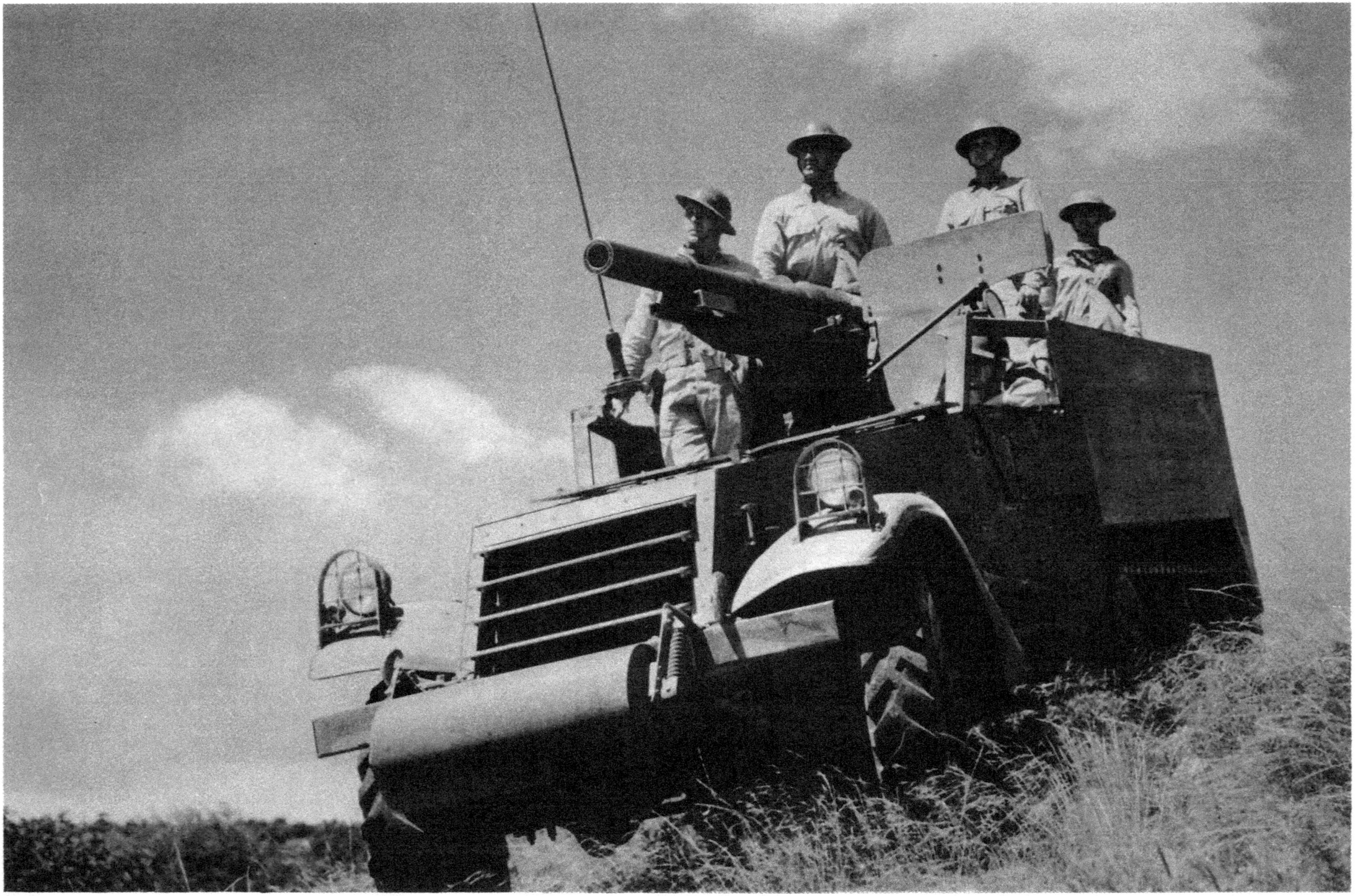

Official Photo: U. S. Army Signal Corps

A tank destroyer mounting a 75 mm. gun, waits for instructions either by radio or bringer. Ft. Hood, Texas

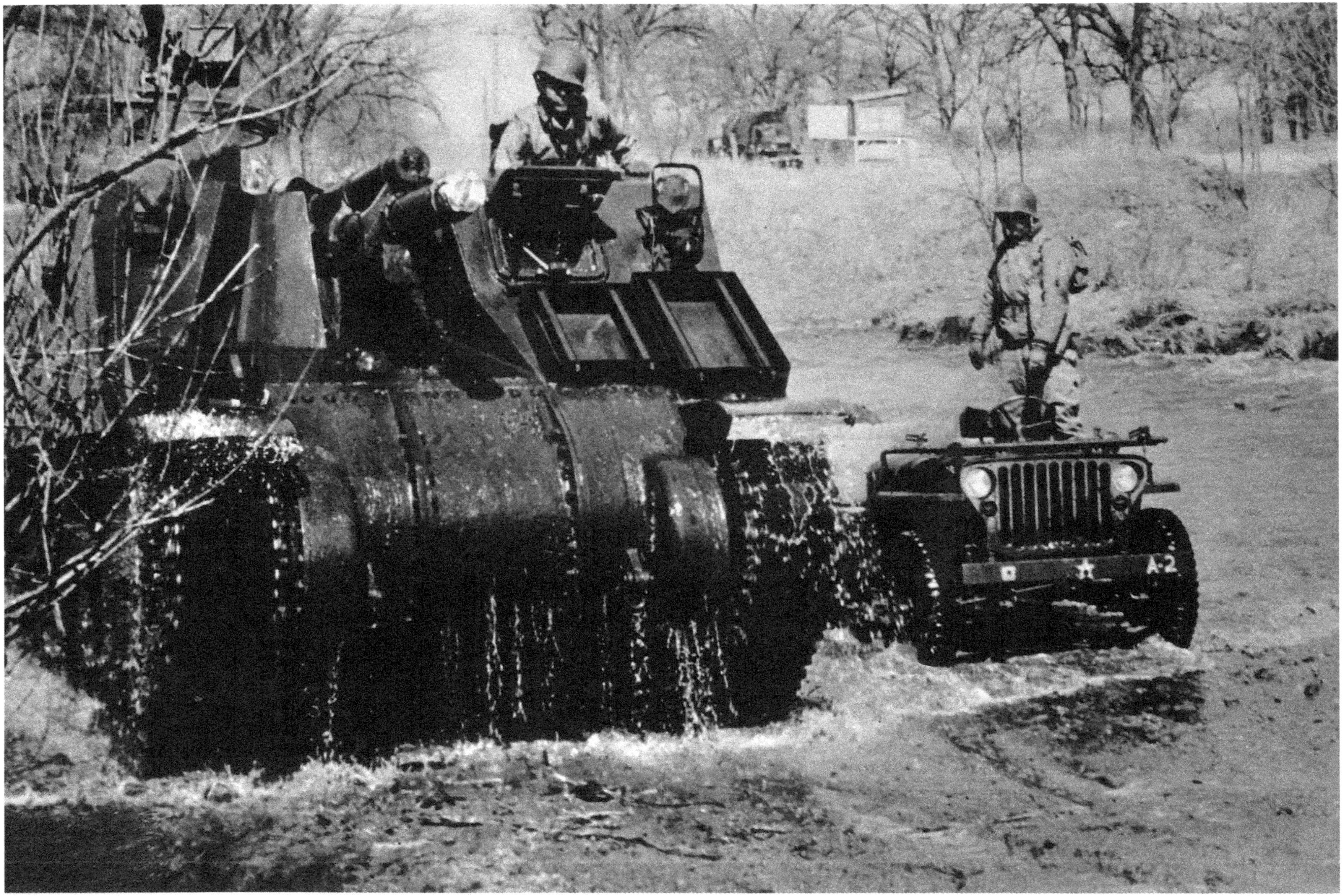
A-2

Official Photo: U. S. Army Signal Corps

M-7, Self-propelled Field Artillery on maneuvers . . . Jeep standing by a dripping M-7 tank destroyer as it fords a stream.

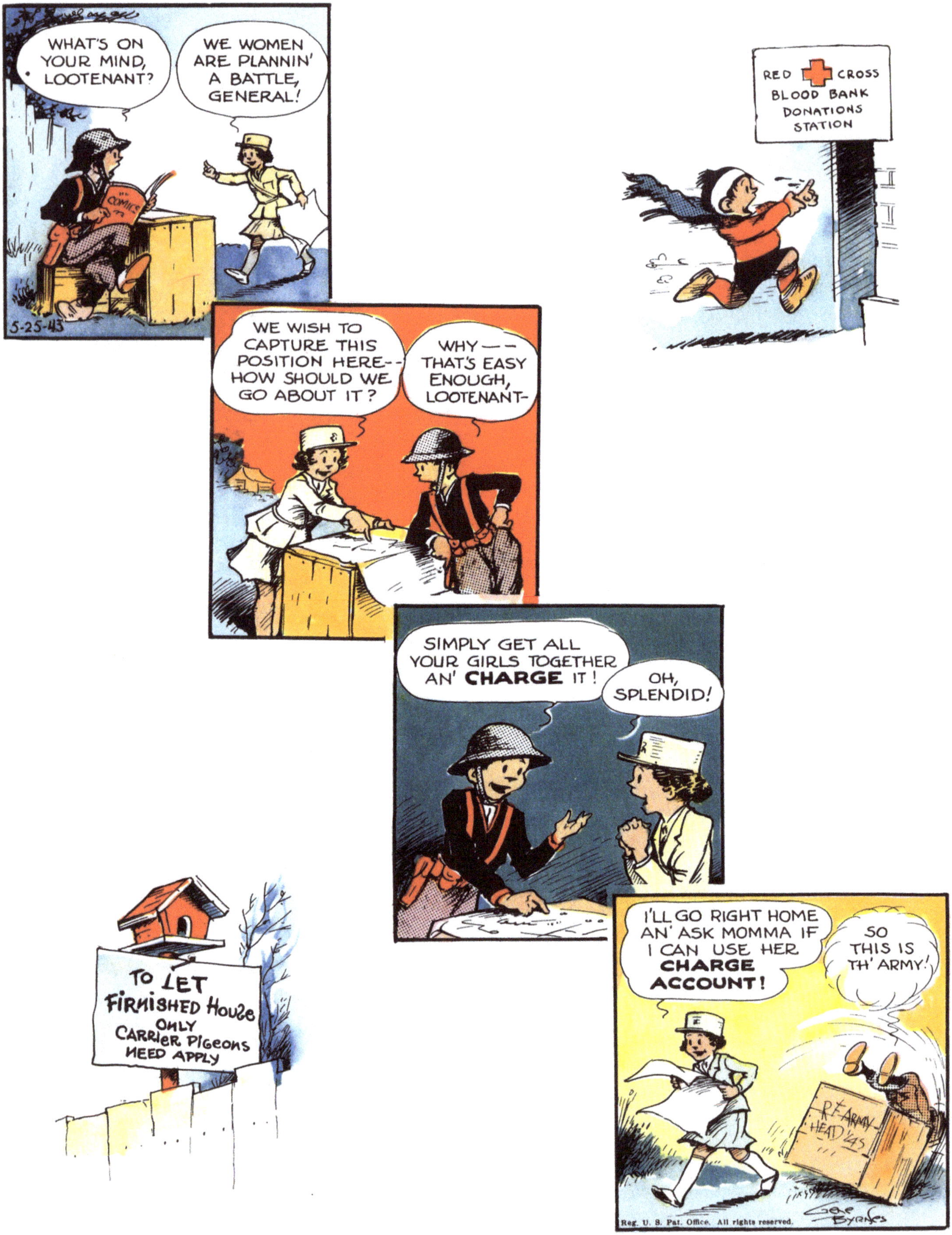

5-25-43
WHAT'S ON YOUR MIND, LOOTENANT?
WE WOMEN ARE PLANNIN' A BATTLE, GENERAL!
COMICS
RED CROSS BLOOD BANK DONATIONS STATION
WE WISH TO CAPTURE THIS POSITION HERE-- HOW SHOULD WE GO ABOUT IT?
WHY -- THAT'S EASY ENOUGH, LOOTENANT-
SIMPLY GET ALL YOUR GIRLS TOGETHER AN' **CHARGE** IT!
OH, SPLENDID!
TO LET
FIRNISHED HOUSE
ONLY CARRIER PIGEONS NEED APPLY
I'LL GO RIGHT HOME AN' ASK MOMMA IF I CAN USE HER **CHARGE ACCOUNT!**
SO THIS IS TH' ARMY!
RF ARMY HEAD '43
Reg. U. S. Pat. Office. All rights reserved.
Gene Byrnes

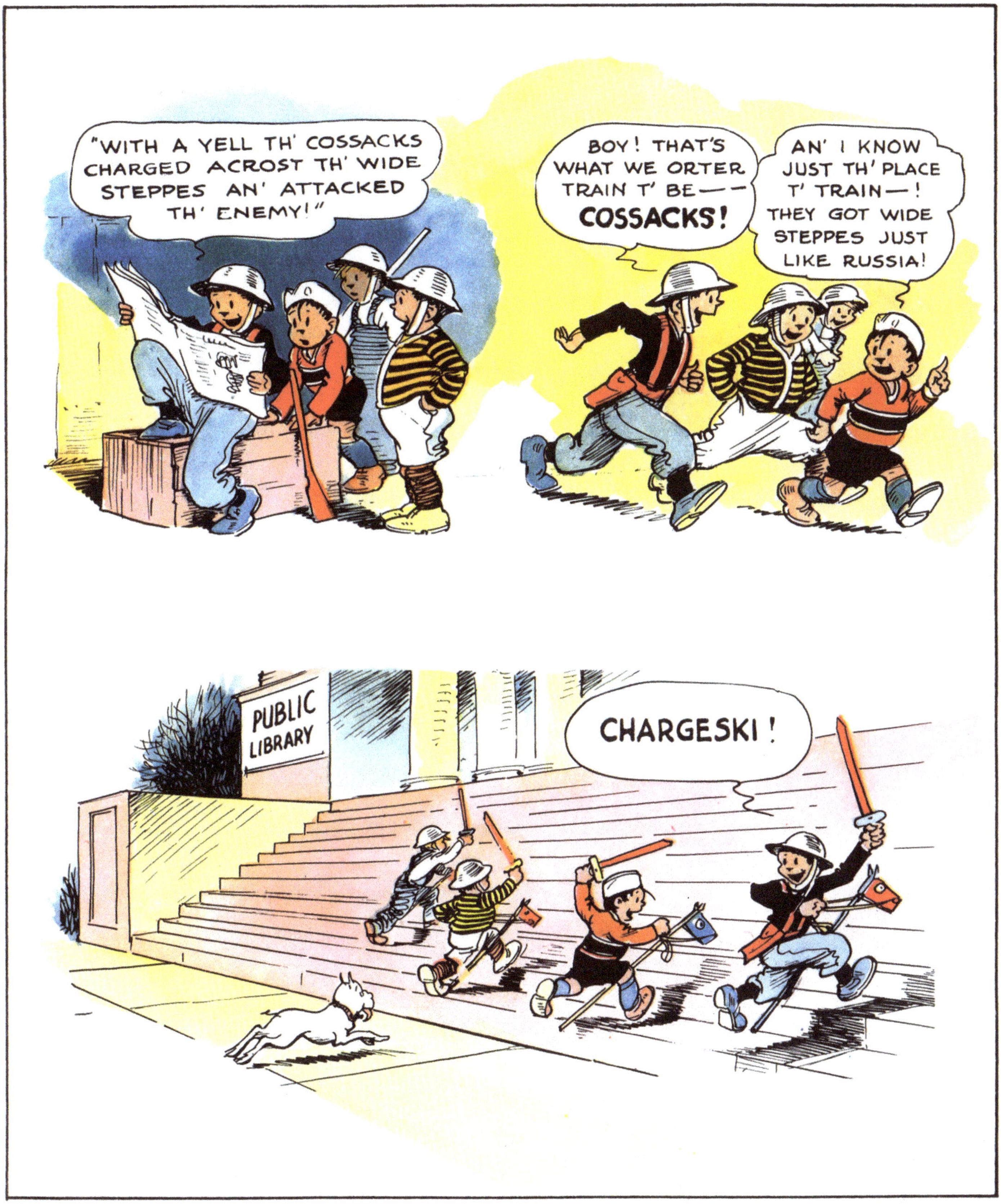
"WITH A YELL TH' COSSACKS CHARGED ACROST TH' WIDE STEPPES AN' ATTACKED TH' ENEMY!"
BOY! THAT'S WHAT WE ORTER TRAIN T' BE— — COSSACKS!
AN' I KNOW JUST TH' PLACE T' TRAIN—! THEY GOT WIDE STEPPES JUST LIKE RUSSIA!
PUBLIC LIBRARY
CHARGESKI!

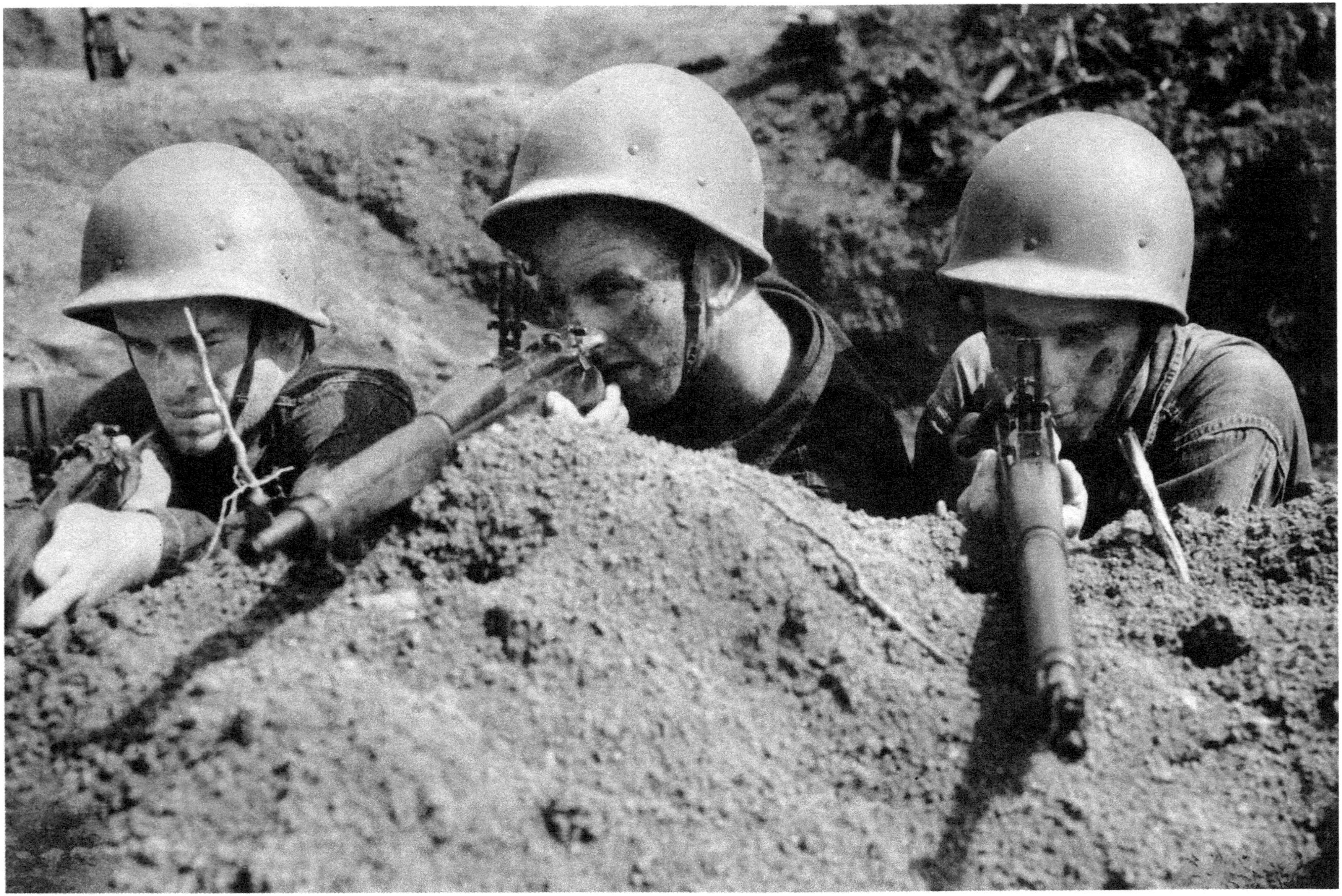

Official Photo: U. S. Army Signal Corps

U. S. troops stationed in the deep jungles of one of the U. S. Army bases in the Caribbean area. The jungle mudders in their hastily dug trenches are lining up the sights of their rifles

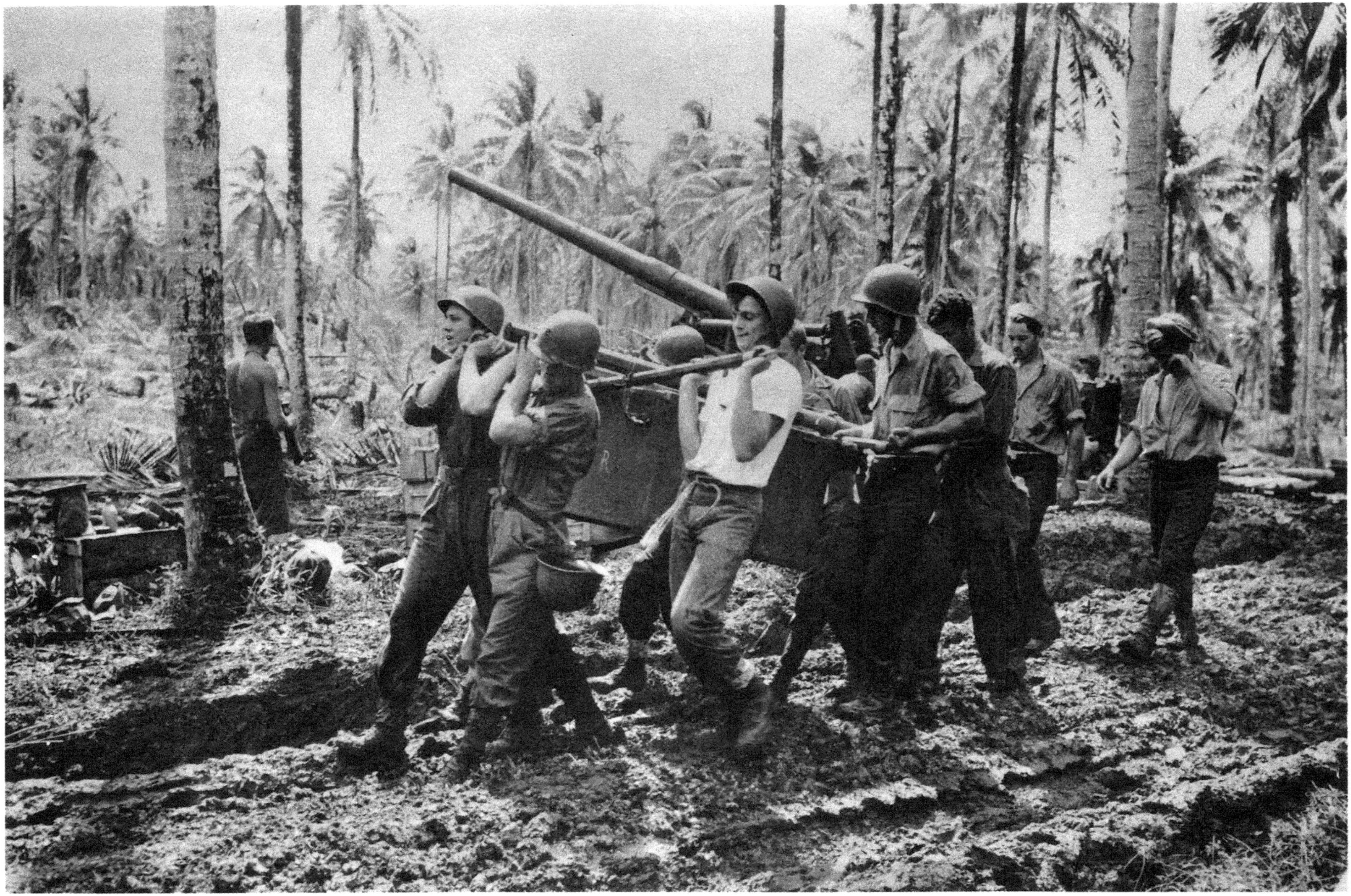

Official Photo: U. S. Army Signal Corps

Marines carry a generator through the mud in preparation for attack on Munda

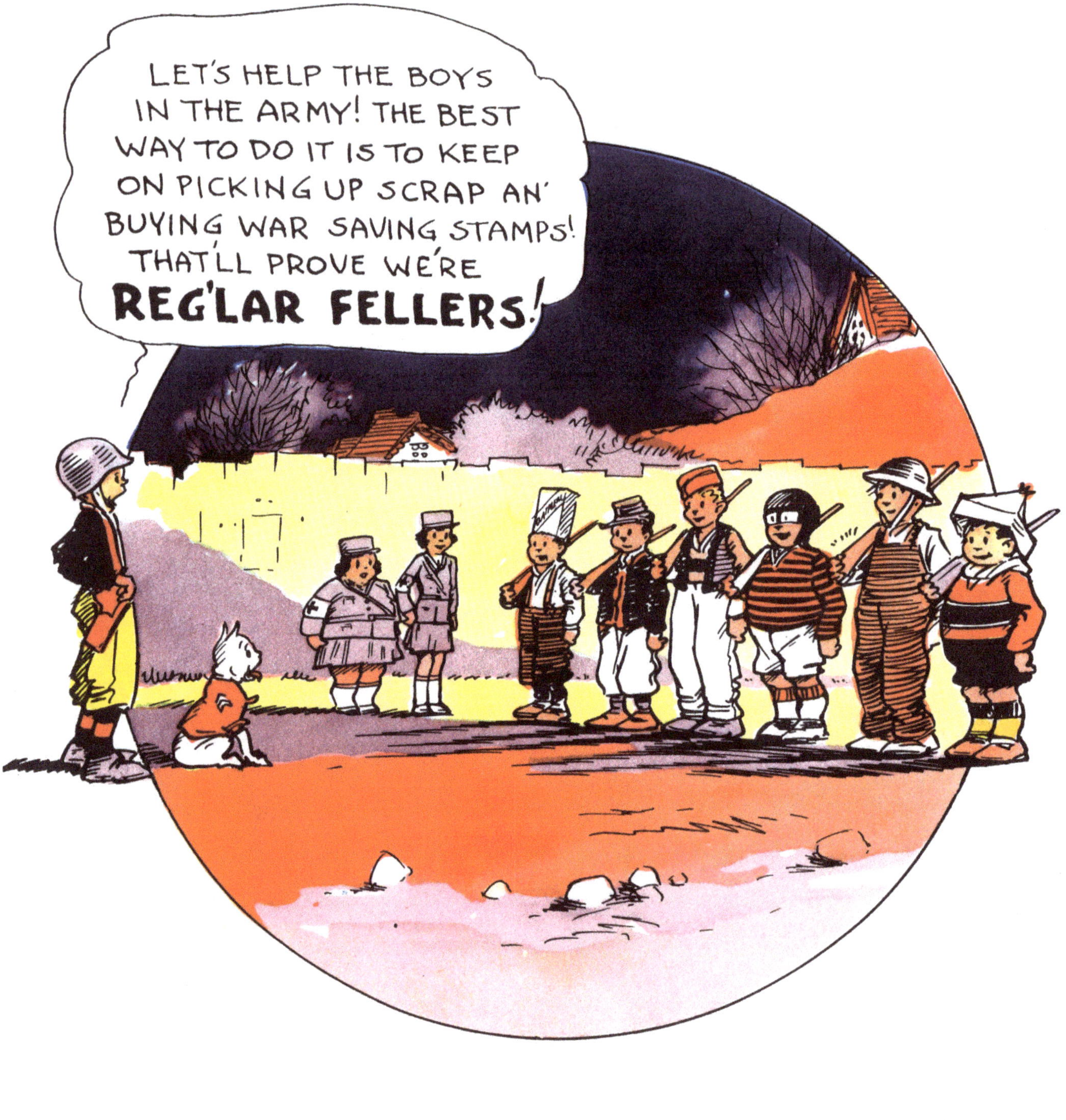
LET'S HELP THE BOYS IN THE ARMY! THE BEST WAY TO DO IT IS TO KEEP ON PICKING UP SCRAP AN' BUYING WAR SAVING STAMPS! THAT'LL PROVE WE'RE **REG'LAR FELLERS**!

CoachwhipBooks.com
Also Available

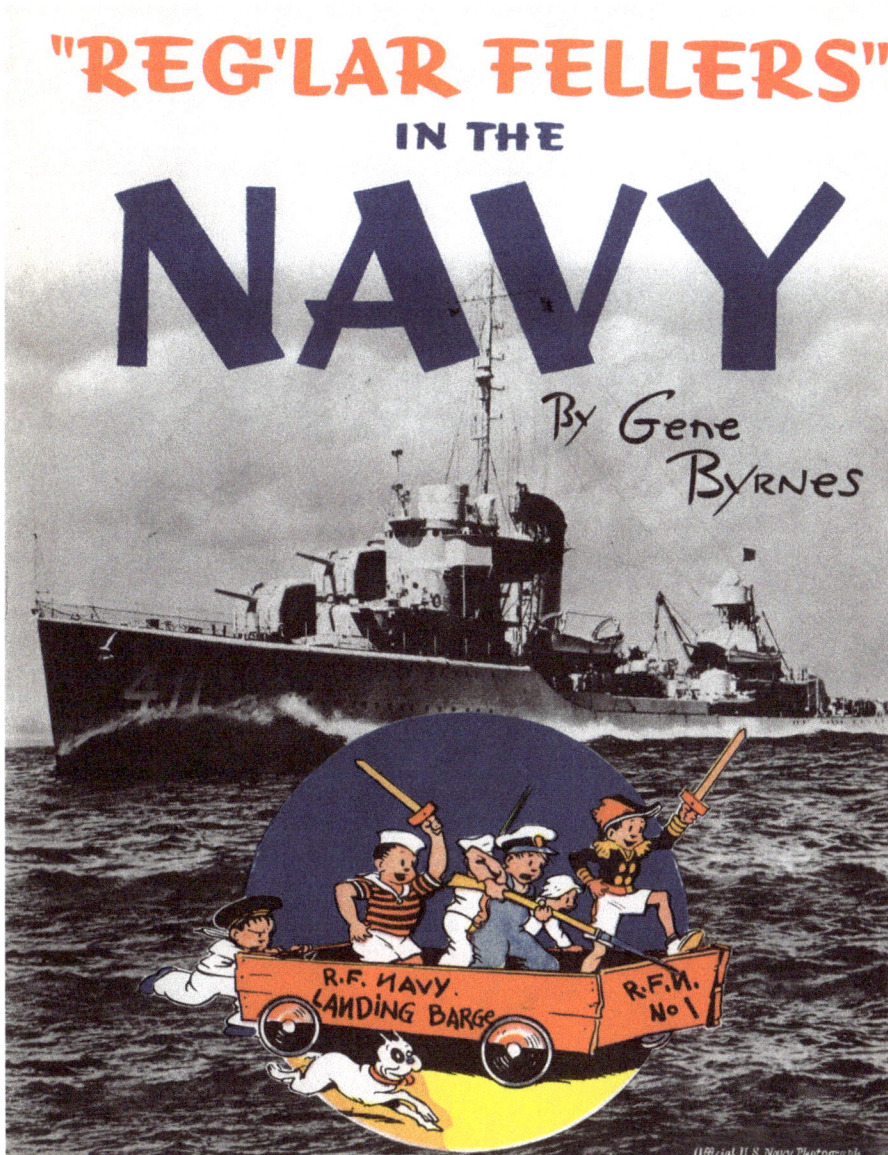

"REG'LAR FELLERS"
IN THE
NAVY
By Gene Byrnes
R.F. NAVY LANDING BARGE
R.F.N. No 1
Official U.S. Navy Photograph

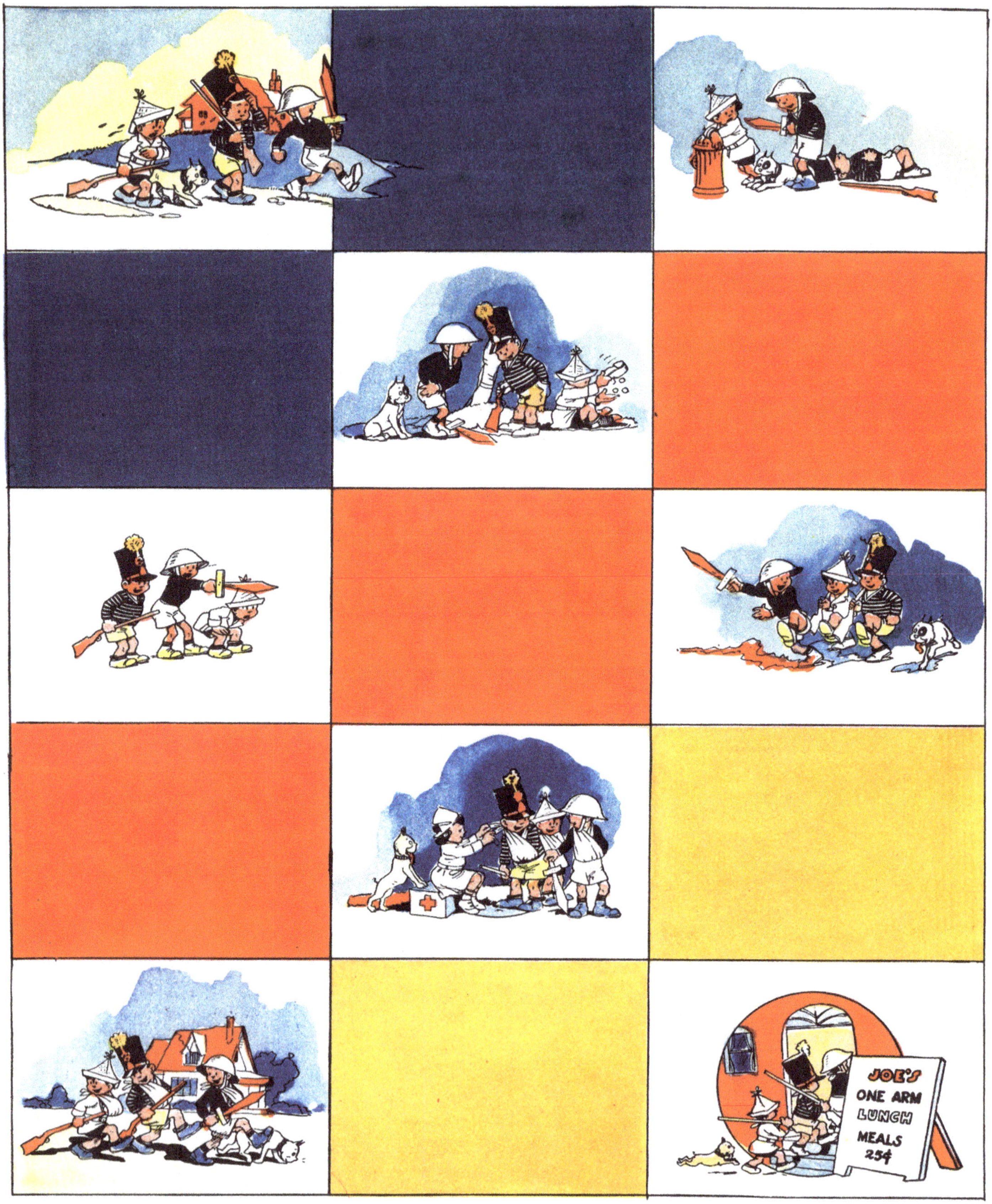
JOE'S
ONE ARM
LUNCH
MEALS
25¢

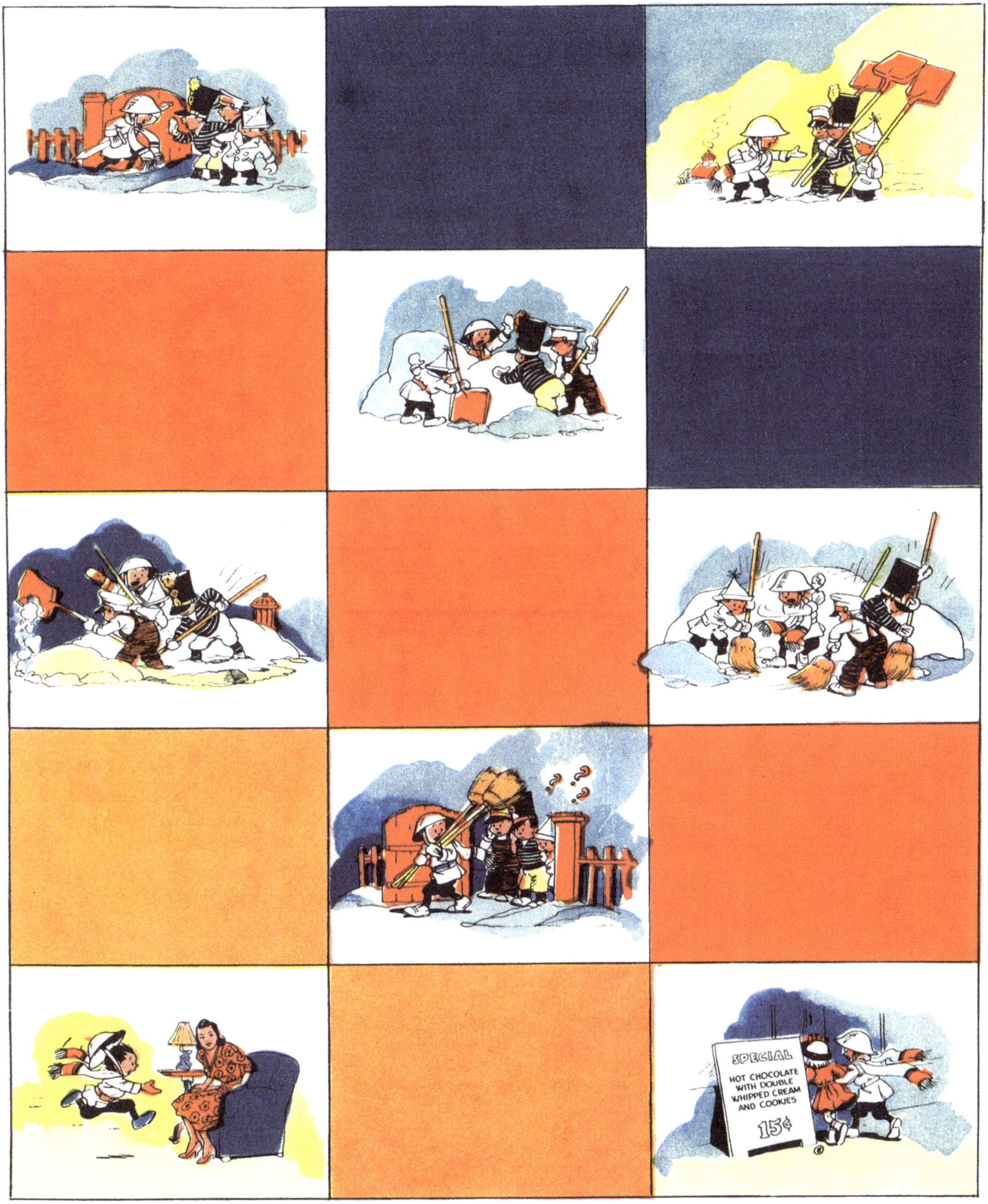
SPECIAL
HOT CHOCOLATE
WITH DOUBLE
WHIPPED CREAM
AND COOKIES
15¢

Coachwhip Publications

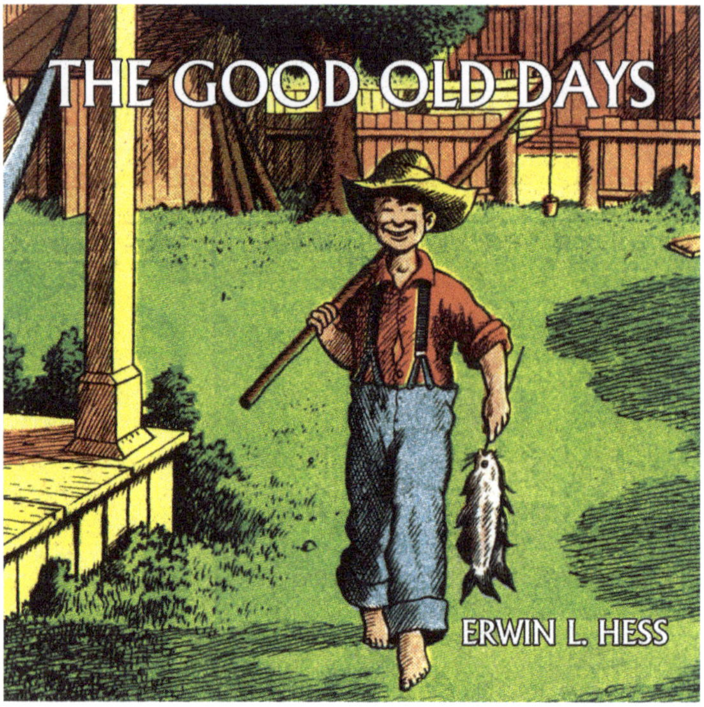
THE GOOD OLD DAYS
ERWIN L. HESS

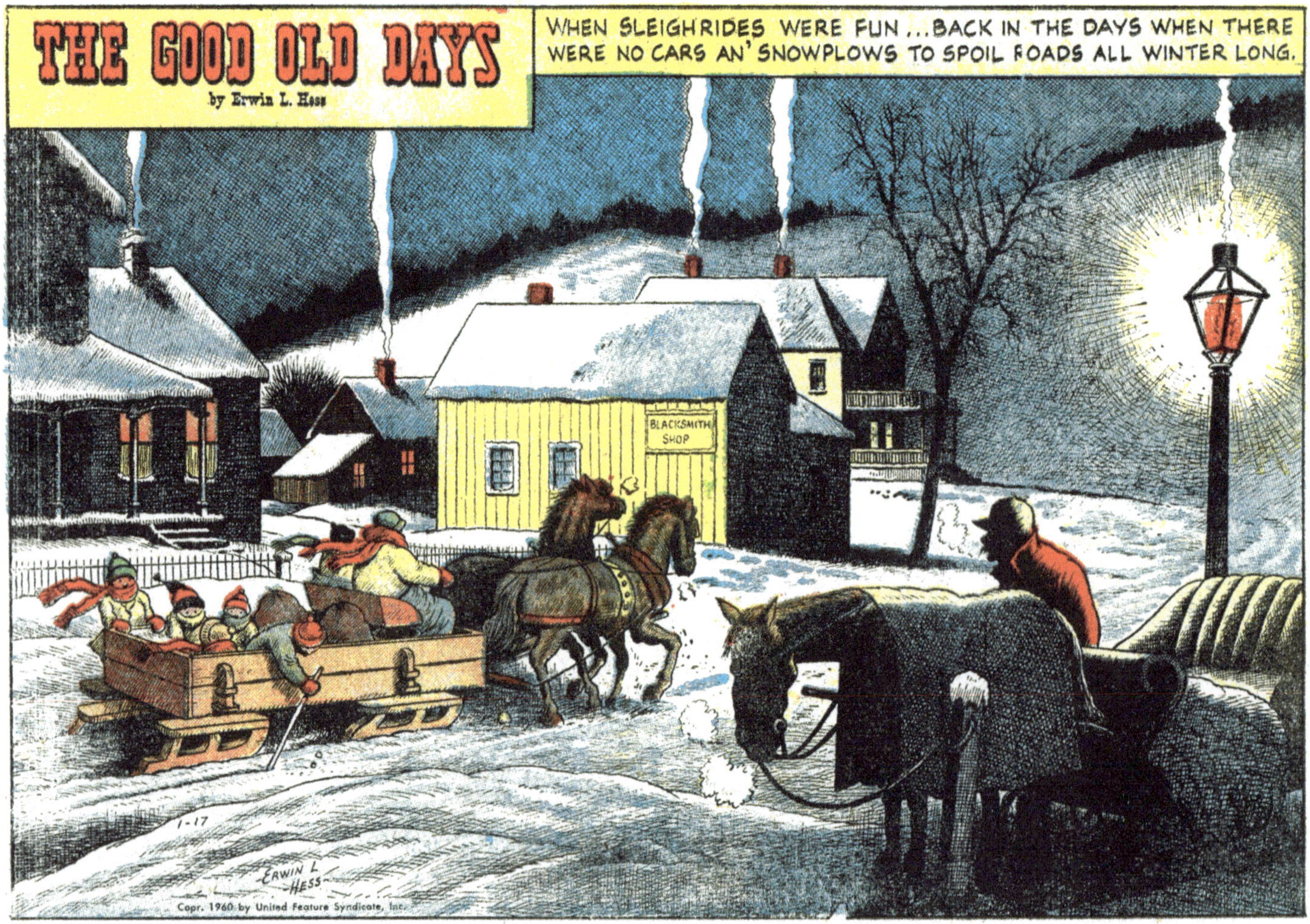
THE GOOD OLD DAYS
by Erwin L. Hess
WHEN SLEIGHRIDES WERE FUN ... BACK IN THE DAYS WHEN THERE WERE NO CARS AN' SNOWPLOWS TO SPOIL ROADS ALL WINTER LONG.
BLACKSMITH SHOP
1-17
ERWIN L HESS
Copr. 1960 by United Feature Syndicate, Inc.

CoachwhipBooks.com

SMITTY
-MY MOTHER THANKS YOU. MY FATHER THANKS YOU. I THANK YOU
CUPPLES AND LEON CO.
PUBLISHERS • NEW YORK
BERNDT

SMITTY—YOU HAVE TO BE SMARTER THAN THE DOG

SO FAR SO GOOD. NOBODY KNOWS I GAVE MY DOG AWAY AND SO FAR, VERA DOESN'T KNOW IT'S MY DOG.
OH UNCLE, WON'T YOU TEACH THE DOG SOME TRICKS?
THAT ISN'T DONE SO EASY VERA - IT TAKES YEARS AND YEARS
I'LL MAKE HIM DO SOME TRICKS
SURE! SURE! LET MR. WISEBOY SHOW YOU HOW IT'S DONE - HE KNOWS EVERY-THING.
???
ALLY OOP! WALK ACROSS TH' ROOM ON YER FRONT FEET
Reg. U. S. Pat. Off., Copyright, 1928, by The Chicago Tribune

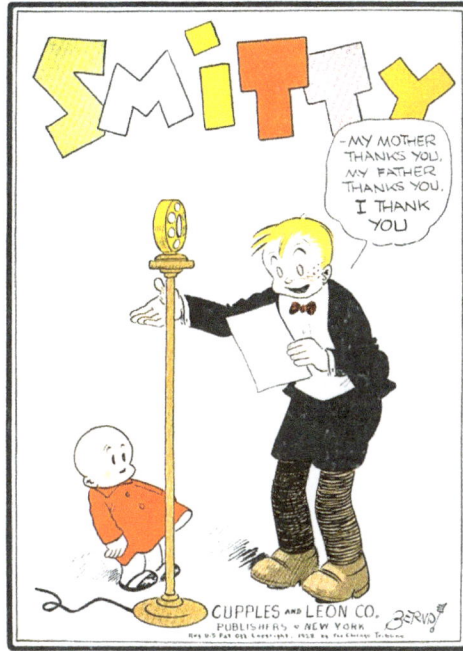

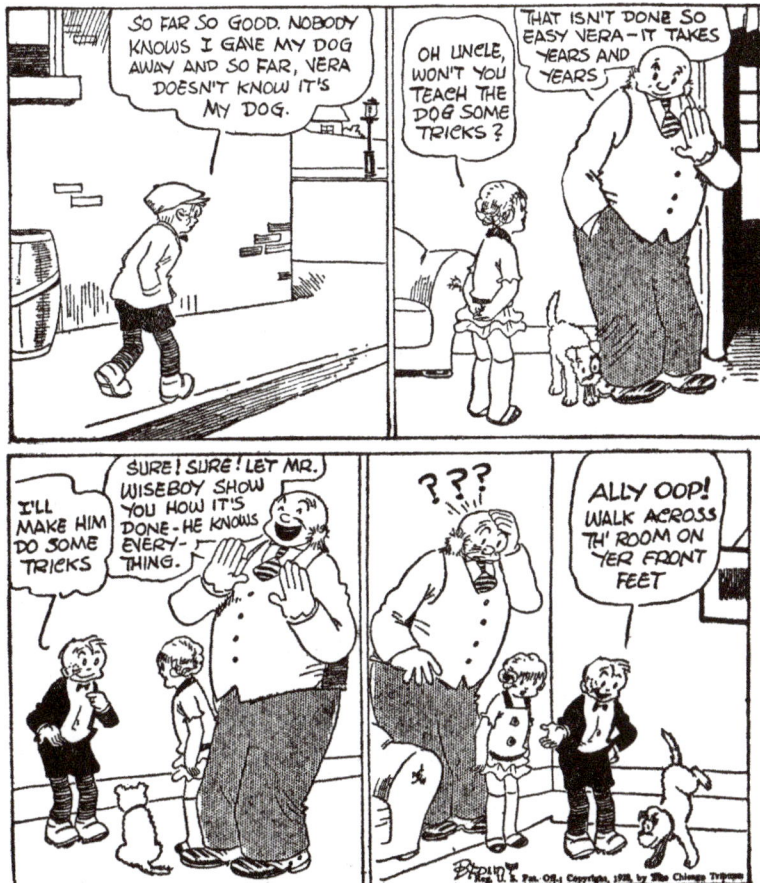

COACHWHIP PUBLICATIONS

JAMES
SWINNERTON
CANYON
COUNTRY
KIDDIES

CATNIP
SWINNERTON

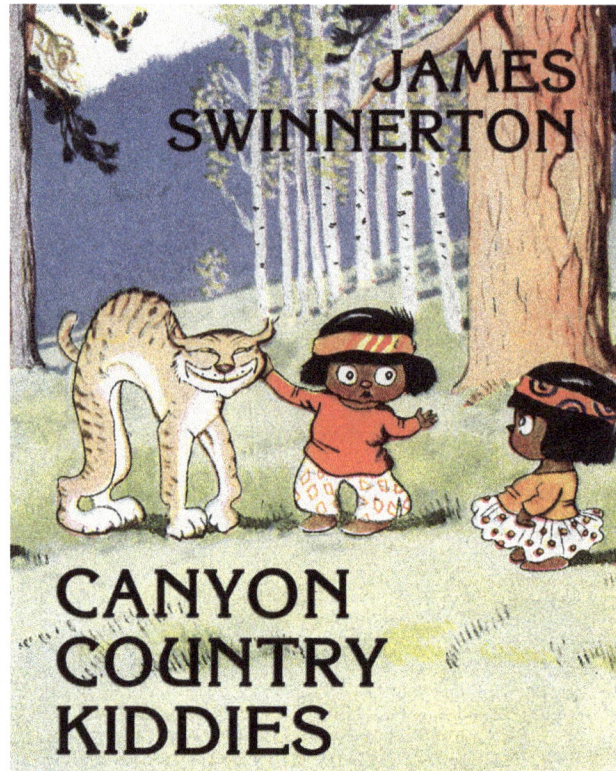

Foolish Questions

RUBE GOLDBERG

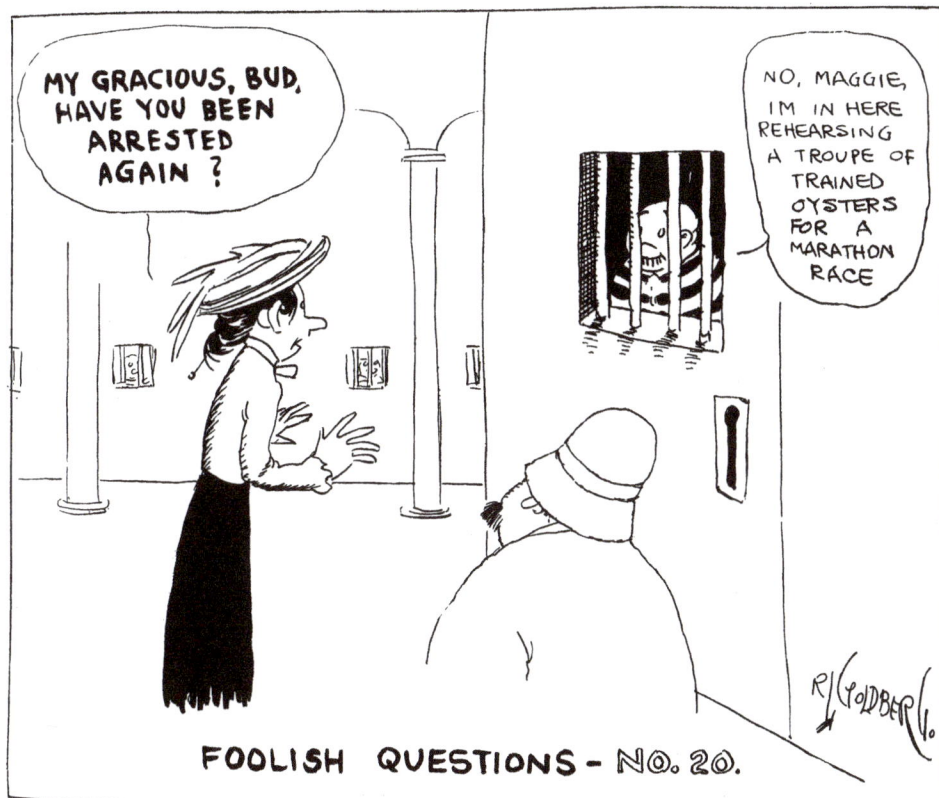

MY GRACIOUS, BUD, HAVE YOU BEEN ARRESTED AGAIN?

NO, MAGGIE, I'M IN HERE REHEARSING A TROUPE OF TRAINED OYSTERS FOR A MARATHON RACE

FOOLISH QUESTIONS - NO. 20.

www.ingramcontent.com/pod-product-compliance
Lightning Source LLC
Chambersburg PA
CBHW061417090426
42742CB00027B/3498
* 9 7 8 1 6 1 6 4 6 2 8 6 4 *